CAMBRIDGE STUDIES IN AMERICAN LITERATURE AND CULTURE

The interpretation of material shapes in Puritanism

The interpretation of material shapes in Puritanism

A study of rhetoric, prejudice, and violence

ANN KIBBEY

Yale University

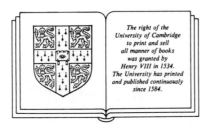

The right of the
University of Cambridge
to print and sell
all manner of books
was granted by
Henry VIII in 1534.
The University has printed
and published continuously
since 1584.

CAMBRIDGE UNIVERSITY PRESS

Cambridge

London   New York   New Rochelle

Melbourne   Sydney

Published by the Press Syndicate of the University of Cambridge
The Pitt Building, Trumpington Street, Cambridge CB2 1RP
32 East 57th Street, New York, NY 10022, USA
10 Stamford Road, Oakleigh, Melbourne 3166, Australia

First published 1986

Printed in the United States of America

Library of Congress Cataloging in Publication Data
Kibbey, Ann, 1948–
   The interpretation of material shapes in Puritanism.
   (Cambridge studies in American literature and culture)
   Bibliography: p.
   Includes index.
   1. American prose literature – Puritan authors – History and criticism. 2.
American prose literature – Colonial period, ca. 1600–1775 – History and
criticism. 3. Theology, Puritan, in literature. 4. Puritans – New England –
History. 5. Rhetoric – 1500–1800. 6. Idols and images in literature. 7.
Iconoclasm in literature. 8. Prejudices in literature. I. Title. II. Series.
PS153.P87K5 1986 818'.1'0809 85–12806
ISBN 0 521 26509 6

British Library Cataloguing in Publication applied for

For S., J., T., and E.

Contents

Acknowledgments

I would like to thank the American Council of Learned Societies, the Social Science Research Council, and Yale University for grants that facilitated the research and writing of this book. I would also like to thank the Library Company and the Presbyterian Historical Society in Philadelphia, Beinecke Rare Book Library at Yale University, Emmanuel College Library at Cambridge University, and St. Botolph's Church and the Boston History Project in Boston, Lincolnshire. All made their full resources available to me and were very helpful in answering inquiries and making photocopies.

I am deeply grateful to those who generously gave me encouragement in the earliest stages of this work and provided many valuable suggestions along the way. I would especially like to thank Sacvan Bercovitch, Katherine Colman, Joan Dayan, Mary Maples Dunn, John Freccero, Jack Getman, Thomas Keenan, J. Hillis Miller, and Michael Zuckerman. Without them, this book would still have been possible, but not probable.

Many colleagues made helpful comments on lectures, seminars, and drafts at various stages, all of which were beneficial in the process of revision. Thanks to Amitai Avi-ram, Danna Blesser, Marie Borroff, Michael Colacurcio, Charles Feidelson, Kenneth Fox, Thomas Greene, Daniel Harris, Keith Hoskin, Dell Hymes, Amy Kaplan, Wendy Kuppermann, Mary Loeffelholz, Elissa Marder, Louis Martz, Ephraim Paul, Martin Price, Jules Prown, Maureen Quilligan, Leslie Rado, Dana Spradley, Keith Thomas, and Thomas Whitaker. Dana Spradley was also a very able research assistant on several matters, as I have indicated in the notes, and did much of the computer programming. Carol Barash assisted as a reader in comparing the editions discussed in section IV of the Appendix. Beverly Cedarbaum and Madeline Colon typed the initial version of the manuscript.

Elizabeth Maguire, Albert Gelpi, Andrew Brown, and Janis Bolster were a patient and insightful group of editors. Their good judgment considerably improved the final version and I am grateful for their efforts.

Finally, I would like to thank my family for many years of abiding support. Their encouragement, their sense of humor, and their trust have been invaluable.

Abbreviations of John Cotton's works cited in the text

AB   *A Modest and Cleare Answer to Mr. Balls Discourse of set formes of Prayer* (London, 1642)

C   *A Brief Exposition of the Whole Book of Canticles, or, Song of Solomon* (London, 1642)

CR   *The Churches Resurrection* (London, 1642)

E   *A Brief Exposition with Practicall Observations upon the Whole Book of Ecclesiastes,* 2nd ed. (London, 1657)

G   *Gods Promise to His Plantation* (London, 1630)

H   *Of the Holinesse of Church-Members* (London, 1650)

R   *An Exposition upon The Thirteenth Chapter of the Revelation* (London, 1655)

T   *A Treatise of the Covenant of Grace,* 2nd ed. (London, 1659)

V   *The Powrring out of the Seven Vials* (London, 1642)

WL   *The Way of Life* (London, 1641)

I

Introductory: figures of prejudice

In 1637, the year in which the Puritans banished Anne Hutchinson for her "mishapen opinions" on religion, the Puritans also initiated a genocidal war against the Pequots, a tribe of Native Americans who inhabited parts of southern and central New England. John Underhill, leader of the Massachusetts Bay Company militia in the war, published a narrative in 1638 revealing the full extent of Puritan violence against the Pequots. The first major battle occurred near what is now Mystic, Connecticut, in the spring of 1637, several months before Hutchinson's state trial. The Puritans surrounded the virtually defenseless Pequots and slaughtered everyone in the settlement, including women and children, by setting it on fire. John Mason, leader of the Hartford militia, "set fire on the west side," Underhill recounted, and "myself set fire on the south end with a train of powder." The human conflagration that ensued was horrific:

> The fires of both meeting in the center of the fort, blazed most terribly, and burnt all in the space of half an hour. . . . Many were burnt in the fort, both men, women, and children. . . . Great and doleful was the bloody sight to the view of young soldiers that had never been in war, to see so many souls lie gasping on the ground, so thick, in some places, that you could hardly pass along.

Those who attempted to escape the flames were shot or stabbed to death. After a second major battle in a swamp near New Haven, the Puritans had succeeded in their intent to destroy the Pequot People, as Mason said, "to cut off the Remembrance of them from the Earth."[1]

When we include the historical fact of the mass killing at Mystic in our perception of who the Puritans were, it raises issues of interpretation that are otherwise obscured in intellectual history.[2] Although the Pequot War was by far the most extreme act of prejudice the early Puritans committed, the social values that inspired it were intrinsic to

I

Puritan culture. Consequently, to isolate the social fact of catastrophic violence as a lapse of cultural beliefs is to fail to understand its relationship to other, nonviolent acts of prejudice characterizing Puritanism. The genocidal war against the Pequots occurred at the same time as the Hutchinson controversy, and although the religious controversy never became a violent confrontation, there were threats and fears of violence on both sides.[3] When we take into account the rhetoric of threat, the distinction between violent and nonviolent acts is more difficult to draw than it first appears. It is equally difficult to distinguish between religious and secular events. Although the Pequot War may seem to have been solely a military campaign – as opposed to the religious disputes of the controversy within the Puritan colony – the war, like the controversy, was perceived as an attack on the enemies of Puritan religion. Captain Mason, for example, attributed the war of extermination to "the LORD GOD" who "was pleased to smite our Enemies in the hinder parts" and "redeem us out of our Enemies Hands."[4] The simultaneity of the war and the religious controversy also suggests that the prejudices of race and gender were linked, but the relationship is a complicated one. To distinguish the war as an act of racial hatred and the banishment of Hutchinson as an expression of prejudice against women oversimplifies events, for the Pequot women at Mystic were the objects of both kinds of prejudice.

Both the war and the controversy demonstrate that prejudice was rationalized by religion in Puritan society, that to a great extent prejudicial and religious beliefs were indistinguishable. The most obvious kinds of evidence are the pronouncements of men such as Mason, who readily cited Scripture and wrapped their own motives in the intentions of their deity. Although this level of rationalization was important, it was in many respects only the outcome of a more profound synthesis of religion and prejudice in the perception of material shapes. As we will see, the Puritan belief in the necessity and righteousness of deliberate physical harm was deeply indebted to the ideology of Protestant iconoclasm in Reformation Europe. The violent destruction of artistic images of people developed into a mandate for sacrosanct violence against human beings, especially against people whose material "image," whose physical characteristics, differed from the Puritan man's own. The association between prejudice and the violence of iconoclasm was strengthened by seventeenth-century concepts of prejudice. For the Puritans and their contemporaries, the word "prejudice" could mean an act of material injury as well as negative prejudgment.[5] For example, Underhill wrote of the Puritans' decision to set fire to the fort at Mystic, "We devised a way how we might save ourselves and prejudice them." Concluding that "we had sufficient light from the word of God for our proceedings," Underhill insinuated that religious violence and prejudicial acts of material harm were inseparable: Prejudice was violent and this violence was holy.[6] The synthesis was further enhanced by another seventeenth-century meaning of prejudice, prognostication. For example, when the minister John Cotton condemned Hutchinson for heresy, he also predicted that she would become an adulteress. Lack of faith in religion, he warned, would lead to unfaithfulness in marriage. However pious she seemed, it would be revealed that her beliefs were actually those of a sexual libertine who advocated "all promiscuus and filthie cominge togeather of men and Woemen without Distinction or Relation of Marriage."[7] In the Pequot War and the Hutchinson controversy, Puritan leaders overtly sanctioned their own acts of violence and the slanders of prognostication, making prejudice indistinguishable from their religious beliefs.

The threats and acts of physical harm, the symbolism of physical identity, and the rationale of iconoclastic violence against people as images – all these aspects of prejudice were informed by a concept of figuration that was qualitatively different from what we usually take "figurative" to mean in literary thought. Puritanism relied on the classical concept of *figura,* an idea that initially had nothing to do with language. In its earliest usage *figura* meant a dynamic material shape, and often a living corporeal shape such as the figure of a face or a human body.[8] This ancient concept of figuration has a modern equivalent in our sense of the human bodily form or appearance as a "figure." For the Puritans, the concept of *figura* was a means of interpreting the human shape, whether as artistic image or as living form, and it comprehended both nonviolent and violent interpretations of human beings. Among its most important qualities, the classical concept of *figura* as it meant material shape defied the conventional metaphoric opposition between "figurative" and "literal." The configuration or shape was simply there, and its defining property was the dynamic materiality of its form. A modern example from abstract art that employs this concept is a mobile: The motion of material shapes continually reconstitutes different figures (or *figurae*) without ever producing a shape that one would distinguish from the others as distinctly literal in opposition to figurative.

In Latin culture *figura* acquired a protean variety of meanings, developing into a theory of figuration that included language and the figures of rhetoric but was by no means restricted to discourse. As Erich Auerbach has shown, *figura* was variously used to mean statue, image, portrait, model, copy, dream image, simulacrum, figment, style, imprint of a seal, geometric form, architectural plan, rhetorical figures, occupation, the acoustic images of speech, and more.[9] Some of these meanings carried the connotation of figurative, fictive, or representational, but the range of meanings that accrued to *figura* was much broader. In early modern Europe the revival of classical learning recovered the complexity and richness of the Latin theory of figuration, a complexity that was owing in part to the kaleidoscopic variety of ways to conceive of the relation between words and referents. Because this theory of figuration did not privilege language, and because *figura* disregarded the conceptual boundaries of "sign" and "referent" that we associate with discourse, the possible combinations of words and things was immense. Although the full range of classical and renaissance meanings of *figura* is relevant to Puritanism, this study is primarily concerned with the concepts of material form that proved to be most important to the American colonists' words and acts of prejudice: the shapes of speech, icons, and the shapes of people.

As the seventeenth-century ideas of prejudice and figuration suggest, linguistic beliefs and values are culturally variable. That is, societies do not necessarily share the same theory of figuration or even grant the same social significance to language. Dell Hymes has observed, "Peoples do not all everywhere use language to the same degree, in the same situations, or for the same things." Consequently, "languages, like other cultural traits, will be found to vary in the degree and nature of their integration into the societies and cultures in which they occur."[10] To explore the social dimensions of language use and its relation to prejudicial violence, we need to understand how, and to what extent, language use contributed to the ways in which Puritan society produced its own sense of social conditions. Exhortations to commit violence were rarely so forthright as they were in the Pequot War, and in general the most exacting social prejudices were not usually conveyed in overt statements. Puritans often sanctioned prejudicial acts obliquely through the representation of violence in figurative language, and by indirectly cultivating an attitude toward material shapes that granted considerable semantic value to material forms. Similarly, Puritan beliefs about social roles and the institution of marriage were preached far more often through the imagery of theological beliefs than by literal statements of doctrine. Though this rhetoric has often been analyzed for its theological content, it has rarely been considered as a means of inculcating social values. As we will see, understanding the persuasiveness of the Puritans' rhetoric from this perspective does not disregard the religious content of their discourse but rather accounts for it in a different way.[11]

As a means of inquiry, I have focused primarily on the works of John Cotton in the period 1620–40, when English Puritans first immigrated to America and Puritan men established their hegemony in Massachusetts Bay. Throughout his life, Cotton gave no evidence of ever having cared whether posterity heard of him or not, and posterity by and large has deferred to his indifference. He is probably best known now (where he is known at all) as Anne Hutchinson's minister, but among his contemporaries he was most respected for his skill in rhetoric, his fidelity to the Puritan cause, and his learning in Hebrew, Greek, and Latin. Cotton was in most respects typical of an Anglo-American Puritan leader. Born in 1584 in Derbyshire, he began his career as dean and catechist of Emmanuel College, Cambridge, in the first decade of the seventeenth century. In 1612, already a noted orator at the university, he left Cambridge to become vicar of the largest parish church in England, St. Botolph's, in the international port city of Boston, Lincolnshire. Here he was married for the first time, to Elizabeth Horrocks. During his years at St. Botolph's, Cotton became widely known for his success as a rhetorician in the pulpit and for his Puritan refusal to perform the rituals of the Church of England. He also appears to have maintained a close association with Emmanuel College, since students came from Cambridge, and eventually from the Continent as well, to study with him in Boston. In 1632 he was threatened with prosecution by Archbishop Laud, and like many other Puritans he went into hiding in London. Cotton's first wife died of illness in 1630, and he was married again in 1632 to Sarah Hawkridge Story (with whom he had five children). After nearly a year in London, Cotton emigrated in 1633 to the Massachusetts Bay Colony, where he became teacher of the First Church of Boston and enjoyed immediate success as a preacher. Within a few years he had become involved in the disputes of the Hutchinson controversy, but despite the crisis, he continued to hold authority in the church and the colony.[12] In the 1640s he was the leading apologist for American Congregationalism, and by the time of his death in 1652 he had become one of the most influential Puritan ministers of the seventeenth century, well known on both sides of the Atlantic.[13]

Cotton was a more sophisticated rhetorician than scholars have taken him to be, but it is not my purpose to assess Cotton himself, or, for that matter, to rescue him from obscurity. In the chapters that follow, the topics I emphasize in Cotton's works and the analytical issues I raise have been selected with a view to their importance for understanding the development of prejudice in early America. Rather than render a biography, either intellectual or historical, I have considered Cotton as an anthropologist might treat an articulate native informant who was directly involved in major events. My purpose is less to understand him as a particular individual than to understand the linguistic and social values that characterized his rhetoric as a member of the Puritan elite. Since the history of iconoclasm, the history of the Pequot War, and the antinomian controversy bear directly on his use of figures, I have also treated these subjects at length.

2

The referential imperative

The use of religion to promulgate social values and rationalize acts of prejudice is relatively obvious in the trial of Anne Hutchinson and the Pequot War, but the same attitude was no less present, and no less important, in the Puritan rhetoric of conversion. Despite their appearance of otherworldly concerns in preaching the soul's salvation, ministers such as John Cotton subordinated belief in the deity to another end: communicating the absolute rightness of their own social ideals. The figures of rhetoric, apart from any scriptural doctrine of an elect nation, were their most important means of persuasion. Figures like the secular imagery of metaphor seem at first glance to be minor, even unrelated to the aims of conversion, but their obliqueness is misleading. As we will see, the social ideas expressed within the figures of rhetoric were the primary exhortations of the sermon. This is not to say that engendering belief in the deity was wholly a fraudulent enterprise, a mere stalking-horse for cultural elitism, for the spiritual pantheon was integral to the Puritan system of social meaning. The act of belief in the deity created contradictions that were intrinsic to articulating and sustaining the prejudicial values of their culture.

Gauging the social import of rhetorical figures in sermons quickly leads to a complex array of considerations about language use. Metaphors, for example, can be interpreted in many ways, and the social values assigned to them can vary substantially from one situation to another. What makes one metaphor didactic, another a casual observation, and another a patently fictive image? The ways in which metaphors interact with other aspects of language use, and cultural assumptions about the power of words in relation to referents, affect the meaning assigned to a particular figure.[1] The social significance of imagery, or any other kind of rhetorical figure, depends on a culture's ideas about language use. In their most general assumptions about

6

language, the Puritans placed considerable emphasis on the power of words to influence an individual's perception of social conditions. This assumption is evident in their self-consciousness about the experience of salvation as essentially a linguistic event. John Cotton, taking Peter's sermon at Pentecost as a paradigm of conversion, describes it as a nearly miraculous transformation of the crowd in response to Peter's words:

> These men at first, did not a little wonder to hear the Apostles speake with strange Tongues, [Acts 2] ver. 12. and mee thinks it is as great a wonder to see this sudden change (by a word speaking:) See in them, what a new tongue, a pricked heart will worke. The same men that even now said, the Apostles were full of the spirit of Wine; now they speake the language of Canaan: before debaucht Ruffians; now, *Men and Brethren;* A work, they had not been wonted to: they that before mocked at new Tongues, had now themselves gotten new Tongues; and it was a greater miracle to have such words in their mouths, then to heare the Apostles speake all the principall Languages in the world.[2]

Not only did speech generate conversion. The hearer's religious experience was itself a linguistic event. "To have such words in their mouths" was to be converted, to undergo the ultimate transformation their religion promised. The phrase "the language of Canaan" is a metaphor suggesting the nature of this transformation. Those converted by hearing Peter's sermon acquired "new Tongues," but they did not actually speak a new language. Rather, the "language of Canaan" designates a particular way of using one's own native language, of learning to use the same words differently.

To put it another way, conversion was an alteration of the hearer's system of reference in response to the preacher's words, a conversion from one system of meaning to another. The Puritan insistence on the need for conversion, and on sermons as the means of it, evinced an awareness that literal meaning is variable. We often assume that literal meaning has stability, but systems of reference are socially variable, even within one culture. What is literal to one person is not necessarily literal to another, and different circumstances may invoke differences in literal meaning from the same individual. Puritans depended on the circumstances of preaching to change the hearer's system of reference and thereby alter the hearer's perception and understanding of social behavior. One might suppose that sermons directly engaged issues of social behavior and that converts were obligated to change their social actions, not just their perception of them. However, Cotton's paradigm is representative of how little Puritans' doctrines concerned social conduct, at least in their sermons on the conversion of the soul. Puritan preachers sought mainly to produce converts who would speak differently because they had come to think differently about the meanings of words and things.

Cotton describes conversion not just as a verbal experience but particularly as an experience of speech: Conversion occurs "by a word speaking." Puritans generally believed that only spoken words, and spontaneous speech at that, could produce conversions. Well known for their staunch opposition to the Anglican practice of writing out sermons and reading them, Puritan preachers themselves spoke extemporaneously or from brief notes, relying quite specifically on speech, not just words, to effect the transformation of conversion. It might seem that Puritan linguistic values granted an absolute privilege to the written word, since their sermons were purportedly explications of biblical texts, and their written notes appear to provide the substance of explication in listing "doctrines," "reasons," and "uses." Michel Foucault implies as much in arguing that the sixteenth- and seventeenth-century world view "presupposes an absolute privilege on the part of writing." He concludes, "Henceforth it is the primal nature of language to be written. The sounds made by voices provide no more than a transitory and precarious translation of it."[3] However, the crucial importance of speaking in conversion shows that Puritans believed written texts were in some way fundamentally dependent for their intelligibility on their incorporation into speech, that sound – however transitory and precarious – was essential.

The importance of speech in the Puritans' culture requires us to recast our ideas about the value they assigned to rhetorical figures in sermons. Figures seem at first to be unimportant because preachers rarely made notes about imagery, simply leaving rhetorical figuration to extemporaneous composition in the pulpit. Such a practice would appear to lend itself to the conventional assumption that rhetorical figures are mere embellishment, something added to the substance of what is being said lexically. However, what was composed spontaneously was the most valued, not the least valued, aspect of language. Puritans believed that when a preacher spoke in the pulpit, he spoke from the inspiration of the deity. Thus the figures of rhetoric were the dimension of language most directly attributed to divine inspiration, and consequently the most authoritative aspect of discourse.

Believing in the need to hear words in order to be converted gives an unusual prominence to material signifiers, to the acoustic shapes of spoken words. This emphasis may seem strange because we are not used to thinking about sound as an important determinant of meaning, and we tend to equate serious figuration with metaphor. The Puritans acknowledged the importance of metaphor, to be sure, but their idea of rhetorical figuration was far more expansive, encompassing a variety of tropes and figures of speech that are unfamiliar to a modern reader. The most important among these are the rhetorical figures of acoustic design.[4] Perhaps because Puritan rhetoric was indebted to classical rhetoricians whose model was the orator, the Puritans were acutely sensitive to the patterns of sound in speech and the capacity of these figures to affect meaning, including the meaning of metaphors.

When Cotton undertakes an explicit defense of rhetorical figures in general, he focuses his defense on verbal schemes, the patterns of actual sounds that are heard when the words are pronounced. Attacking the idea that the plain style either can or should be devoid of figures, he describes how the topic of vanity is "amplified by many ornaments of rhetoric" in Eccles. 1.2, "*Vanity of vanities, saith the Preacher: vanity of vanities, all is vanity.*"[5] He enumerates eleven different rhetorical figures in Solomon's words: the trope hyperbole and then ten figures of speech involving rhythm and the repetition of letters, syllables, and words. His catalogue of verbal schemes leaves no syllable unturned: the same sound continued in a sentence; the sound at the end of one sentence repeated at the beginning of the next; the same sound employed at the beginning and end of a sentence; the same sound repeated at the beginnings of sentences; the same sound repeated at the ends of sentences; interlaced repetition of sounds at the beginning and middle, and the middle and end of sentences; sentences with the same number of syllables; the same sound continued and increased by degrees through the verse; the repetition of sounds that are similar but not quite the same (E5–6). The rhetoric is so woven with verbal patterns that it is wholly figural, implying a continuous relation between sound and meaning.[6]

Cotton's theory of rhetoric does not separate discourse into figurative and nonfigurative usage. Because the figures of acoustic design are inextricable from the material fact of speech, all language use is figurative in some way. This idea was a common one in classical rhetoric, and Cotton himself probably drew directly on Quintilian, who uses *figura* in this sense in the *Institutio Oratoria* to introduce his theory of rhetorical figuration:

> The first point for consideration is, therefore, what is meant by a *figure* [*figuram*]. For the term is used in two senses. In the first it is applied to any form in which thought is expressed, just as it is to bodies which, whatever their composition, must have some shape. In the second and special sense, in which it is called a *schema,* it means a rational change in meaning or language from the ordinary and simple form, that is to say, a change analogous to that involved by sitting, lying down on something or looking back.[7]

Since the shapes of words, or any combination of them, or any parts of them, are *figurae,* to use language is to compose in figures. Asking a rhetorician to avoid using figures is like asking a musician to avoid playing notes, for material shapes are an intrinsic, inescapable feature of speech. Even in speech devoid of the obvious adornment of metaphor and image, there will always be the audible shapes of syllables. Quintilian's second and more restricted usage of *figura* refers to verbal schemes such as Cotton enumerates.[8] He uses the analogy of bodily positions to explain how the schemes relate to his more general concept of figuration: Particular motions of the human body give it a different shape without changing the fundamental shape of the body itself. He mentions that some rhetoricians call rhetorical figures "motions" and that he himself thinks of schemes as "certain attitudes" or "gestures" of language.[9] Though verbal schemes are easily recognized as figurative discourse, Quintilian also concludes that "in the first and common sense of the word [*figura*] there is nothing that is not figural [*nihil non figuratum est*]."[10] That is, all discourse is figural, whether it is schematic or not, and Quintilian means this materially, concretely, in the sense of the dynamic material shapes of speech. Whether *figurae* are just inevitably there or put there in the more conscious and purposeful designs of a practiced orator, the material shapes of language make all speech a figuration.

Hyperbole, the one trope Cotton lists among the "ornaments" of Solomon's words, describes the general effect of figures of sound. The "reasons of the Repetition of this vanity; and the Holy Ghosts manner of speech," he explains, are "to shew the excessiveness of the vanity" (E7). Cotton's sense of hyperbole as a sustained alteration of meaning follows Quintilian's view that tropes can be understood as "modes." Modes alter meaning substantially, for "the changes involved concern not merely individual words, but also our thought and the structure of our sentences."[11] As a mode rather than a particular instance of a figure, a trope is a generic term for a quality of sustained alteration. It indicates the effect of using a variety of figures in a certain way, rather like composing in a particular key in music. The hyperbolic mode can incorporate a wide array of tropes and figures, all geared toward the expression of augmentation or diminution, or both.[12] For example, Solomon exaggerates his diminution of the value of "earthly things" by his hyperbolic exclamation that "all is vanity." Hyperbole does not define, name, or classify. It amplifies, diminishes, augments, emphasizes, enhances, understates, attenuates.[13] More than any other trope, it lends itself to the idea of figures as gestures, and it gestures most persuasively, Cotton argues, through the designs of sound, the patterned arrangement of acoustic shapes.

Cotton's theory of rhetoric proposes that the function of reference in language is complex and often indirect, for the meaning of speech is dependent not only on such tropes as metaphor but also on the formal qualities of material signifiers. The idea is perhaps easier to comprehend if we consider a modern visual analogue to the Puritan concept of sound design. We respond to the aesthetic form as well as to the lexical meaning of store signs, and we do so in a way that acknowledges our sensitivity to the variegated means by which reference is communicated through material figuration as well as literal meaning. The shape of a sign, its style of graphics, and its colors semantically convey as much as the lexical meaning of the words on the sign, and perhaps more than the words. We respond to neon lights very differently from the way we respond to antique lettering, for instance, so much so that each kind of sign means something different even if it has the same lexical meaning on it. In the interpretation of prose, however, we characteristically ignore the material signifier by assuming that the function of reference in prose is simple, reducible to the lexical meaning of words.

For Cotton, such simplicity of literal meaning was achieved only by the careful use of rhetorical figures, the speech equivalent of graphics and lighting. The clarity of meaning that implies a straightforward equivalence between words and things was fragile and continuously problematic because the function of reference in language was multidimensional. Puritan preachers conceived of literal meaning as a rhetorical construct, as a pliable figure and not a given of language. Even literal meaning was dependent on the interplay of signifiers and the use of tropes, so much so that the function of reference could depend substantially on the relation of words to each other in discourse. Indeed, reference often depended more on the composition of words than on the existence of a tangible referent to refer to. Since literal meaning could not be taken for granted, it needed to be preached, divinely fixed, made absolute by the inspired eloquence of the orator. In his sermon rhetoric Cotton sought to fix literal meaning with the force of a referential imperative asserted through the figures of his rhetoric.

To take an example, the longest and most complete record of Cotton's rhetoric of conversion, *The Way of Life,* is a transcript of about fifty sermons he preached sometime between 1627 and 1632 while he was vicar of St. Botolph's in Boston, Lincolnshire. The first sermon shows how conversion was initiated and demonstrates many characteristic features of his rhetoric. Cotton seems to use figures sparingly, but a close look at his use of language shows that it is just as figural as his lectures on Ecclesiastes suggest it would be, for there is no such thing as an undesigned sentence in his sermons. Plain though his style may be, its plainness and clarity are a measure of his unusual skill, for his rhetoric is an intricate form of figural expression, even and especially in its most apparently styleless, or literal, moments.

The topic of his first sermon is the need for prayer, a more interesting subject than it might seem at first glance, since the Puritan idea of prayer was autobiographical narrative. Cotton is adamant about the inviolable connection between conversion and the linguistic performance he calls prayer: "No Prayer, no Grace; little Prayer, little Grace; frequencie of Prayer, argues power of Grace" (WL10). Prayer, as personal narrative, is the rhetorical form of the Puritan "self," the means of creating a subjectivity that confirms the existence of the deity. In this initial sermon Cotton is far less concerned with what is said in any prayer than with converting the hearer to engage in this activity in the first place. The value of prayer is the reality it grants to its supposed audience, the deity, by direct address. Once the hearer is persuaded "to cry, Abba, Father" (WL4), the preacher has succeeded in his intentions, for this direct address expresses the belief that the referents of the spirit world named in the sermon are actually out there, exterior to the language of the preacher and informing that language with the power of absolute truth in its capacity to name referents. Converts who pray speak their own place in this system of reference, participating in its rhetoric and the "power" it offers by invoking the deity in relation to themselves.

Given his primary topic, Cotton's choice of text appears odd, for it lends itself far more readily to a discourse on the providential history of seventeenth-century England as a new Israel, a common idea in Protestant thought: "And I will poure upon the house of David and upon the Inhabitants of Jerusalem, the Spirit of Grace and of Supplication" (Zech. 12.10). At the end of his sermon Cotton does return to the idea of an elect people, but he begins by interpreting these words in a flagrantly ahistorical way. He effaces prophet, lineage, and Jerusalem by emphasizing the words "grace" and "supplication," ignoring the history in the text to arrive at his topic of prayer. Scriptural narrative recedes as he substitutes the airy *dramatis personae* of the soul's private spiritual life: the deity as "Father," "Son," and the "Lord Jesus," and the convert as a "child of God" (WL1–4). Cotton also fragments the grammatical coherence of the Scripture text in his appropriation of single words and short phrases that are rearranged for the statement of doctrine: "The Spirit of Grace is a Spirit of Supplication" (WL3). He employs the biblical words "spirit of grace" and "supplication," but more for their nominal meaning and acoustic shape than for the logic within the text. Thus the relation of the sermon to Scripture is primarily one of topical and acoustic resemblance, rather than logic. These biblical words reappear throughout his sermon, and as his own speech gradually discloses the meaning he assigns to them, they in turn continually endow his rhetoric with the authority of Scripture. In subsequent sermons "pierced," "mourn," and "bitterness," words that appear in the latter part of Zech. 12.10, serve the same purpose. Interwoven with Cotton's own rhetoric, these acoustic images symbolize the authoritativeness of his sermon.

By invoking and then dismissing the larger social and historical context at the outset as irrelevant, and by violating the grammatical coherence of the text, Cotton destroys what the scholastic exegetes had called the "historical-grammatical sense." The hearer, already deprived of any reference to ordinary life in Boston, is further isolated from alternative frames of reference by Cotton's emphasis on selected words and phrases. The effect of his exegesis is to intensify the immediacy of the social and material situation of his preaching, the relation between the minister and the hearers in St. Botolph's church, for his interpretive exclusions make his own spoken words especially authoritative. In this conceptual vacuum the function of reference can begin to depend indirectly but substantially on signifiers, the material shapes of words as signs. Since the referents are intangible abstractions, and they often are in Cotton's sermons, the hearer is all the more receptive to the interplay of signifiers. In the absence of other material knowledge about these spiritual referents, the sound design of his words becomes the primary sensory evidence that these referents – Father, Son, and child of God – actually exist. The Puritan injunction to hear sermons is in effect an injunction to respond to the material relation of words to each other as acoustic shapes, accepting these words as the material symbols of the deity.

Cotton's most important figural means of persuasion is the scheme of paronomasia. From the Greek *para-* (beside) and *onomazo* (to name), paronomasia is a sequence of words sounding almost alike. A rhetorical scheme of near repetition, paronomasia usually involves complete words. Although Cotton recognizes the conventional definition of this figure, he also defines paronomasia much more broadly in his lectures on Eccles. 1.2: "the repetition of like sounds, yet somewhat differing" (E6). Because he includes letter and syllable repetition as well as patterns of complete words, he subsumes virtually all other verbal schemes in his concept of paronomasia (other schemes merely designate specific patterns such as alliteration). His willingness to extend the idea from words to "like sounds" reflects his own practice of deriving phonic themes of letter and syllable repetition from the scriptural words he selects for his biblical acoustic theme. That is, Cotton interprets the Scripture text acoustically as well as exegetically. By developing phonic themes from biblical words, he provides his rhetoric with an additional, even less cognitive, claim to derivation from Scripture. For example, the statement of doctrine serves as an opening chord announcing the phonic themes of sibilants (/s/-like sounds) and /p/.[14] The following illustration of sound design is quoted in a line form resembling verse with graphics added below the line to indicate some of the acoustic patterns:

> The Spirit of Grace is a Spirit of Supplication.
>
> A spirit of Prayer;
>
> so God describes the spirit he promiseth to give his people:
>
> a spirit of Supplication,
>
> that is,
>
> humble Prayer. [WL3][15]

In its general outline, the acoustic emphasis in this example reflects the topical and argumentative emphasis of the sermon as a whole, the experience of the "spirit" as it leads to articulation in "prayer," a transposition from /s/ to /p/. Following the classical wisdom on the use of figures, not to appear to strain for an effect, the acoustic imagery seems to arise naturally from the *figurae* of the words themselves. The "spirit of grace" and "supplication" readily lend themselves to a theme of sibilants, and Cotton later introduces additional phonic motifs through brief quotations from Scripture.

The web of verbal schemes combines with isocolon (rhythmically complete phrases of approximately equal length) to give greater coherence within each line, and among several lines at once. The isocolon (represented by the verse form) complements syntactic forms, enhancing the grammatical unity. Cotton varies the isocolon, but not indiscriminately, for lines of equivalent length occur in sets of two or three. In the example just given, the pattern of isocolon alternates between long and short lines except for the variation in the fifth line. In general, Cotton adheres to Cicero's advice to create a rhythm that will "move freely, but not wander without restraint."[16] The figures of isocolon and phonic themes of consonant sounds are not the only kinds of figures he uses, but even these verbal schemes involve almost every word.

As Cotton begins to amplify his doctrine, he develops the motif of sibilants, particularly where the words are pivotal to his doctrine. For example, at the end of the first "reason" and the beginning of the second, "spirit of grace" is embedded in a pattern of emphatic repetition:

> so that thus it becomes a spirit of Prayer,
>
> because it so fits us with a sense of our own estates.
>
> This will appeare more especially,
>
> if you adde this second reason;
>
> and it is taken from the estate of the spirit of Grace
>
> in those in whom it is received;
>
> and what is that?
>
> It is a spirit of life in Christ Jesus, Romans 8.2.
>
> the same spirit of which he speaks, verse 15. [WL6]

The sibilants are varied, both in the range of phonetic variation and in the variation of placement within each word, but their general pattern in Cotton's rhetoric is quite regular. They occur about three times in every nine syllables, acting as a motif alluding to the acoustic figures in the initial doctrine.

Cotton maintains an effect of plainness by interweaving a variety of phonic repetitions, so that the effect of each figure is muted by others that cross it. For example, grace

> is freely bestowed on us without any desert of ours,
>
> yea without so much as our desire. [WL4]

Or, as the first reason explains,

> Wheresoever God gives the spirit of Grace,
>
> that heart grows forthwith sensible
>
> of all its former ungraciousnesse.
>
> It is so deeply sensible of that. [WL4–5]

Among the devices Cotton uses are the repetition of "without"; the paired "desert" and "desire"; the /g/ theme of "God," "gives," "grows," and "ungraciousnesse"; and /r/ in nonalliterative positions. The general effect of these verbal patterns is to enhance the assumption of referentiality, the belief that the spirit world is real, because they exaggerate the material coherence of the words: They sound like they have meaning.

Cotton usually introduces a new phonic theme by alliteration (the repetition of a sound at the beginning of words), to emphasize it. He brings out its relation to meaning by varying the figures in coordination with shifts in topics. In the early part of the sermon, in addition to the sibilant theme derived from "spirit," there is also a /g/ theme that is emblematic of what one ought to desire: "God" and his "gracious gift" of "grace" in the "Gospel" (WL1–3). When Cotton broadens the experience of grace to include conviction of sin, it is reflected in the aural pattern:

> as soone as ever the spirit of Grace visits our hearts,
>
> we begin to see that we were borne children of wrath. [WL5]

Just at the point where sibilants have begun to appear inevitable, not there in any meaningful capacity, they yield to a new pattern of /w/ and /b/. Cotton develops /w/ as an aural figure of evil, of "wickednesse," the "world," and the unregenerate "will." The schemes of /b/ are associated with regeneration, "to be reborn." With each systematic variation in the phonic pattern, Cotton strengthens the relation between sound and meaning, between signifiers and referents.

Even if one believes that signifiers are meaningless, they do not sound like it in this rhetoric. Because the acoustic imagery is consistently related to lexical meaning, the aural figures are associated with the ideas expressed and thus appear to bear an intrinsic relation to meaning. Words seem to fall into place, but Cotton achieves this effect because the rhetorical design emphasizes the relation of signifiers to *each other,* not the relation of signifiers to referents. At the same time, the signifiers do not call attention to themselves because these figures do not invite consideration in their own right. The patterns of aural repetition depend on cumulative effect, and a single figure rarely appeals so dramatically to the ear that one would pause to think about it by itself. The sound design seems inadvertent, present more by accident than by intent, but it is just this kind of plainness that a rhetorician strives to create, what Cicero called the "loose but not rambling effect" of "careful negligence."[17] In its general composition, the rhetoric is not as rough or colloquial as we might expect from a plain stylist because Cotton sustains verbal patterns to create an incantatory effect. Cicero advocates only an intermittent use of verbal figures to generate "the concinnity that enlivens [*illuminat*] a group of words."[18] Cotton employs such figures throughout, enlivening his whole rhetoric with a shimmering quality, the tremulous hyperbolic clarity of words that glow faintly with the aura of genuine meaning. The rationale of material coherence, the webbing of isocolon and phonic repetitions, encourages a rhythm of comprehension that tells the mind, through the ear, how to think about a word or phrase relative to other words. By subtly but relentlessly appealing to the ear to tell the "eye of faith" what to "see plainly," the acoustic design gradually makes the function of reference seem unproblematic.

Once Cotton establishes the convergence of phonic patterns and theological topics, he exploits the association to accommodate more complex referents. At the climax of the first reason, he employs another version of the classical *figura,* called a figured controversial theme. In brief, this is an insinuation beyond the stated meaning, a figure "whereby we excite some suspicion to indicate that our meaning is other than our words would seem to imply; but our meaning is not in this case contrary to that which we express, as is the case in *irony,* but rather a hidden meaning which is left to the hearer to discover." It can be used well, Quintilian observes, when it is "unsafe" or "unseemly" to speak "openly."[19]

In Cotton's case, it is theologically unseemly. He appears to preach a belief in the goodness of grace and the evil of Satan, but in the way he interweaves /g/, /w/, and /s/ alliterations he hints at an accompanying act of belief, one that accepts both "Satan" and the "self" who is a "servant of sin" as valued believers. While the alliterations of /g/ and /w/ are firmly opposed, "God" and "*g*race" on the one hand and "*w*ickednesse" on the other, the alliterated /s/ floats ambiguously between the two, oscillating between the /g/ and /w/ alliterations in a variety of schemes that form hesitant linkages with both. Ethically, the /s/-alliterated words are a perplexing mixture: They include "*s*ee," "*s*ervant," "*s*pirit," "*s*ensible," and "*s*oul" – but also "*s*elf," "*s*in," and "*S*atan." Both within the alliterative repetition itself and in the gestures of schematic contextual variation, /s/ accrues a more complicated association. It is less a phonic emblem of the "spirit of grace" as an unmitigated good than a theme connoting the valued reality of the spiritual world, good or evil. Cotton does not confront the ethical ambiguity in the referential meaning. Instead, he gives it shape in the aural design.

The figures of sound convey only a general impression, and one might doubt it was there at all if it were not for a much more explicit statement elsewhere. In his notes on Ecclesiastes Cotton explains the extent to which Satan is distinguishable from what is evil. Atheism, not Satanism, is the ultimate opprobrium. Disbelief in the reality of the spiritual world is the "root of Atheisme, and will make us worse than the devils: For they believe there is a God, and tremble, *James* 2.19" (E188). From this perspective, "Satan" is an estranged ally of the deity, and valued as such. Though evil in an ethical sense, he has ontological value as a referent in the population of the spirit world.

A similar ambiguity informs Cotton's idea of the self, the topical focus of the controversial theme. In conversion, the soule begins to loathe it selfe,

and to abhor it selfe,

and to complaine and confesse its wickednesse before God. [WL5]

The ambiguity of /s/ figures reflects the contradiction in the concept of the "selfe." Wicked and loathesome, it is also saved, for its creation by confession is an act of grace. The appearance of /s/ in ending positions in the final line imitates the way the "soule," the "selfe," is drawn toward the last word, "God," by the act of prayer in the lexical meaning. Prayer to "God" is the correct act of belief that "Satan takes possession of us" whenever the self "wittingly and willingly commits any knowne sinne" (WL5). Thus the self reinterprets its past as well as its present and future within the dichotomy of "God" and "Satan" as referents. Atheism is never a real possibility – it only seems that way to the unconverted.

Cotton's rhetoric indirectly comprehends belief in Satan as a misdirected act of faith, not disbelief, a misunderstanding rather than a rejection of the deity. As he is aware, it is the refusal to believe in his spirit world that fundamentally challenges the referential meaning of his words, rejecting "selfe," "God," and "Satan" altogether. Nonetheless, Cotton does not commit the referential meaning of his words to an exhortation to his hearers to believe in "Satan" or the "selfe." To say that this is not even what he really means is exactly the point. His figured controversial theme gives the material shape of sound to the contradiction of "Satan" as the estranged ally of the deity, to the contradiction of the "selfe" as, at once, loathesome and saved, and to the contradiction of "wickednesse" as simultaneously evil and virtuous. But this does not mean that Cotton's aural figures say something different from his theology, turning the meaning of words as metaphor or irony might be said to do. As Quintilian observes, such figures do not function ironically. They gesture at "hidden" meanings whose hiddenness is part of their meaning.

Cotton's use of acoustic themes appears extremely manipulative if one believes that signifiers are arbitrary, and Puritans often indicated their awareness of this possibility by leveling this charge against their Anglican opponents. They vindicated their own practice by their doctrine of divinely inspired speech. In Cotton's synthesis of religious beliefs and classical rhetoric, figures of speech are not only the shape and form of discourse, they are – as shapes – cognitively significant. The reason that figures of speech are "no vanity" to him derives from his belief that signifiers are meaningful shapes that participate in the semantic dimension of words. In the Christian providential universe, acoustic images are divinely purposeful signs, not arbitrary signs, and however attenuated or oblique their signification as figures might be, there is some intrinsic meaning to be discovered in the relation between the audible figure and the referent. Generalizing from a discussion of Hebrew proper names in Scripture, Cotton explains that words as signs are divinely, and therefore significantly, related to their referents, for "God is not wont to give names to things but according as he findeth them, or purposeth to make them" (E4). The hidden manipulations in the gestures of rhetorical figures may be in the profane world only the sinister and debased practice of conniving rhetoricians, but Puritans argue that these same devices can also be understood as the means by which words gesture beyond their stated meaning to disclose a spiritual, divinely created, hidden meaning. Believing that the original languages of Scripture were a key into the nature of words as significant forms, Cotton understood these significant forms to include the "Holy Ghosts manner of speech" (E7)–hence his lectures on Ecclesiastes and his own use of paronomasia.[20]

In the seventeenth century the belief in purposeful relations between signifiers and referents found a justification not only in religion but also in a natural philosophy of quasi-mystical analogies based on the principle of resemblance. In this philosophy the things of the created world were believed to be related to each other by an intricate web of dynamic analogies. Similitude, emulation, and sympathy were among the more important kinds of resemblance.[21] Cotton does not discuss this philosophy at length, but it appears in his works. For example, it informs his explanation of differences in individual character: "The mind of man, as Philosophers have observed, is somewhat assimilated into the nature of the Object which it studieth, and is conversant about: as Mariners who are conversant about winds, and seas, and storms, are more boysterous. Shepherds and Herds-men more bruitish" (E12). Men come to resemble the qualities of the natural environment in which they work because they are influenced by the analogies that inform the natural world.

As a philosophy of language, belief in mystical resemblances probably depended, at least in part, on the philosophy of Plato's *Cratylus*. In this dialogue Socrates proposes that words are not arbitrary at all but meaningfully, if strangely, related to their referents: "And Cratylus is right in saying that things have names by nature, and that not every man is an artificer of names, but he only who looks to the name which each thing by nature has, and is able to express the true forms of things in letters and syllables." Socrates suggests that the composition of a word "imitates the essence" of the referent it names, and that if words were understood in this way, as natural names, it would be possible to "know how to apply them to what they resemble." The quality of resemblance between the word and its referent provokes a long discussion of various Greek words as he and Cratylus explore the possibilities of hidden resemblances. At the climax of this dialogue, Socrates imagines a continuous perfect linguistic act, beginning from single letters:

> We shall apply letters to the expression of objects, either single letters when required, or several letters, and so we shall form syllables, as they are called, and from syllables make nouns and verbs, and thus, at last, from the combination of nouns and verbs arrive at language, large and fair and whole. And as the painter made a figure, even so shall we make a speech by the art of the namer or the rhetorician.

"Or," he adds, "by some other art." The *Cratylus* concludes with Socrates' expressing considerable skepticism, and not only a skepticism about the rhetorician. He implies that his explorations into the composition and meaning of words may only be an entertaining fancy, a utopian vision of language. Rejecting the idea of a divine namer, he warns that the ancient original namers may simply have been wrong in their knowledge of things, and so he casts doubt on the validity of his ingenious arguments from ancient Greek words. He warns Cratylus that a right knowledge of words does not necessarily constitute a right knowledge of things, that possibly it amounts only to the acquisition of a fundamentally wrong perception of the world.[22] Cotton, however, draws no such conclusions as Socrates. Fully accepting the idea of a divine namer, Cotton interprets Scripture texts as an exemplary use of language, and divinely inspired preaching as a rhetoric that discloses the true meanings of words.

The Cratylist philosophy of significant figures provides an important perspective on the rationale for the plain style in Puritanism. Rhetorical figures must be subdued, not because of any distrust of rhetoric as such but because the gestures of sound design participate in signification. The coherence of a verbal sign is achieved by a sound design that does not call attention to itself at the expense of the other semantic properties of words, for its purpose is to communicate the full significance of the things named by the words. Consequently, the misuse of rhetoric lies in the separation of signifiers from the other properties of words. A manner of speech that calls attention to itself alone is a "vain" use of the material shapes of words, because it forcibly divides the manner and matter of speech, violating the holistic character of the sign as figure. With the subtle figuration of the plain style, however, the rhetorician incorporates the philosophical significance of words as material shapes, revealing the full meaning of his words through his attention to the concinnity of words.

Because Cratylism is concerned with semantics, with the relation between words and referents, it might appear at first to engage issues about the material world exterior to language and the social conditions of language use. But as Socrates warns, and his own meditation on Greek words demonstrates, Cratylism has the opposite effect. It fundamentally concerns the relation of signifiers *to each other,* minimizing or ignoring the relation between words and referents. Since Cratylism asserts that there is a meaningful relation between the signifier and the referent, signifiers by themselves convey knowledge about the referents. Thus a rhetorician can easily conclude that the interplay of signifiers by itself can disclose this knowledge in the absence of referents. It is no accident that the preferred scheme of Cratylist orators was paronomasia, and Cotton's unusually expansive interpretation of this figure is indicative of the profound credence he gives to the *figurae* of speech. His rhetorical strategy at the beginning of the sermon considered here is also Cratylist in that it nullifies consideration of the material world exterior to language, or even the material world portrayed in biblical narrative, focusing cognition on the interplay of acoustic images and the spirit world to which they refer.

The material shapes of signifiers are seductive even to those who do not accept Cratylism, and that, perhaps, was the value of aural design to preachers who sought to persuade the unconverted. One does not need to believe the philosophy or religion that attributes semantic value to signifiers in order to respond to the sensation of coherence apart from the lexical meanings of the words. Once the hearer responds aesthetically to the sound design, the patterns of analogy between sound and meaning draw the hearer on to accept the function of reference in the lexical meaning of the words as well. For Puritans, there can be no appeal to the senses apart from the mind because of "the combination and concatenation of all the faculties of the soul in pure nature, like as links in a chaine; draw one draw all, break one and break all" (E233). Since Cotton assumes the interrelation of faculties within the individual, he believes that the mind, will, and affections can be drawn on to persuasion together if the speaker can capture the attention of the ear. Although Cotton's rhetoric is composed to articulate a referential imperative, to command belief, he rarely uses an imperative in grammatical construction. His preacherly exhortations are almost wholly figural, for he trusts to the figures of his rhetoric to "set forward the end of the discourse, to wit, to affect the heart with the sense of the matter in hand" (E8). The minister's words convey "the sense of the matter" figurally, communicating the imperative of a system of reference that is initiated and sustained by the experience of hearing signifiers.

In the way he combines aural design and theological meaning, Cotton creates a major contradiction in his sermons. When considered as the Puritans considered rhetorical figures, as a dimension of reference, as usable rather than superficial embellishment, sound design exploits the hearer's aesthetic sensibility to promulgate a religion that doctrinally repudiates the intrinsic value of material forms. That is, the means by which the Puritans articulated their otherworldly beliefs was deeply committed to the intrinsic meaning of material, concrete *figurae*. The contradiction in Cotton's sermons generates what Gregory Bateson has termed a double bind situation.[23] A double bind is created when there is a contradiction between a statement in the overt lexical meaning of words and an injunction at a more abstract or formal level of communication. Bateson explains, "Posture, gesture, tone of voice, meaningful action, and the implications concealed in verbal comment may all be used to convey this more abstract message."[24] In Cotton's rhetoric, even as his hearers are being told theologically to turn away from the world, to transcend it and believe in the existence of the spirit world of the deity, they are also being told to respond to and accept the sensible, material world by responding to the physical sounds of his words as audible shapes. In conversion, hearers are bound simultaneously by the otherworldly system of reference in the spiritual meaning and by the materiality of audible shapes that leads them to believe the spiritual message.

Although Bateson implicitly acknowledges that the function of reference is multidimensional, including the level of abstract communication, he privileges the lexical meaning, calling this the "primary injunction" and designating the abstract or formal level as "secondary." However, there is no reason to presume that the overt meaning of words is privileged in communication, especially if the bind is in fact double. In their research on the inducement of hypnotic effects, Milton Erickson and Ernest and Sheila Rossi have proposed an interpretation of the double bind that does not privilege overt lexical meaning. They argue that the abstract, meta-level of communication in a double bind appeals to the unconscious, that it involves a power of suggestion to which the recipient responds involuntarily and without being consciously aware of the conflict between levels of communication. In the double bind, what is stated in the overt communication "is restructured or cast into another system of reference in the metacommunication." Metacommunication invokes an alternate system of reference that serves as a new context for the lexical meaning. The vulnerability of the unconscious to the hypnotic suggestions of metacommunication makes response involuntary. The recipient of a double bind message can be induced to accept an alternate system of reference, recasting lexical meaning, without consciously choosing to do so. Erikson, Rossi, and

Rossi describe metacommunication as a "comment on the primary message," but here they follow Bateson more closely than their own theory warrants. They demonstrate that lexical meaning is not necessarily privileged and that the extent to which metacommunication determines the content of a "message" depends on the circumstances of a particular linguistic event and the cultural values informing it.[25] Metacommunication may not be "secondary" at all, but instead may be the "primary message."

This theory indicates how significant the audible shapes of rhetoric can become for the function of reference, and it brings out the implications of the rhetorician's assumption that all discourse is figural in a material sense. The gestures of verbal schemes are a significant dimension of rhetoric because the abstract designs of sound can be a substantive part of semantics in discourse. The aesthetic forms of words, their acoustic figural construction, can determine in part what the content of a message will be because literal meaning to an important extent is an effect of rhetorical *figurae*. In general, the linguistic values in Puritan theology give substantial weight to metacommunication by attributing it to divine inspiration and insisting on the need to hear sermons. Moreover, the psychological observation that one can respond to the abstract level of communication without choosing to do so (as in hypnosis) is paralleled in the Puritan religious belief that no one could voluntarily choose to become a convert. We need not equate Puritan preaching with hypnotic effects in order to recognize that Puritans believed that conversion was an involuntary experience, induced by the special conditions of sermon rhetoric. Cotton's choice of the Pentecostal sermon as a paradigm for conversion to the "language of Canaan" and his portrayal of conversion as only slightly less than miraculous imply that he granted considerable importance to aspects of communication that we might describe as hypnotic.

By attributing rhetorical figures, and hence all that the preacher says, to the Holy Ghost, Puritan theology denies the presence of the orator as a social being and thus seems to grant no social power whatsoever to the preacher. As Cotton explains it, lay Protestants should think of their ministers as "mere Conduit-pipes" for the Holy Ghost (WL358). The more of a rhetorician Cotton becomes, the more invisible he becomes as orator, for the more it all seems to come from the words themselves and from a deity who uses ministers the way he uses words, as a material vessel in the fallen world through which the order of things, words, and people is redeemed and given expression. The spontaneity of delivery only adds to the sense of Cotton's nonpresence as a speaker, maintaining a basic dogma of Protestant religion, that converts enjoyed a socially unmediated relation to their deity. However, this seemingly egalitarian theology actually asserts a hierarchical, authoritarian relation between the speaker and the hearer.

The theological justification for Puritan rhetoric defines a specific manner of hearing for the listener, one that requires the obedience of the involuntary act of conversion. Theologically, because rhetorical figures are the "Holy Ghost's manner of speech," the mystical communication of semantic value, they need no interpretation from the hearer, only acceptance. If anything, interpretation by the hearer is an offensive act of rebellion and disobedience. To comprehend is to be guided by the acoustic design without question, to accept the words as a "child of God," to "receive" the words and be "obedient to the Word" expressed in the minister's discourse.[26] Rhetorically, whether one considers the effect of sound design to be the Ciceronian illumination of words, an incantatory hypnotic effect, or what one critic has called the "powerful illusion" of Cratylism, this aspect of metacommunication appeals to the hearer on a level of its own irrespective of the lexical meaning of the words.[27] Cotton's discourse is still quite intelligible, of course, but the sound design is prominent enough to generate a contradiction between the abstract designs of material signifiers and the overt meaning of the words as they refer to spiritual life. It is the entire contradiction of the double bind, not just the panoply of spiritual beings, to which the hearer is converted. The contradiction of Cotton's rhetoric, to accept the material patterns of acoustic figures as divine illumination while turning away from the material world as corrupt, is never described as a quality of the rhetoric itself. Rather, the contradiction is displaced onto the converted hearer, whose contradictory, sinful-but-redeemed nature is offered as the rationale for the rhetoric. Cotton's religion justifies this exploitation of the hearer as right, appropriate, and a redemptive act.

Cotton preaches a contradictory relation to the material world not only in his use of acoustic figures but also in his use of metaphors. Puritan religion defined metacommunication far more broadly than Bateson's theory does, for the Puritans included rhetorical figuration such as metaphor in the aspects of speech inspired by the deity.[28] Rhetorically, the second "reason" in Cotton's sermon is devoted to the interpretation of metaphor, and his use of this trope leads to the dramatic climax of the sermon. He represents the conversion, or turning, of the soul by the metaphor of a newborn child, turning the literal meaning of words denoting people and things in the observable world to represent the theological idea of spiritual regeneration. The hearer accomplishes initiation into the spiritual life portrayed by understanding the metaphor that describes it.

To persuade the hearer to accept the interpretation of metaphor he offers, Cotton continues to rely on sound design. The banality of the image and the increasing intensity of acoustic figures in the second reason suggest that metaphor was something of a threat, that meaning needed to be carefully turned to produce conversion. In the steady crescendo of closely structured periods, the schemes of transverse repetition, and chiasmic reversals, Cotton guides the hearer's understanding of the image he introduces:

> yet such a spirit of *life*, as is an imperfect *life*, a weak *life*,
>
> as of a child new borne, true *life*, but very weak,
>
> being pained and bruised in the birth, it cryes out bitterly;
>
> so a new borne babe in Christ,
>
> as soone as it hath received the spirit of Grace,
>
> it feeles it selfe in a cold and naked condition,
>
> and thereupon feels its own weaknesse and hunger. [WL6]

The schemes of /b/ in the second, third, and fourth lines announce the image but they also enclose it, confining the impact of a visual image that proves to be scarcely more than a glimpse. As "child" modulates to the abstract subject "it," the phonic theme of /b/ modulates to /k/ in an analogous aural design. The two phonic themes are interwoven in lines 3 and 4, where an inversion occurs. The phonic order of "cryes out bitterly" is reversed in "babe in Christ," a reversal that marks the turn from literal to figurative meaning. After line 4, /b/ is dropped and /k/ becomes dominant as the visual image of the child recedes, and the figure operates as a metaphor for the dilemma of the regenerate soul.

The metaphor continues in another circular period with more complex schemes of transverse repetition employing slanted rhyme:

> An imperfect *life* strongly desires reliefe,
>
> and if it be afflicted with any sense of death,
>
> it will exceedingly struggle and strive, and wring every way,
>
> if it be possible, to preserve the *life*. [WL6]

The word "life," which begins and closes the period, is joined together with the phonic theme of /r/ in the word "reliefe" at the end of the first line, emphasizing what conversion promises. Together, these acoustic themes predominate over the ominous undertone of another theme implied by the aural likeness of "strongly desires" and "sense of death." The theme of /r/ is omitted only from the second line; it appears twice in "strongly desires" and not at all in "sense of death." The last phrase, "preserve the life," conjoins the main phonic themes of the period, /p/, sibilants, /r/, /v/, /l/, and /f/, omitting /d/ in the assertion of the victory of life over death.

In the midst of these carefully woven phonic patterns, Cotton briefly alludes to the visual image in the third line, "struggle and strive" and "wring every way," to emphasize a sense of conflict, but the culminating moment of anguish gives way to an abstract closure, the preservation of a figured, spiritual life. When Cotton amplifies the last phrase, "to preserve the life," the metaphor as visual image becomes even more vague and the religious conflict it represents becomes the focus:

> so we no sooner receive a spirit of Grace,
> but we find our selves compassed about with a body of death,
>   Romans 7.24.
> Now all *life* when it is compassed about with *death,*
> it will so strive to preserve it self,
> that you would think the *dying* man to be the most *lively.* [WL6]

The period turns on a chiasmic reversal (life/death/dying/lively), circumscribing the central phrase, "to preserve it self." Cotton implies a radical inversion of the ordinary sense of life and death, an inversion produced by belief in his figurative meaning. The primary life-and-death conflict of the "self" is spiritual, figurative and not literal.

Finally, the dualism of the convert's experience is brought out fully with repeated antitheses that are emphasized by contrasting sounds in the vowels and consonants of opposing words:

> So there is no Christian soul that receives a spirit of Grace,
> but finds it selfe compassed about with enemies,
> the flesh lusting *against* the spirit,
> so as there is a great strife in him, Galatians 5.17.
> Faith strives *against* doubting, his heart being changed;
> his heat and zeal *against* coldnesse;
> humility and meeknesse *against* pride and wrath;
> and thus he strives earnestly for the preservation of his life. [WL6–7]

"Compassed" by these weighty antitheses, the "soul" is firmly locked into the oppositions of its new subjectivity. The rhetorical design of hyperbolic antitheses implies an authoritative closure, a catechistic finality to the concept of the "selfe" in conflict.

The concluding use of the image occurs in the periodic sentence that is the climactic midpoint of the discourse:

> Now then you shall need no more to make a Prayer;
> for if once a man grow to be sensible of his own weaknesse,
> he hath matter enough to complaine of to God and himselfe,
> he sees what he stands in need of,
> he wants faith, and a soft heart, an humble spirit, and zeale for Gods
>   glory;
> *now he wants every thing;*

> so as (that I may so speak)
> he can tell God stories of his misery,
> and that with some earnestnesse, and heartinesse,
> as a man struggling for his life;
> can now plead for any thing that might make him live in Gods sight,
> and the Spirit teacheth us all this. [WL7]

"Now" that the rhetoric has created the right kinds of "wants," it leads to spontaneous prayer: "he hath matter enough to complaine of" expressed in autobiographical "stories of his misery" addressed "to God and himselfe." The pun expressing both lack and desire, "now he *wants* everything," is the focus of the period and the turning point of the entire sermon, the center of the rhetorical experience of grace.[29] It marks the transfer of meaning from the literal child in the image to the figurative child, the self.

But is it all as evident as the aural design implies? To be guided by the sound design is to follow the figurative usage of the image in its portrayal of the soul's life, and consequently to lose sight of the mental image *qua* image. The sermon invites the hearer, the "self," to ignore how this use of metaphor makes contradictory claims on the literal meaning in the content of the image. The metaphor describes a child who in the visual image struggles to gratify the wants of the flesh to preserve its natural, physical life. At the same time, it also refers to the spiritual "child," the newly regenerate "self" who struggles to repudiate the wants of the flesh, its "enemies" in the antithetical conflict of the "flesh lusting against the spirit." The main function of this metaphor is brought out in the pun on "wants." Whereas the sense of the lack of virtue depends on the concept of the soul as fundamentally sinful, the implication that the self's desires are entitled to gratification depends on the logic of the initial image, the incontrovertible needs of the cold and hungry child.

Metaphor is often described as turning the meaning of a word from a literal to a figurative sense. What distinguishes Cotton's use of metaphor, as he hints by the repeated gestures of acoustic reversals and antitheses, is a particular kind of turn, one that sets the figurative meaning against the literal. Metaphor need not contradict in its figurative sense what is described in the visual image, but it does here. Cotton's use of metaphor is itself an example of the "flesh lusting against the spirit" because the intelligibility of the figurative meaning depends on the validity of the literal. That is, the a priori understanding of the natural child's struggle is the means of conceptualizing the spiritual "child's" struggle. In reasoning from what is known to explain what is unknown, the metaphor assumes and therefore affirms the validity of the literal meaning it asserts. At the same time, the religious, figurative meaning repudiates the validity of the literal meaning in the image. Thus the figurative sense is yoked in conflict with the literal: It cannot get along with it and it cannot get along without it. By relying on the image to make the spiritual life intelligible, Cotton simultaneously validates and repudiates its literal significance. Thus his use of metaphor generates the double bind that he then proceeds to lament as a condition of the hearer, not the rhetoric.

This contradiction is exactly what characterizes the religious "life" of the convert: "We no sooner receive a spirit of Grace, but we find our selves compassed about with a body of death." The material and social world, including the convert's own participation in this world, becomes a "body of death," for belief in the reality of the spiritual world generates an antagonism between the spiritual sense of figures and the literal sense on which they depend for their intelligibility. In effect, the hearer is told to accept the contradiction in the rhetoric as a given, as axiomatic, and think only about its consequences for the divided "self" that is generated by it, expressing these thoughts in an autobiographical narrative of confessional prayer.

The social ideas informing Cotton's metaphors become more apparent if we consider them in light of Quintilian's theory of metaphor. In Quintilian's narrowest definition, metaphor is a trope "designed to move the feelings, give special distinction to things and place them vividly before the eye."[30] He is more expansive, however, when he considers metaphor from a social perspective. Metaphor is not so much a question of literal and figurative meaning, although it may be reduced to this, as it is a case of proper and transferred usage. In a metaphor "a noun or a verb is transferred from the place [*loco*] to which it properly belongs to another where there is either no proper [*proprium*] term or the *transferred* [*translatum*] is better than the proper [*proprio*]."[31] The proper, conventional meaning of a word is its ordinary social usage, what Quintilian calls its "natural and principal signification [*a naturali et principali significatione*]."[32] In its metaphoric usage, a word is taken out of its usual place, its social domain of ordinary signification, and used in another domain (thus the English phrase "borrowed speech").[33] Quintilian's willingness to assert a "natural" signification implies a solidity and stability in proper signification that the use of metaphor enhances. Because a metaphor draws attention to the transferred meaning, not the locus from which the image is borrowed, metaphor implies that one can more or less take for granted the proper signification of the words that compose the mental image. Thus metaphor indirectly asserts a stable social consensus about proper meaning, agreement that words adequately represent referents in the domain of discourse from which the metaphor is derived. Since it is a temporary borrowing, and since a good metaphor should "shine forth" in discourse, it also validates proper usage by calling attention to its own impropriety as such.[34]

What Quintilian considers secondary in his discussion of metaphor, the stability of proper meaning, becomes major in Cotton's rhetoric. Taking full advantage of the structure of metaphor, Cotton exploits the concept of assumed propriety in metaphor to preach consensus on social conduct through imagery. By using social behavior as a source of metaphor, he indirectly defines what kind of social behavior is proper, what social meanings can be taken for granted. Moreover, when a metaphor describes social conduct, the contradiction between proper and figurative meaning it asserts fuels the convert's perception of sin. For example, Cotton exhorts the hearer to imitate the Father as well as the Son, calling attention to his metaphoric descriptions of the deity as a patriarch (WL4).

In another sermon, when he tells converts to "run to God as our heavenly Father," he elaborates an image of how this "Father," the deity, will treat the convert:

> God will ponder all the petitions of your soules, and weigh well what you have said, and he knowes what you aime at in asking this, and that blessing: and though he may seeme to deferre it, he better knowes your need of it, then your selves doe, and when he seemes most to crosse it, then doth he most abundantly answer it.[35]

The proper meaning asserted in the image presents an ideal view of a father's superior knowledge, judgment, and prerogatives, an implicit injunction about how fathers ought to act and how they should be deferentially treated by those who must "run" to them for what they "need." The force of exhortation lies in the discrepancy between rhetoric and theology. Cotton's theology supposes a sinful and corrupt hearer who is quite possibly a father himself. The convert who is a father need only appraise the difference between the social content of the image and his own behavior to discover the measure of his sins. Cotton does not exhort the hearer to make this connection between metaphor and behavior, but he does not need to, for the rhetoric requires it. To believe that the deity is the ideal father portrayed is simultaneously to attribute proper signification to the social image of the father that describes the deity. In effect, Cotton preaches proper and figurative meaning at the same time, creating the insinuation that Puritan fathers actually should be this social ideal, and that other members of a household should treat them as if they actually were as the image describes them. Because the metaphor asserts a proper meaning in which the function of reference is assumed to be descriptive, stating what already is rather than what ought to be, the prescriptive force of the image lies in the preacher's refusal to acknowlege the difference between the image and the human reality, except in the religious idiom of sin. That is, since Cotton's rhetoric assumes that the proper meaning is literal, what difference there is in social reality becomes the convert's burden of sin. The grander the attributes of the deity, the greater the sin and the more need for sermons and prayers that affirm the authority of the cleric.

In other sermons Cotton himself occasionally takes account of the proper as well as the transferred meaning in his metaphoric tropes, overtly recognizing the descriptive value of his social analogies. For example, he develops the traditional metaphor of marriage to describe the relation between Christ and church members, who are spiritual "spouses to Christ." He proposes that one "use" of his sermon is "to allow the lawfull use of gladnesse and mirth in dayes of marriage and espousals; for from hence is the similitude fetched."[36] Although the sermon is almost entirely concerned with transferred meaning, Cotton also preaches in conclusion on the proper meaning of the image. Developing the same metaphor of the Puritan woman's role in another sermon, Cotton advances the doctrine that churches should "propagate" other churches, and that "private converts" should also "seek the conversion of others," because this is the "conjugal duty of a church" to Christ. Among his "reasons," Cotton gives the following: "It is the most conjugal duty of a wife to be fruitful to her husband in breeding and bringing forth children to him."[37] The imperative that women bear children as a "duty" to their husbands is not his main doctrine, but because the metaphor is the logical basis of the theology, social injunctions such as these are intrinsic to his religion. Acknowledging the proper as well as the transferred significance of his social imagery, he preaches literal "conjugal duties" as well as figurative ones.

While Cotton's acknowledged social analogies carry substantial weight as religious exhortations, he is most dogmatic where he is most oblique. Preaching an idea overtly implies a sense of contingency, a need to persuade. The use of metaphor, however, asserts that persuading is not necessary, for the figure is understood to rely on already accepted conventions. Cotton thus indirectly defines social consensus by his choice of metaphors even more strongly than by his analogies, co-opting the collective agreement implied by consensus. He often introduces an image as an analogy and then develops it as a metaphor, just as he does with the image of the newborn child in the first sermon, where he shifts from simile to metaphor when he moves toward the dramatic climax of the sermon. Thus, although the imagery of ordinary life in his sermons may seem inconsequential, it is the primary means by which he sanctions social behavior. Cotton rarely preaches overtly about ordinary social conduct in *The Way of Life,* and it would be extremely difficult to reconstruct daily life in Boston, Lincolnshire, from the doctrines of his sermons, but the topic continually appears where it is most prescriptive, in the social content of his imagery describing the soul. When social behavior is consigned to metaphor, Cotton need never address, much less defend, the kinds of social conduct he preaches. Like the sound design of his sermons, his images are exempted from inquiry, protected from critical thought by the act of belief.

Cotton's metaphors seem to be poorly chosen considering Quintilian's dictum that a good metaphor should "shine forth," proclaiming its figurativeness. Like other Puritans, Cotton makes frequent use of metaphors that describe family roles, and his images often seem banal from an aesthetic point of view.[38] The most ready explanation, of course, is that Puritans wished their metaphors to be useful much more than they wished them to be aesthetic. And useful they are. In the figures of the deity as a father or son, the church as a mother or wife, and the convert as a child, servant, or wife, the imagery represents the ascribed roles of Puritan households, the dimensions of power and obligation in family relationships. Because these figures, drawn ostensibly from ordinary social reality, assert a simple and unproblematic function of reference in their proper meaning, they have a quality of plainness about them in unobtrusively announcing an equivalence between sign and referent, a plainness that proves to be strongly exhortative precisely because the imagery does not shine forth. Rather, it constrains the imagination of the hearer to the social values portrayed. When Cotton says, for example, "Is it not apparent that that servant hath provoked his Master very deeply?" (WL195), attention is easily drawn to the spiritual conflict between the offending convert and the irate deity because there is a ready assumption that the situation of a servant who offends a master is familiar to everyone from social experience. Hearers are not asked to contemplate the social and economic complexities of relationships between masters and servants. Through the use of metaphor, they are invited not to. The banality of these images strengthens the assertion of a straightforward function of reference in the literal meaning, thereby strengthening the force of the referential imperative in sanctioning particular kinds of social behavior. The aesthetic imagination is not just aesthetic, as the Puritan polemics on the plain style suggest, for metaphors that shine forth do something more than provide amusing novelty: They threaten the social conservatism of the sermon rhetoric.

How, then, do these dull metaphors establish the discrete categories of proper and transferred loci? And how is Cotton able to bring attention to spiritual life if the metaphor does not transport the imagination to the transferred meaning? Puritan metaphor seems never quite to make the leap that Quintilian advocates, and yet the capacity to fix signification depends on the differentiation of proper and transferred meaning. Puritanism achieves this differentiation in part by following traditional hermeneutics in its transfer of the whole concept of propriety to spiritual meaning, inverting the classical frame of reference. Cotton's use of metaphor, like the tropological sense of Christian theology in general, reinterprets the concept of proper meaning in classical metaphor to conform with religious idealism. To be converted is to reverse one's notion of proper meaning, to believe that the spiritual sense is normative and that socially constituted proper meaning is derivative. Theology consistently treats metaphor as directly appropriate, and not borrowed in the sense of derivative or transferred. Insofar as religious idealism successfully inverts the criterion of appropriateness, metaphor becomes a rhetorical expression of the Christian's alienation from life in the secular world. The spiritual meaning of metaphor conveys an eerie sense of alienation from the material and social world because it posits ordinary proper meaning in the context of its rejection. It is the antagonism, the contradiction of a transferred meaning logically turned against the proper, that establishes the necessary difference and distance between domains of signification.

The Protestant commitment to live in the world as well as transcend it, articulated in the metaphors of the soul's life, extends religious sanction to secular life, and thereby recasts the significance of social conduct. Cotton acknowledges in later sermons of *The Way of Life* that "it is a double life which we live in this world" (WL284). Puritanism sanctions not only the soul's interior "spirituall life" but also "the outward and temporall life . . . which wee live in the flesh." The latter includes the whole of the Puritan's ordinary secular life, "that whereby we live, as members of this or that City, or Town, or Commonwealth, in this or that particular vocation and calling," and "that, by which we doe live this bodily life, I meane, by which we live a life of sense, by which we eate and drinke, by which we goe through all conditions, from our birth to our grave, by which we live, and move, and have our being" (WL284, 436). The double bind is thus expressed theologically in the Puritan "double life." Its dualism corresponds to the transferred, figured meaning of "spirituall life," on the one hand, and to the domains of ordinary signification from which images are drawn, on the other.

In effect, Cotton sanctions a double standard of proper meaning, expressed most concisely in the first sermon by the pun at the center of his discourse. The "wants" of the convert are the cognitive turning point where spiritual and literal meaning meet. As the unification of radically different and still distinguishable meanings in a single concrete symbol, the pun does not privilege either of the meanings it expresses. Different meanings not only share a single signifier, the same acoustic shape; they also share the single usage of a single signifier, collapsing time, place, speaker, circumstance, all the usual criteria of differentiation in classical appropriateness. In the pun the argument from the acoustic shape of the words reaches its greatest intensity, for it is the shape of the signifier that asserts that two contradictory concepts of proper meaning can be acknowledged simultaneously. Rhetorically, the pun structures the way in which spiritual and ordinary propriety collide in the polarized "self" of the Puritan convert, who must live both a "spirituall life" of the soul and an "outward and temporall life" at the same time.

The simultaneous generation of proper and transferred meaning, in which both meanings are sanctioned, implies a concept of metaphor that differs from Quintilian's basic idea of tropes as a transfer of meaning from one locus of discourse to another.[39] Recall that Cotton selects hyperbole, not metaphor, to characterize sermon rhetoric in his lectures on Ecclesiastes. To understand the significance of Cotton's liking for hyperbole, we need to delve further into Quintilian's theory of tropes. Quintilian's theory tends toward the metaphoric mode, so much so that he is able to distinguish metaphor and trope only by interpreting metaphor as a trope specifically intended to summon a vivid mental image. His basic concept of a trope is a more general definition of metaphor that omits the characteristic of the visual image and emphasizes the idea of substitutive discontinuity between two "places" (loci) of discourse. Quintilian explains briefly, "By a *trope* is meant the virtuous alteration [*cum virtute mutatio*] of a word or phrase from its proper meaning to another," and more expansively:

> The name of trope is applied to the transference of expressions from their natural and principal signification to another, with a view to the embellishment of style or, as the majority of grammarians define it, the transference of words and phrases from the place which is strictly theirs to another to which they do not properly belong.[40]

Whether one understands the idea as the substitution of one word for another or one context for another, the metaphoric mode asserts, by substitution, a discontinuity between a word and its contexts, and between proper and transferred meaning. It cultivates a recognition of discrete domains of signification, two different "places" of word usage, in asserting that the transferred usage is not the proper meaning but something else that has been substituted for it.

Since metaphor focuses on the transferred rather than the proper meaning, the way in which literal meaning could be considered figural is obscured. It is just this issue that hyperbole addresses. Among the tropes Quintilian discusses, hyperbole appears the least amenable to his metaphoric concept of proper meaning.[41] Hyperbole calls attention to the socially variable quality of proper meaning by challenging assumptions about fixed appropriate usage. Where metaphor assumes that propriety is fixed and objective, the stable measure against which one can contrast and recognize the variability of transferred meaning, hyperbole depends on the ways in which propriety is socially variable, and thus hyperbole readily lends itself to the idea that all discourse, even literal meaning, is figural. In the use of hyperbole, literal meaning is something that can be exaggerated or diminished, stretched, bent, and so on. Hyperbole demonstrates the ways in which proper meaning, including literal meaning, is not fixed but changeable, and (Quintilian worries) it exploits social difficulties of distinguishing between the loci of proper and transferred usage. The exaggerations of hyperbole depend on the oscillations of proper signification and often do not distinguish literal from figurative meaning, do not announce the substitution of another, figurative sense in place of a literal meaning. Indeed, the successful hyperbole often depends on an incapacity to distinguish proper and transferred usage. Hyperbole demonstrates how much lexical meaning depends on social consensus, however achieved, for its stability and its capacity to name the actual things in the referential world convincingly and persuasively. If proper meaning is socially determined, it is also socially variable and, potentially at least, no more fixed or objective than transferred meaning. Thus, whereas metaphor tends to minimize the problematic aspects of proper signification, hyperbole focuses quite directly on its instability.

Hyperbole suggests a concept of appropriateness quite different from that of metaphor because the pliability of a proper meaning occurs in the same place, positing a single locus, rather than two separate domains of discourse. In exaggeration, proper and figurative meaning are not distinguishable as discrete categories, and thus hyperbole challenges what the locus of proper meaning is and how it is determined. The questions about propriety emphasize the social conditions of the use of words – the speaker and hearer in a particular social situation confronting uncertain expectations about the constraints of proper usage. From the perspective of the hyperbolic concept of appropriateness, it seems naive to accept what the metaphoric mode assumes, that literal meaning is objective, fixed, or stable, or discontinuous with figurative meaning. Rather, it is the *use* of metaphor that *creates* the distinction for which the metaphoric mode claims a prior existence. A use of metaphor simultaneously declares a literal as well as a figurative meaning and a discontinuity between the two that defines the domains of signification for each. Thus the hyperbolic mode suggests a combinatory concept of metaphor rather than a substitutive one: Metaphor is a trope that fixes literal meaning by using that meaning figuratively. The polarization of literal and figurative meaning generated by metaphor is a single figure, a single verbal act expressing dualism, when understood from the perspective of the hyperbolic mode.

The fact that Cotton singles out hyperbole in his lectures on Ecclesiastes suggests the importance of the hyperbolic mode for his own rhetoric. In *The Way of Life* his use of metaphor is essentially hyperbolic, and his doctrine similarly reflects the priority of the hyperbolic mode. By preaching that social mores must be spiritually determined, he preaches the need for belief in the transferred spiritual meaning to guarantee the fixity of proper signification. Social consensus, he warns, is extremely unstable, for although Puritans are not opposed to "legall rights," he argues that "the Lawes of men" are not enough to secure ordinary life for the convert, "unlesse we *claime* it by some Evangelicall right" (WL452). "A Christian man looks for a *Christian right to his civill blessings*," and a convert needs this right to "*receive and enjoy* an estate of prosperity" (WL542, 453). His interpretation of the secular world implies that proper meaning is precarious and fragile, so much so that ordinary life must be lived "by faith" (WL437), guaranteed by the absolute power of the deity. The social agreement implied by "natural and principal signification" is not enough for the Puritan. Only the proper meaning that is generated simultaneously with transferred meaning is stable.

To put it another way, Cotton invokes spiritual authority to make ordinary life safe for Puritans. He treats instability as a condition exterior to his rhetoric, but his own words do much to create and sustain belief in chronic instability. He creates uncertainty about proper meaning to return it to the convert in the metaphoric form of a fixed literal meaning, a referential imperative whose stability depends on a conceptual polarity created by the metaphors of the soul. The minister renders social meaning uncertain by making it contingent on the theology of the soul, and simultaneously gives it a new kind of certainty, that of divine authority. Once the hearer grants reality to the system of reference in the minister's discourse, the convert receives both the anxieties of unstable meaning that make him dependent on the rhetoric and the belief that the secular way of life described in the imagery is a privileged existence. If Puritans must have an "Evangelicall right" to ordinary life, then, once acquired, this right potentially frees them from uncertain criteria like "the Lawes of men." Since their own secular way of life is guaranteed by the figurative language of salvation, the sinful convert's plea for grace is simultaneously an affirmation of belief in the absolute superiority of Puritan mores.[42] Thus the supposed transcendance of conversion merely leads the Puritans back to the "natural life" they already live.

Ethically, conversion is made an absurdity because the concept of propriety sanctioned by the figurative language is the rhetorician's idea of social convention. Proper meaning in rhetoric is not, as Cicero takes care to point out, an ethical idea. It concerns what is customary, decorous, or appropriate.[43] Cotton's sermons make a religious virtue of social conventions, using the spiritual sense to preach proper signification in the social world with divine authority. Cotton specifically rejects the notion that ethics, casuistry, or moral reform has anything to do with conversion. His social imagination on this point extends no further than individual acts of "lust" such as drunkenness, adultery, and "whoredome," but even these are irrelevant to conversion (WL24, 301). Although he believes that converts refrain from the "life of lust," refraining does not constitute conversion. At one point he sardonically suggests that if moral reform is all that people expect from religion, they ought to restore the Old Testament sacraments, for the reform of immoral behavior such as cursing or lying would come about much more quickly "if it were to cost us a sheep or a lamb" (WL34). He preaches at length on the difference between the "conscience" and the "heart," but only to declare that conscience is irrelevant to conversion (WL140–49).

From the perspective of social values and behavior, nothing happens in conversion, and that is the point. Conversion is a conversion to a way of thinking, not a conversion to different social behavior, except for the verbal rituals of prayer and church ordinances. In the "life we live in the flesh" (WL289) the lives of the regenerate and the unregenerate are so much alike that they are indistinguishable:

> It is first a reproofe to all the sons of men, that have not yet attained to this grace of faith; let a man be never so lively in the life of sense, that he can relish his meate and drinke, and sleepe, and walke, and talke, &c. yet all the actions of his life, without the life of faith, is but a dead life; when a man is most lively in the life of sense, it is but the action of a dying man; let a man live the life of reason, and so as that he can discourse never so wisely and judiciously, and that he can converse with all sorts of men, and transact businesses in great dexterity, yet it is but a dead life. [WL301]

Cotton's criticism of the unregenerate concerns not what they do, or even what they value in the world, but the "dead" lack of faith with which they do it. He inveighs against the unregenerate "life of sense and reason, and carnall wisdome" (WL480), of "living to a mans *owne wisdome and reason*" (WL269), because it is a life that is lived without the intervening rhetoric of the soul.

At the conclusion of his first sermon in *The Way of Life,* Cotton indicates how much his cultural elitism depends sheerly on the physical characteristics of words to compel belief. Disdaining arguments from ethics or social behavior, he appeals to the acoustic resemblance at the level of signifiers to attribute quasi-divine authority to the prayers of converts. His rhetoric is structured not by logic but by the phonic theme of /p/ and paronomasia, cognitively joining words that merely sound alike. The "*spirit* of Grace," through "*pleading*" to the deity, "leads us on to a *spirit* of *power*" in "*prayer*" with a "*purpose*." To make it "more *plaine*," Cotton reiterates that the ability to pray is "a *spirit* of *power*" and that "the *Spirit* of God is a *spirit* of *power*" (WL9). Following a reference to "Gods *people*," Cotton adds the "*promise*" of the deity to his verbal theme, warning converts to have a "*patient eare*" for the re*proofe*" of the deity through the words of the sermon, for "then the *promise* is evident, I will *poure* out my *spirit* u*pon* you" (WL12).

The acoustic resemblance of "power" and "poure" becomes the focus of Cotton's rhetoric as the "spirit of supplication" is again transmuted into a "spirit of power":

It may serve to teach those that have received the spirit of Grace,

how to maintaine and keep alive the spirit of Prayer,

for we have daily need of praying,

and of making supplication,

of earnest prayer,

humble and hearty prayer,

what for our friends, our enemies, our children, servants, brethren,

Churches abroad, Kingdomes we live in,

we shall be able to *poure out* supplication to God in behalfe of them all,

if he *poure upon* us a spirit of Grace. [WL13]

The paronomasia culminates in the twice-quoted biblical *figura* of "poure" as acoustic figure and metaphor coincide to divulge the source and the means of the "spirit of power."[44] The deity who will "poure out" in Prov. 1.23 and who will "pour upon" in Zech. 12.10 here shares this biblical acoustic image with the elect who "poure out" their prayers. The phonic theme of /p/ is omitted only from the expansive clause of lines 7–8 where Cotton enumerates "them," the numerous unconverted.

Because the metaphor from the biblical text does not commit Cotton to any particular theological or historical idea, he is free to give this acoustic figure whatever meaning he chooses through the associations of paronomasia. Implicitly, the prayers of converts are a priestly intercession "in behalfe of them all" – friends, enemies, servants, children, England, and churches outside England. Exploiting the oscillations of the hyperbolic mode, Cotton rhetorically associates the elect with the divine power of salvation. Although he does not actually attribute this power to them theologically, he makes the locus of spiritual authority ambiguous through the use of acoustic imagery. Paronomasia renders the locus of propriety unclear because, without negating the point of departure, the chain of acoustic figures ultimately arrives somewhere else. Once Cotton establishes the scriptural locus of an acoustic figure, he can modify its shape and connect it to his own discourse without relinquishing the sanction of the biblical locus of meaning. Juxtaposing one acoustic figure with another, his verbal schemes gradually shift the locus of propriety by diffusing a sense of place, rather than marking any distinct change between one figure and the next as metaphor does. The Puritans are not the deity, but they have a mystical communion with the deity that gives them peculiar access to sacred "power." It is "poured out" on them more abundantly than on others through the divinely inspired mutations of paronomasia. If Puritan elitism seems arbitrary, it is, and the arbitrary claim to the power of salvation is nowhere more clearly expressed than in the muddled figures of paronomasia.

Cotton's religious belief in Puritan social conventions is most apparent in the farewell sermon he delivered at Southampton in 1630 to the first emigrants of the Massachusetts Bay Company departing for New England. A manifesto for the new colony, the sermon was published in London shortly afterward as *Gods Promise to His Plantation*.[45] Although contemporaneous with *The Way of Life,* the Southampton sermon seems radically different because many of the referents of his words are worldly rather than spiritual: merchants, colonists, the Massachusetts Bay Company, the New England territory, and the economic conditions of England and New England. Although Cotton reminds his hearers that they may reap the benefits of the "land of Canaan" only if they are converted, "in Christ" (G6), for the most part social behavior is here presented directly, without the intervening structure of metaphor and the tension of the double bind that generates a sense of sin in

The Way of Life. The result is a sweeping approbation of the economic and social values of the emigrants.

The inanity of Cotton's reasoning is the effect of absolute belief in Puritan propriety undisguised and untroubled by self-contradiction.[46] He uses the same rhetorical devices as before, but their arbitrariness and speciousness are far more obvious. Again, Cotton depends first and foremost on the *figurae* of rhetoric to argue his case for the Puritans as an elect people. The text for the sermon is 2 Sam. 7.10, *"Moreover I will appoint a place for my people Israell, and I will plant them, that they may dwell in a place of their owne, and move no more"* (G1). The sermon is a discourse on planting that ranges across an impressive variety of literal and figurative meanings, held together by little more than the chain of paronomasia in /plant, planted, plantation/. Variations of /plant/ develop in a slow crescendo toward the concluding section on the superiority of the Puritan church. To move is to "transplant," to "plant a Colony" is a good reason to move, and a person may "transplant himselfe," if providence allows, to "such Plantations" (G8–9, 11). He distinguishes between other "severall plantations" and "Gods plantation," and includes a digression on a literal "plant" to amplify the deity's words as a metaphor elaborating what it means to "plant a people" (G13–14). He warns that others have been "planted before" unsuccessfully, and that to survive it is necessary to engage in "planting the Ordinances of God," because the deity "plants us when hee gives us roote in Christ" – conversion – in order to "plant us in his holy sanctuary" (G15). Cotton exhorts his hearers to "have speciall care that you ever have the Ordinances planted among you," for the deity's Scripture has revealed that "every plantation that he hath not planted shall be plucked up." Thus he charges "all that are planted at home, or intend to plant abroad, to looke well to your plantation" (G16–17). Finally, converts themselves are "plants" who must take religious care of their children, "the plants that spring from you" (G19). He introduces widely different meanings of planting that blend a variety of literal and figurative significations: planting the Israelites in Canaan, planting the soul in Christ and in the church, planting the church in New England, planting progeny, and, finally, planting the settlement as an economic enterprise, one in which planting in the ordinary literal sense will be necessary.

Although typological analogies between the history of Israel and the history of the Puritans inform the rationale of *Gods Promise,* these historical analogies are plausible to Cotton because of an argument that is acoustic rather than historical or moral. Cotton depends on paronomasia, the analogies of audible shapes, to disclose the analogies among people and events. Unlike typological *figurae,* the acoustic chains of paronomasia do not imply a progressive sequence of figures, and the absence of progression accounts for the strangely ahistorical quality of this sermon. Israel and New England seem oddly contemporaneous because the scheme of paronomasia renders insignificant the intervening time and distance through the figural analogies of words. The continuous reappearance of /plant/ gradually blurs the geographical, social, and historical differences among people. Israelites, Englishmen, and American emigrants blend together in the indeterminacy of locus that paronomasia creates, diffusing the sacredness of Scripture to sanction the Puritan secular enterprise in New England, the "land of Canaan" (G6).

Cotton has pretensions to casuistry when he considers reasons for emigration, but his "reasons" merely describe the social values of converts. The "procurement" of "good things," for example, forms an entire category of viable "reasons" for emigration (G8–10). Almost any reason is a good reason to go, and one is reminded of Franklin's quip, "So convenient a thing it is to be a *reasonable Creature,* since it enables one to find or make a Reason for every thing one has a mind to do."[47] Cotton demonstrates his awareness of the figural sanction of social behavior when he approves that "some remove and travaile for merchandize and gain-sake," attributing this reason for emigration to a rhetorical figure in a parable: "Yea our Saviour approveth travaile for Merchants. *Matth.* 13.45, 46 when hee compareth a Christian to a Merchantman seeking pearles: For he never fetcheth a comparison from any unlawfull thing to illustrate a thing lawfull" (G8). Since figurative expressions are never drawn from "any unlawfull thing," he argues, the images of metaphor in spiritual discourse are prescriptive. Thus Puritan merchants may seek anything of value in New England with the assurance that they are enacting a sacred image. The general rule Cotton supplies describes the structure of meaning in his own sermons on the soul's life, but his choice of a biblical image here deflects attention away from the rhetorical figures of his own discourse. As he flaunts the absurdity of his exegetical reasoning, he protects his actual means of persuasion from direct analysis.

The concluding exhortation to the emigrants unabashedly displays the Puritans' sense of values in its anticipation of the cultural exchange that awaits them in the New World: "Offend not the poore Natives, but as you partake in their land, so make them partakers of your precious faith: as you reape their temporalls, so feede them with your spiritualls: winne them to the love of Christ, for whom Christ died" (G19). Although cast as a fair trade, this exchange of "temporalls" for "spiritualls" amounts only to economic exploitation and cultural imposition. While the Puritans appropriate for themselves the land and other "temporalls" of the New England territory, they offer in return an

endless supply of "spiritualls." The Puritans' desire to be on the receiving end of "temporalls" indicates where their religious sentiments ultimately lie, but Cotton is not wrong about their need to purvey "spiritualls." Through the metaphors of the spiritual realm, the Puritans
generate a social imperative, one that persuades them of the fixity and
certainty of their own system of reference.

3

Iconoclastic materialism

Because Puritans placed considerable faith in language alone to define
and order their world, their verbal rituals have generally received more
attention than their iconoclasm. It is well known that the Puritans were
iconoclasts, but this aspect of their religion has been greatly oversimpli-
fied and their motives for destroying images in the church have been
much misunderstood. Puritan iconoclasm, no less than Puritan rhetoric,
granted substantial importance to material shapes. As we will see, what
historians and critics have misconstrued as a categorical opposition to
images was actually a devoted, if negative, act of reverence, and a very
self-conscious one at that. Although iconoclasm appears to have been a
rejection of all images, in their own way the iconoclasts believed very
deeply in the power of icons. Simultaneously adoring and destroying,
they both rejected visual shapes and endowed them with sacred meaning, adopting an attitude toward visual figures analogous to their reliance on material figures of sound. Since the iconoclasm of the Protestant Reformation in Europe strongly influenced seventeenth-century
ministers such as Cotton, and since Puritan violence owed much of its
rationale to the acts and beliefs of iconoclasts, it is worth while to
explore in depth the European sources of Anglo-American beliefs.

Iconoclasm was a frequent occurrence during the Reformation in
Europe, something of a trademark of the presence of Protestants in a
city. Where Protestants preached, church art was smashed, burned, and
generally desecrated. Although iconoclastic crowds were usually violent, they were neither spontaneous nor random in their assaults on
material shapes. Rather, they were usually well organized in their rituals of destruction, systematically attacking material objects associated
with the practice of Catholic religion. In England iconoclasts periodi-
cally received the sanction of legal and ecclesiastical authority to remove
images from churches and to renovate or demolish church buildings for

secular purposes. Iconoclasm was widespread in England during the first century of the Reformation, and the Puritans were among the most zealous of the destroyers. Indeed, iconoclastic beliefs accounted for much of what was "Puritan" about them.[1]

Many Puritan acts of iconoclasm were violent, but Puritanism is hardly reducible to sheer vandalism. Ideologically, what distinguished the Puritans from other English iconoclasts was their extension of iconoclastic motives to nonviolent symbolic acts. Puritans were notorious for refusing to kneel at the Lord's Supper, and Puritan clerics additionally refused to make the sign of the cross in baptism or wear the surplice when performing religious rites. For Puritans, such practices involved the rationale of iconoclasm because these gestures of the body were construed as images. As they conceived it, their own disobedient refusals were nonviolent acts of iconoclasm intended to destroy the idolatrous image of the Anglican cleric. For them, physical assault was only one aspect of a more far-reaching iconoclastic repudiation of the English church, and the nonviolent refusal to kneel at an altar was no less an act of iconoclasm than smashing an altar. By the late sixteenth century, when many images had already been destroyed, nonviolent acts of iconoclastic disobedience to Anglican authority became the Puritans' most characteristic trait. This is not to say that they repudiated violence, for the great outbreak of destruction unleashed by Puritan victories in the English Civil War proves how deeply they could still believe in it. Nonviolent symbolic acts, however peaceful they may seem, remained closely tied to the rationale for material destruction.

As Natalie Davis has argued, Protestant iconoclasm was informed by an obsession with the right use of material objects.[2] What historians have not recognized is the peculiar way in which this obsession involved, as it were, the right use of people. Although human beings and material objects may seem to us to be mutually exclusive categories, iconoclasm depended on a presumption of likeness between people and objects. The Puritan belief that the cleric's clothing and ritual bodily gestures were imagistic suggests how nonviolent iconoclasts conceived of people as material shapes. The idea was also intrinsic to violent iconoclasm. The belief that human beings and material objects had something in common is particularly evident in iconoclasts' descriptions of violent acts against themselves. As Phyllis Crew has noted, in the Netherlands, executions of Protestant preachers by Catholics were construed as acts of violence against sacred material shapes: "And to finish the game . . . they have, against the express commandment of God, erected an infinity of beautiful images, paintings, and statues. . . . Finally, to sustain such an enormity by force, they have burned the true and living images of God, living men, in order to make sacrifices to their images and dead idols."[3] Protestant iconoclasts were true idols, "living images" who were counterparts of the "dead idols" of Catholic art. In this strange commonality of people and icons, human beings and material objects were interchangeable, as other iconoclasts demonstrated when they "hung images of saints from the gibbets erected to execute iconoclasts."[4] Iconoclasts and church art were perceived alike as material shapes of religious significance. The violence committed against iconoclasts, no less than the violence they perpetrated, was understood as a response to a religious image.

In iconoclasm the *hominis figura* of classical thought became a material shape with iconic value, and as the outrage of the persecuted iconoclasts implies, they attributed special religious significance to their own human shapes. Iconoclasts engaging in the destruction of idols were interpreted as *figurae* with religious meaning. As we will see, they believed in the "living image" that was the person of the iconoclast, and this belief was accompanied by a negative reverence for the "dead" icons they so ardently smashed. This peculiar linkage of sacrosanct violence and people as material shapes constitutes the beginnings of what would become the Puritan version of social prejudice. Because iconoclasm concerned the significance of human beings as material shapes, because it sanctioned material harm, and because it thrived on the confusion between people and objects, the iconoclastic dimension of Puritanism strongly influenced the development of prejudice.

How did the iconoclasts come by their belief in icons? According to their street invectives as well as their preaching, their beliefs about the sacrament of the Lord's Supper and their corresponding hatred of the Catholic Mass it replaced were crucial to their motives. Among the main targets for the iconoclasts were the material objects used in the performance of the Catholic sacraments. Historians, interpreting iconoclasm as a kind of populist religious movement, have been skeptical that men such as John Calvin could have shared the beliefs of local preachers and violent crowds, or that this population could have shared Calvin's beliefs on the doctrine of the sacrament.[5] However, people need not have taken their ideas directly from Calvin in order to have shared some of his basic assumptions, particularly if these tenets of belief were preached to them by men who were familiar with Calvin's sacramental theory. As for Calvin himself, he was very much a partisan of iconoclastic ideology. The way in which Calvin raises this issue in his *Institutes of the Christian Religion* is important because it shows how early Protestants related their theory of the sacraments to their iconoclastic belief in living icons.

Like other iconoclasts, Calvin seems at first to express an unequivocal opposition to all images when he displays his hostility to Catholic "idolatry," as in this denunciation: "Whatever men learn of God from images is futile, indeed false"; or in this interpretation of scriptural prohibitions against images: "We see how openly God speaks against all images, that all who seek visible forms of God depart from him."[6] Nonetheless, although he often seems to oppose images categorically, he actually had a deep commitment to certain kinds of visual form. When Calvin says what he would prefer to see in a church to replace visual art, stating his own views in positive terms, he describes the Protestant sacraments as live, iconic art:

> When I ponder the intended use of churches, somehow or other it seems to me unworthy of their holiness for them to take on images [imagines] other than those that are living [vivas] and iconic [iconicas], which the Lord has consecrated by his Word. I mean Baptism and the Lord's Supper, together with other ceremonies [aliis ceremoniis] by which our eyes must be too intensely gripped and too sharply affected to seek other images forged by human ingenuity.
> Behold! The incomparable boon of images, for which there is no substitute, if we are to believe the papists! (113–14)[7]

What Calvin favors are "images" that are "living and iconic" (a crucial point that is lost in Ford Lewis Battles's modern English translation of iconicas as "symbolical"). The Protestant icon is the actual performance of religious rites such as the Lord's Supper: what one sees as the participants enact the sacramental events and other church rituals.

The living and iconic images of the sacrament, Calvin argues, are an art superior to all other images in the church. With eyes riveted on these Protestant performances, the good Christian will neither need nor seek out "other images." His sardonic conclusion shows that he believed he had indeed found a substitute for visual art and, moreover, that religious art had all along been an inadequate substitute for the living and iconic images of Christianity. Like the iconoclasts, Calvin himself conceived of Catholic visual art and Protestant sacramental rites as competing icons. In arguing for living images, for live art, he collapsed the distinction between art and life, just as the iconoclasts did when they perceived themselves as persecuted art objects. Calvin's use of the words vivas and iconicas defines the spiritual propriety of material shapes, justifying the attack on the images of Catholicism by sanctioning living icons, Protestants themselves, as the proper visual art of the church. His choice of iconicas (meaning "exact image") emphasizes the artistic realism that informs his concept of an image.[8]

The way in which Calvin defines legitimate representational art suggests that he felt that representational art had the threatening power to simulate the living. He seems at first cautiously in favor of the general idea of representational art, distinguishing between the artistic image and what it represents, and he protests against being thought a categorical iconoclast: "I am not gripped by the superstition of thinking absolutely no images permissible. But because sculpture and painting are gifts of God, I seek a pure and legitimate use of each" (112).[9] Discussing what kind of religious visual art he finds acceptable, strongly implying that he finds it far more acceptable outside the church, he allows representations of "histories and events" because they can be instructive (112). He opposes "images and forms of bodies without any depicting of past events" (112). The artist must represent the context, the limited temporality of his images, depicting figures engaged in "events" whose historicity, whose pastness, is recognizable.[10] Such figures are acceptable to Calvin both because they convey the idea that the artist is a mere copyist of living icons and because historicized figures are safely "dead" in their depiction and thus distinguishable from the living.

Calvin's fear of visual art is more evident where he discusses the kind of representation he most opposes. He despises visual representations of the deity itself, for "God's majesty is sullied by an unfitting and absurd fiction, when the incorporeal is made to resemble corporeal matter. . . . [E]very statue man erects, or every image he paints to represent God, simply displeases God as something dishonorable to his majesty" (101). Any artistic *figura* is an offense to spiritual propriety, he argues, because the deity cannot be envisioned by the human imagination (103). The proper limit of visual art, he claims, is that "only those things are to be sculptured or painted which the eyes are capable of seeing: let not God's majesty, which is far above the perception of the eyes, be debased through unseemly representations" (112). This injunction suggests that Calvin's opposition to Catholic art was in part an opposition to a mimetic concept of art. Although he does refer to the living images of the Protestant sacrament as representations of the deity, this is the least interesting aspect of the sacrament for him. The efficaciousness of the sacrament depends on something more than representation. When he calls the material objects of the sacrament "symbols," "signs," or "marks" of the deity's power (1385–86), he interprets these material shapes as fetishes that enable the perceiver to locate the mystical presence of the deity's power.

Calvin's brief discussion indicates that, despite his attacks on Catholics for their visual literalism, it is Calvin *himself* who is idolatrous in his own perception of Catholic art. His literal-minded injunction that visual art should involve only subjects "which the eye is capable of seeing" exemplifies the realism of iconoclasm, its confusion of art and life. Calvin's theory of visual art is that of a materialist who fears that he can think no further than he physically sees. Although he seems to express utter disbelief in artistic images when he condemns them as "dead matter" (103), his contempt is proportionable to the threat he feels in the capacity of these images to simulate life. Quoting Augustine, he explains the vulnerability of the onlooker: "For the shape of the idol's bodily members makes and in a sense compels the mind dwelling in a body to suppose that the idol's body too has feeling, because it looks very like its own body" (113). Visual figures invite sensual pleasure, he warns, because the mind imagines that the image, like the viewer, is alive (112–13). Even images that are not "licentious" are a threat. Although images "do not speak, or see, or hear, or walk," they can seem capable of these acts because "they have mouth, eyes, ears, feet" and thus "seem to live and breathe." An icon has the power to "compel the mind" to make a fetish of the image. Calvin argues that Scripture warns not only against "the worship of idols," but "against idols themselves," because there is "very much danger" in them (113). He candidly summarizes, "Men's folly cannot restrain itself from falling headlong into superstitious rites" (113). Images have such power over people that the mere presence of the image compels fetishistic adoration. Calvin assumes that this response to an image is a universal quality, and thus, whatever Catholics may say about the value of representational art, he insists that they believe in their images as a fetishist believes in icons.

Calvin felt threatened by religious statues and paintings exactly because he feared the power of a visual figure to enthrall, contain, or constrain his own concept of the deity. It was not that a "resemblance" of "God's majesty" in "corporeal matter" was incredible, or that he found it ludicrous to worship an image. Rather, it was precisely because such a visual image *was* plausible that the sheer presence of visual forms in Catholic religion became so threatening, became perceptible as inducements to worship the image itself as the *figura* of the deity's presence in the world. Calvin's reasoning implies that Protestant iconoclasts believed it necessary to attack the visual images in church sculpture, glass, and painting not because they disbelieved these images but rather because they believed quite strongly in their power. Despite their strident claims that it was the Catholics who worshiped "dead matter," the iconoclasts needed to kill these images by disfiguring them to guarantee that they were dead. Because the imagination of the Protestant invested spiritual power in the material shapes of religious ritual, the *figurae* of Catholic religion could be rendered powerless to captivate the Protestant only if the material shape itself was recognizably destroyed and represented as such. This attitude would account for the execution style of many iconoclasts, who destroyed the heads of statues rather than the entire image. In the Lady Chapel of Ely Cathedral, for example, the statuary was within easy reach, but while the iconoclasts systematically smashed all the heads, they also systematically left the rest of the bodies of the figures intact.[11] An observer in the Netherlands wrote of the iconoclasts, "They hammer away mainly at the faces."[12] In thus beheading the offending images, iconoclasts symbolized the need to kill images that were believed to be somehow alive and dangerous.

The intensity of their general belief in the iconic value of material shapes is apparent in acts of desecration that suggest the need to destroy beyond visual recognition any religious shapes – not just images of people – by using them for something else, something materially functional, in order to destroy fully a threat of power inhering in the *figura* itself. Altar stones became "paving stones, bridges, fireplaces, or even kitchen sinks," basins for holy water were used to salt beef, and a triptych was used as a pig trough.[13] In their satiric reinterpretation of material shapes and forms, and in their acts of violence, the iconoclasts expressed how intensely, fearfully, and negatively they revered visual form. Their execution of visual art objects and their reshaping of material forms for a different use demonstrated an ardent, if negative, belief in the power of visual figures. Fearful of their own weakness for idolatry, they were motivated by an intense need to see only the true icons of their deity in the church.

While Calvin's beliefs about the iconic nature of the sacrament are clearest in his discussion of art in the church, his sacramental theory in the more conventional sense was informed by the same ideas. In opposing the Catholic doctrine of transubstantiation, Calvin made the material bread in the sacrament essential to his religious beliefs, calling this the "earthly part" of the sacrament (1375). Beliefs about the bread as a material substance were intrinsic to his rejection of Catholic doctrine, and we can gauge the importance of this belief from the tenacity of Protestants such as Calvin on this issue. Transubstantiation, he maintained, not only denied the true nature of Christ; it also denied the true nature of sacramental bread. Calvin insisted that the sacramental bread remained "true" bread even after its consecration. Arguing against "that fictitious and fantastic transubstantion" which he found absurdly "literalist," Calvin opposed the idea that bread and wine materially changed into the body and blood of Christ, that is, the idea that the bread and wine were substantively annihilated (1374, 1383). If the bread became only an empty form, an appearance or a "mask" (1398), it could not be sacramental: "The nature of the Sacrament is therefore canceled, unless, in the mode of signifying, the earthly sign corresponds to the heavenly thing. And the truth of this mystery accordingly perishes for us unless true bread represents the true body of Christ" (1376).

In the sacramental "mode of signifying," there had to be a correspondence between material elements and Christ in which the bread remained "true" to itself. To be sacramental, it had to be true bread. Though the controversy over transubstantiation seems to have been about the nature of Christ, it equally involved the nature of the "earthly part" of the sacrament, the bread. Without the bread, the efficacy of the sacrament was "canceled" and the mystery perished.

The Protestant opposition to transubstantiation focused on the unchanging materiality of the bread. However, the shape, the *figura,* of the bread as a visible material object was also important to Calvin. Remarking on what kind of bread could be used in the sacrament, he insisted that only "common bread," the bread of ordinary daily life "intended solely to feed the stomach," could be appropriate (1375). The commonness of the true bread was essentially an iconoclastic idea because it was a rejection of a representational image of bread, the wafer of the Mass. Substituting one *figura* for another, and again repudiating the concept of representational objects, Calvin advocated "common" bread, the kind of bread people actually ate in their daily lives. His belief not only emphasized the material use value of the sacramental object; it also declared a stylistic imperative: the plainness of literal-minded realism. Both in his rejection of transubstantiation and in his rejection of the *figura* of the wafer, Calvin articulated a paradigm of the sacramental object that deeply influenced English Puritanism, for it was this sense of realism that Elizabethan Protestants took to heart in fashioning their living icons of common plainness. Thomas Norton, translating Calvin's *Institutes* into English in 1561, emphasized the *figura* of common bread as a stylistic mandate for the human living icon. Where Calvin wrote of *imagines* that were *vivas* and *iconicas,* images that were living and iconic, Norton rendered the phrase as "lively and natural images."[14] Interpolating from the necessity for common bread in the sacrament, Norton transposed Quintilian's linguistic concept of "natural and principal signification" to make it a means of interpreting objects. As Norton's translation implies, the sacramental bread was a paradigm for iconic people as well as objects.

Whether or not Elizabethan Puritans got their ideas specifically from Calvin, they expressed Calvin's kind of sacramental realism in their opposition to Catholic art. Perhaps the best example of the Puritan belief in common bread can be found in the architectural design of Emmanuel College. This Puritan stronghold of Cambridge University was in part a reconstruction of buildings that had belonged to a Dominican Priory. As F. H. Stubbings has shown, Emmanuel College architecturally expressed its Puritanism by converting the old Dominican church into the buttery, hall, and fellows' parlor for the new college. Thus did common bread replace the wafer of the Catholic sacrament. The first fellows of Emmanuel, roughly a generation older than Cotton, were noted for their self-conscious realism in celebrating the Lord's Supper. Not only did they refuse vestments, they took the sacrament while sitting in a common way at a common eating table, and there is good reason to think that the architectural innovation was a quite self-conscious act of edification. The avowed purpose of Emmanuel was quite similar to that of the old Dominican order: to produce an educated, preaching clergy. In this sense the new Puritan college, begun in 1584, was a symbolic reinterpretation of the Catholic cleric. In the substitution of the buttery and eating hall for the church, the Puritans expressed their Calvinistic sense of sacramental realism over against the Catholic doctrine of transubstantiation.[15]

It is easy to see a similar motivation in the iconoclastic act of Cotton's predecessor at St. Botolph's, Thomas Wooll, who not only refused to wear his surplice but used it for a seat cushion instead.[16] In this satiric protest, characteristic of iconoclastic symbolic acts, what was falsely sacred was returned to a profane condition when it was given a material use value. Where sacramental realism invested common things with a spiritual value ordered to a sacred teleology, the inverted rite of the iconoclasts de-sacralized false *figurae* by destroying their visible forms and returning their material substance to a common use in the physical, material world. This kind of iconoclasm expressed a materialistic dis-figuring of false religious images by adapting Calvin's sacramental logic: If it was a seat cushion, it was no longer a true surplice, and the mystery accordingly perished. The emphasis of sacramental theory in Puritanism concerned the shape and function of the material objects in question. For Puritan iconoclasts, the crucial issue was less the opposition to transubstantiation, which they largely assumed, than the need for proper material shapes, for common bread to replace the wafer.

Calvin's belief in living icons and true, common bread implies a wholly positive valuation of the icons he believed appropriate to Christianity. However, to understand the value he attributed to them, it is necessary to take account of the reversal of propriety in the sacramental act. The ritual negates as well as sanctifies the sacramental *figura,* creating a double bind, because the religious power of the elements is referred to the "spiritual" presence of Christ. Calvin distinguished himself from Catholic transubstantiationists, on the one hand, and Protestant memorialists, on the other, by his doctrine of the "spiritual" presence of the body of Christ in the sacrament of the Lord's Supper. He believed that the resurrected "true and natural body" of Jesus Christ had ascended to heaven and remained there. However, although the fleshly body of Christ was absent, Christ was still mystically present in the sacrament. It was the spiritual presence of Christ that gave the sacramental icon its religious value (1370–71).

The doubleness of the bind was the simultaneous assertion and denial of the religious power of the bread. Its materiality was necessary for the "mystery," but not by itself enough to make the event a sacrament. The true bread, while remaining such, was also transformed. Calvin describes it as a conversion:

> Some of the old writers used the term "conversion" sometimes, not because they intended to wipe out the substance of the outward sign, but to teach that the bread dedicated to the mystery is far different from common bread, and is now something else. . . . For because they say that in consecration a secret conversion takes place, so that there is now something other than bread and wine, as I have just observed, they do not mean by this that the elements have been annihilated, but rather that they now have to be considered of a different class from common foods intended solely to feed the stomach, since in them is set forth the spiritual food and drink of the soul. This we do not deny.
>
> If there is conversion (these men say), one thing must be made from another. If they mean that it is made something which it was not before, I agree. [1375]

To convert the true bread, to make it sacred, is to declare it inadequate within its new teleology, to declare that it needs the spiritual presence to be sufficient for its new, religious use. Although perfectly satisfactory as "common" bread, as material food, it is insufficient as "spiritual" food. From Calvin's idealist perspective, of course, when "common" bread is "made something which it was not before," it is made something better, since it is the greatest privilege to be "joined" to the mystical body of Christ. But from a secular perspective, the "common" bread has only been distorted and made to seem something other – and something worse – than it is. What was satisfactory and intelligible is now contemptible and mysterious, not by itself worth eating.

Bread is deprived of its "common" material integrity in the act of consecration, made incomplete in order to be completed by the "spiritual presence" that makes its materiality sacred. The religious virtue of the bread is solely its capacity as a fetish to exhibit or display the spiritual presence. It "not only symbolizes the thing that it has been consecrated to represent as a bare and empty token, but also truly exhibits it" (1385). A true fetish, but an "empty token" at the same time, it has a sacredness that always remains derivative, never inhering in the essence of the material element alone: "The symbol differs in essence from the thing signified (in that the latter is spiritual and heavenly, while the former is physical and visible)" (1385). The bread is never more than a material locus, because it never acquires the "essence" of the thing signified. Calvin's concept of the sacramental bread as "physical and visible," a "bare and empty token" without the valued spiritual "essence," reduces the material elements to the physical dimensions of concrete objects. Without the redemptive grandeur of the spiritual presence, they are contemptible things, sheer physical objects whose reality is fully defined by their materiality and their visible shape. The doctrine of the spiritual presence thus debases the *figura* even as it makes the sacramental object the privileged locus of religious power.

Calvin's analysis of sacramental bread is very similar to Karl Marx's analysis of commodities in the capitalist market. In Marx's theory, exchange value is the counterpart of the spiritual presence. Both Calvin and Marx perceive a contradiction between the ordinary use of an object and the value (spiritual or exchange) that it acquires upon consecration/circulation. Moreover, both Calvin and Marx warn of the dangers of fetishizing the object itself, and perhaps Marx wrote more accurately than he knew when he associated this system of thought with Protestant religion. Protestantism, Marx observed, is "the most fitting form of religion" for "a society based upon the production of commodities," but there is no indication that he knew how closely his own analysis of commodities paralleled Calvin's analysis of sacramental objects. Although Marx perceived analogies between religious and capitalist thought, he argued that "the religious world" is the "reflex of the real world," not realizing the extent to which Protestant theologians such as Calvin valued material objects in their theology and conceived of material objects in a way directly analogous to the concept of commodities in the market.[17]

Like Marx's theory of commodities, Calvin's theory of the sacramental object potentially defines a society – in this case, a corporate institution, the church as a mystical body. In Calvin's terms, people are reduced to the status of material objects because sacramental theory interprets the conversion of people by means of the paradigm of the conversion of bread. Just as in other versions of Christianity, Calvin adopts Paul's rhetoric of Christians as "bread" in 1 Cor. 10.17: "We being many are one bread and one body: for we are all partakers of that one bread" (that is, of Christ as the "bread of life" in such passages as John 6.35). In the symbolism of the sacrament was the interpretation not only of Christ's body but, more important, of the convert's body. For example, John Jewel, an early English Protestant, explains it this way:

> For that was not Christ's meaning, that the wheaten bread should lay apart his own nature and receive a certain new divinity, but that he might rather change us, and . . . might transform us into his body. For what can be said more plainly than that which Ambrose saith, "Bread and wine remain still the same they were before and yet are changed into another thing."[18]

How the bread is "converted" to its sacramental purpose is a paradigm for how people are converted, for what happens to them in their experience of the mystical "spiritual presence" of Christ. In accepting the sacrament the Christian accedes to the self-definition implicit in the sacramental bread and wine he swallows. Theologically, the original sin that plagues his own human essence is the social counterpart of the inadequate common bread, and to be "joined" to the mystical body of Christ likewise becomes the source of the convert's positive value.

As common bread, the "natural" man believes that his own life is reducible to a version of sacramental bread, repudiating his subjectivity in conversion and perceiving himself as a vessel of the deity's power. To express this lack of acknowledged subjectivity, the model Christian of Cotton's sermons on conversion adopts Paul's phrase from Gal. 2.20: "Not I, but Christ liveth in me." Cotton expands on Paul's "not I, but . . . me" to emphasize the expression of social subjectivity as an absence: "not I; as if it were too broad a word for a Christian man to speake" (WL277).[19] Converts, like common bread, are inadequate in themselves when understood from the perspective of spiritual propriety. Because the individual can never be more than an image or *figura* of religious truth, that truth always exceeds the Protestant's own manifestation of it: The individual can, like the elements of the sacrament, "exhibit" religious truth, but not *be* it. The Christian speaks of being "in" Christ but never of individually becoming the mystical body itself, for the individual only participates in a religious collective subject that transcends human limits, uniting Christians to the mystical Christ and to other "members" of the corporate "body."[20] In the convert's self-perception, one's own social subjectivity is mere common bread, always subordinated to the essence of the mystical Christ that sacralizes the material shape.

Despite the spiritual condition of being a sacramental object, the Protestant continues to live in the common social world. In common society the Protestant claims a privileged, sacramental subjectivity with respect to people who are not members of the mystical body. Paradoxically, the debased and sinful *figura* that needs saving in the church becomes the *figura* of privileged truth in the common social world. Since the Puritan social subject is ideologically subordinated to the religious collective subject that makes the individual sacramental, the Protestant claims the privileged social subjectivity of a fetish while acting as an "empty token" at the same time – thus the duplicity of the living image. Calvin's sacrament declares converts to be simultaneously contemptible and sacred, inadequate as common bread but the locus of revelation as sacramental icons.

In Calvin's view, it is language that creates the subjectivity of Protestant society as the mystical body of Christ, and specifically, the consecrating words of the sacrament. Since the verbal act of consecration is addressed to the other communicants, not to the material elements, the cleric's words are an expression of the social entity defined by those who partake in the sacrament, who act as living icons. Again, the paradigm of the conversion of the bread is important. The spiritual presence of the mystical Christ that transforms material shapes into icons is evoked only by the consecrating words: "The bread is a sacrament only to those persons to whom the word is directed: just as the water of baptism is not changed in itself, but as soon as the promise has been attached it begins to be for us what it was not before" (1377). The point is not only that the power of evocation resides in the words. It is also by means of words that the communicant understands the religious mystery of the sacrament. The bread does not divulge its own mystical secret. The only way a communicant can know what is there is to hear and understand the words that reveal the sacredness of the material shape.

According to Calvin, sacramental speech is particularly characterized by the trope of metonymy, the substitution of one name for another (from the Greek *meta-* and *onomazo,* a change of name).[21] Calvin emphasizes the explanatory power of this trope because he does not appeal to the historical life of Jesus Christ to explain the religious significance of the bread. Instead, he appeals to the classical trope of metonymy to interpret "This is my body," the words of Christ spoken by the cleric to consecrate the bread. The substitution of the word "body" for the word "bread," he proposes, "is a metonymy, a figure of speech commonly used in Scripture when mysteries are under discussion" (1385). For Calvin, metonymy is *the* figure of the deity's rhetoric in Scripture, the normative mode for describing the general character of divine intervention in the world:

> For as the sacraments agree in many respects, so in this metonymy they all have a certain common ground with one another. Accordingly, as the apostle teaches that the rock from which spiritual drink sprang forth for the Israelites was Christ [1 Cor. 10.4]—because it was a visible sign under which that spiritual drink indeed truly was, but was not discernible to the eye—so the body of Christ today is called bread, inasmuch as it is the symbol by which the Lord offers us the true eating of his body. [1386]

The metonymy indicates that which is not "discernible to the eye" in the "visible sign," the spiritual presence of Christ. By substituting one name for another, by renaming the visible, metonymy locates the invisible but "true" presence of Christ in the material world.

Apprehensive that his interpretation will be misunderstood, that figurative will be construed to mean fictive, Calvin emphasizes that the relation between the thing named (the body of Christ) and the thing renamed (the bread) is not fictive because the trope signifies the reality of Christ's presence, albeit mystical and spiritual: "Those things ordained by God borrow the names of those things of which they always bear a definite and not misleading signification, and have the reality joined with them" (1385–86). Consecrating tropes are true because the material shapes of bread and wine "have the reality" of the mystical Christ "joined with them." However "misleading" they may seem to the uninitiated, the tropes of the sacrament express this reality. Moreover, they invoke it, enacting what they declare. The consecrating power of sacramental tropes extends beyond the capacity for representing spiritual truth to include the power to make true what the tropes signify.

Since Calvin chooses metonymy as the normative religious trope, it is worthwhile to explore the structure of meaning it articulates. Metonymy can seem misleading because, unlike metaphor, it is not characterized by resemblance. Instead, it expresses relations that seem arbitrary, and the more arbitrary the relation, the more striking the metonymy.[22] In the tropes of the sacrament, it is the perceived *lack* of resemblance between body and bread, the nominal *in*appropriateness of the word "body," which indicates that the consecrating word is figurative. The verbal act of substitution is a layering of names that expresses a skewed reference. Calvin's preference for nonrepresentational figures is again evident, for the renaming of metonymy is not likely to invoke a visual image, or if it does, it is a visual absurdity. Because it describes an apparently arbitrary association, it does not depend on the concept of a figure as a resemblance or imitation of something else.

Sacramental metonymy seems to be a purely verbal phenomenon, but it actually depends on the visual sense quite directly for its intelligibility, because the consecrating trope presupposes a juxtaposition of words and referents. It is the juxtaposition of the word "body" and the referent bread in the situation of the sacrament that conveys the idea of skewed reference, indicating the renaming. Thus the trope depends on a visual apprehension of the material object renamed, yoking words and visible referents together for the comprehension of both. Calvin's insistence that the substance and *figura* of the bread remains what it is, that it is not transubstantiated, is an insistence on the truth of skewed reference. For him, it is the discrepancy between the spoken word and the visible referent, expressed by metonymy, that marks the presence of the mystical Christ.

The concept of appropriateness articulated by metonymy is contradictory, in that it asserts both the metaphoric concept of two discrete loci and the hyperbolic concept of a single locus of meaning, the joining that the layering of metonymy signifies. That is, metonymy expresses a conflicting concept of proper meaning by its indeterminate "joining" of the locus from which the metonymy is taken and the unspoken locus of the renamed object. By preserving the act of nominal substitution, a recognizable renaming, sacramental metonymy expresses a temporary conjunction of loci and the concomitant tension of proper meaning. The unresolved locus of proper meaning in metonymy not only asserts a conflict between the spoken figure and the unspoken name it replaces. Because the assumed proper meaning in metonymy remains unspoken, this trope can also be interpreted as expressing a conflict between words and things, between figure and referent, as sources of meaning. Is propriety determined by the locus the word names, or by the locus of the object renamed?

Calvin raises this question by making common bread essential to his doctrine. He attempts to resolve the conflict of proper meaning by asserting that sacramental metonymy expresses a fundamentally unequal relation dominated by the spiritual presence, not the bread. The trope signifies the temporary fusion of two radically different loci, the superior "heavenly" domain of the resurrected Christ and the vastly inferior "earthly" domain of the common bread. In the religious reversal of propriety that locates the primary injunction in the spiritual domain, the bread becomes an empty token, lacking the essence of the mystical Christ it signifies. However, Calvin's rejection of transubstantiation also assigns religious significance to the material objects, the sacramental *figurae*. Calvin's deity requires true bread, true wine, live participants, and (Puritans like Cotton would emphasize) the actual sounds of consecrating words. Thus, whereas Calvin may seem to assert a secure hierarchy of proper meaning in his concept of metonymy, his belief in the material bread maintains the conflict of proper meaning as a religious principle, asserting that it is necessary and intrinsic to belief.

The paradigm of Calvin's sacramental theory is reproduced in his attitude toward the images of Catholic art. As we have seen, although he is disdainful of material images in the church, he is also deeply apprehensive about a pervasive weakness for "idolatry." And with good reason. The conflict of meaning in sacramental metonymy grants an intrinsic power, however subordinate, to material shapes. One has only to reverse the metonymy to locate the primary injunction in the *figura,* the object. As Calvin himself acknowledges in describing the nature of transferred meaning in metonymy, Scripture offers just such cases of reversed metonymy. Analyzing the use of the trope in the Bible, he observes, "Not only is the name transferred from something higher to something lower, but, on the other hand, the name of the visible sign is also given to the thing signified" (1385). Calvin argues that it does not matter whether the Holy Ghost is called a dove or a dove is called the Holy Ghost – either version of metonymy names the same mystical relation. He is never in doubt, or so he claims, that the primary meaning is always the mystical Christ. Nonetheless, it is the awareness that the substitution of names can take place in either direction that creates the possibility of idolizing things in the material world, of becoming dove worshipers, for example.

Although Calvin attempts to rationalize the reversed metonymies in Scripture as equivalent statements, his fears of idolatry and his belief in living icons suggest that equivalence is hardly the result. Rhetorically, a reversal of metonymy changes meaning significantly. Since metonymy asserts that the primary injunction comes from the locus of the figural name, reversing the locus of the name reverses the hierarchy of propriety expressed by the trope. Quintilian's brief remarks about metonymy are instructive on this point. He describes metonymy as a device "employed to indicate an invention by substituting the name of the inventor, or a possession by substituting the name of the possessor." And he adds, "If, however, the process is reversed, the effect is harsh."[23] In Calvin's terms, when the name of "something lower" is transferred to "something higher," the hierarchy of proper meaning is reversed and spiritual propriety becomes a function of *figurae.* The effect is indeed harsh, for material shapes become the possessors of the deity's spiritual truth. In the attribution of the name of "bread" to converts, it is just this kind of reversal that occurs. The conceptual interchangeability of the common bread with the convert's own material body creates a reductive materialism that conceives of human beings as nothing more than "physical and visible" objects. This concept of the social-material world reduces people to the status of fetish objects, just the sort of reduction Calvin invites when he boasts that the Protestant sacrament offers a vision of living icons. Emphasizing people, words, and objects as holy *figurae,* Calvin emphasizes their dynamic material shapes as they "exhibit" and "mark" the spiritual presence, not the act of transcendance that the sacrament supposedly inspires.

The concept of living icons also expresses a metonymic relation between a live human being and an artistic representation of one. The violence of iconoclasm attempts to resolve a conflict of meaning between artistic representations, the false idols that simulate life, and actual people, the "lively and natural images" who are the true *figurae* of Protestant religion. The conflict expressed in the juxtaposition of the word "body" and the referent bread becomes a conflict between fetish objects in iconoclastic violence. Iconoclasts perceive themselves as the true figures who must reshape–rather than rename–representational significations in their struggle for the determination of meaning. The sense of iconoclastic violence as subverbal, as a loss of figurative imagination, comes from the manner in which they interpret the sacramental paradigm. Acknowledging their own status in the sacrament as silent objects, as "bread," the iconoclasts take the sacramental objects, not the figurative words, as the primary locus of propriety in their iconoclastic rites. By the actions of their own sacramental, iconic bodies, the iconoclasts reshape other *figurae* into something they were not before. In this physical and visible conversion of material objects, iconoclasts affirm the primary significance of material shapes, implicitly asserting that the material shape of common bread is not only essential to the sacrament but privileged in it as the locus of signification. The commonness, the realism, of sacramental bread becomes a paradigmatic sanction to transform false religious objects into something that can be used in common life, a way of returning the material substance to the profane, ordinary existence from which it came. These symbolic acts reinterpret the temptations of Catholic or Anglican art and ritual as false metonymy and therefore as a power that can be reversed by dis-figuring the sacralized objects in a reverse sacrament. Because common bread may be construed as profane or as sacred, as contemptible object or as sacramental icon, iconoclasts attribute the former to the objects they despise and appropriate the latter concept to themselves.

Iconoclastic violence fully adopts the paradigm of sacramental metonymy in its most iconic sense. The literal (or possibly, original) name that is suppressed in renaming is interpreted as in fact silent. The word "bread" has no materiality, no audible shape, in the actual performance of the sacrament and therefore no direct iconic value. Theologically, sacramental metonymy implies the priority of the spoken figure over the unspoken name it replaces. Iconoclasts, reversing the hierarchy of propriety, privilege the object and accept the silence of the name of the object as true. For them, metonymy expresses a conflict between figuration and objects, rather than a conflict between names. It is a conflict in which figures, linguistic or artistic, are likely to be false, and objects as referents are the primary source of proper meaning. The nonviolent symbolism of the Puritans basically shares this paradigm, attributing major significance to their own nonverbal ritual acts as living icons. In the refusal to kneel at the Lord's Supper, wear the surplice, or use the sign of the cross in baptism, Puritan clerics grant religious meaning to themselves as perceptible material shapes in the church. Where Puritanism does take cognizance of the name of the object in its metonymic reversal, acknowledging that a body is not, finally, bread, the ordinary or common name of the object acquires sacramental value. It becomes the primary locus of meaning, either as the sanctified silence concealed by the metonymy of spoken words or as the cult of the literal, nonrhetorical plainness of ordinary language.

Much of sixteenth-century Puritan belief can be traced directly to Calvin's paradigm of the sacraments. For example, William Perkins, an influential Puritan at Cambridge in the late sixteenth century, follows Calvin closely at many points in "A Reformed Catholike," "A Warning Against the Idolatrie of the Last Times," and "A Golden Chaine."[24] Perkins asserts the Calvinist doctrine of the spiritual presence over against the doctrine of transubstantiation: "We differ not touching the presence it selfe, but onely in the maner of presence. For though we holde a reall presence of Christs body and blood in the sacrament, yet doe we not take it to be locall, bodily, or substantial, but spiritual and mysticall" (1.583). He also follows Calvin on the necessity of interpreting Christ's consecrating words figurally: "These words must not be understood properly but by a figure" (1.585), specifically, the trope of metonymy (1.72). Referring to the act of consecration as a "mutation" of the sign, Perkins rejects the idea that this is accomplished "by changing the substance of the thing" and understands it similarly as a reorientation to spiritual propriety. The sign/thing is "severed from a common to a holy use," not changed in substance but transformed from its "common" use to a spiritual use (1.72). Perkins similarly extends his interpretation to the whole performance of the ritual, defining the sacramental "sign" as "either the matter sensible, or the action conversant about the same" (1.72). In his sacramental theory, then, Perkins can fairly be called a Calvinist.

Perkins's discussion of Catholic "idolatry" develops into a comparison of true and false images that also relies heavily on Calvin. Taking essentially the same tack, Perkins also sounds thoroughly anti-imagist at times: "Now God hath not bound himselfe by any word to be present at images, and to heare us when we call upon him, at them, or before them" (1.661). However, as with Calvin, there are major exceptions to his categorical refusal of visible shapes, and the communicants of the sacrament are the principal ones: "Christians themselves are the images of Christians," Perkins declares in his condemnation of idolatrous visual art (1.580). He prefers the deity's created, living images of Christianity to any of the figures of visual art: "Now the meanest man that can bee, is a more excellent image of God, then all the images of

God or of Saints that are devised by men" (1.582). Perkins also distinguishes between false images and the viable icons of the deity by arguing that although the icons of the deity are visible shapes, they are not representations in the sense of an actual image or picture of the deity: "The Formes in which the Sonne and Holy Ghost have appeared, were not their Images, but onely sensible signes and pledges of their presence" (1.660). Again, biblical history falls outside the category of acceptable visualization as Perkins relegates this subject to representations of what the eye can see, limning Calvin's argument that this kind of visual art is legitimate *outside* the church: "We hold the historical use of images to bee good and lawfull: and that is, to represent to the eye the actes of histories whether they be humane, or divine: and thus we thinke the Histories of the Bible may be painted in private places" (1.580). In these respects, Perkins treats the topic of idolatry very much as Calvin did.

Despite their reliance on Calvin's theology at many points, Elizabethan Puritans are by no means wholly derivative in their thinking, and in one crucial respect they go substantially beyond Calvin's *Institutes* in their justification of icons. What distinguishes Elizabethan Puritans such as Perkins from Calvin is the use of the Second Commandment to justify the Protestant belief in images. Calvin's rather furtive belief in icons becomes an open declaration in Elizabethan Puritanism. Perkins unabashedly proclaims his belief in icons by interpreting the Second Commandment very strangely, as a mandate for ordained images. The commandment that forbids "graven images," he explains, contains an important qualification *against* categorical opposition to images: "In the second commaundement it is not simply said, Thou shalt not make a graven image: but with limitation, thou shalt not make *to thy selfe,* that is, on thine owne head, upon thine owne will and pleasure" (1.580). Repudiating the images of human imagination, Perkins contrasts such false images with true images, which are ordained by God: "In one case it is lawful to make an image to testifie the presence or the effects of the majesty of God, namely, when God himselfe gives any speciall commandement so to doe" (1.580). For Perkins, the Second Commandment justifies the Calvinist belief that Protestant sacraments are a "lawful" image. Thus the rallying cry of the iconoclasts, the prohibition against graven images, became the open sanction of the Puritans' belief in themselves as living icons.

Although the Lord's Supper remains the paradigm for commanded images, Perkins makes possible a more general and overt belief in living icons, for he implies that there are many more images commanded by the deity in Scripture. At the same time, perhaps sensing the immense possibilities for expanding the Protestant belief in images, he attempts to limit the applicability of the Second Commandment by emphasizing the importance of the temporality of the image. Even viable sacred "images" must be understood as "signes not forever, but onely for the present time, when they appeared: and therefore neither signes nor images of Gods presence now" (1.660). An image can be sacramental only if it is contemporaneous with those who perceive it. Expanding on this idea, he brings together a wide variety of mystical figural appearances in Scripture: not only the troublesome dove but also the brazen serpent and the images of Abraham's and Daniel's visionary experiences (1.581, 1.660). His willingness to equate historical events, the images of visionary experience, and the objects of the sacrament suggests that he is intending to account for the whole range of figural phenomena in Puritan beliefs. However, neither the sequence of events nor the notion of typological fulfillment is important.[25] His concept of sanctioned *figurae* acknowledges temporality, but his paradigm is the sacrament:

> When God appeared in the forme of a man [to Abraham, Gen. 18, and to Daniel, 7.9], that forme was a signe of Gods presence onely for the time when God appeared, and no longer; as the bread and wine in the Sacrament are signes of Christs bodie and blood, not forever, but for the time of administration: for afterward they become againe as common bread and wine. And when the holy Ghost appeared in the likenesse of a dove, that likenesse was a signe of his presence no longer then the holy Ghost so appeared. [1.581]

Perkins emphasizes the idea of a recurrent spiritual presence in the material shapes of the temporal world, but his main point is that each is a living image only for a specific period of time. Among his examples, however, "Gods presence" in the sacrament is distinctive because it uses the same *figurae* again and again in an event that is repeated indefinitely. His argument depends on the temporal and spatial constraints of the performance of the sacrament itself: The elements are sacramental only "for the time of administration," invested with the mystical presence of Christ only during the sacrament. Outside the situation of the sacrament, they are without iconic significance.

Despite the constraints he describes, Perkins himself occasionally generalizes beyond the administration of the sacrament in "The Arte of Prophecie." He extends the iconic quality of the sacramental performance to preachers, venturing that a minister should consider himself a "type," a living icon, in all aspects of his life: "Because the doctrine of the word is hard both to be understood and to be practised, therefore the Minister ought to expresse that by his example, which hee teacheth, as it were by a type. . . . For the simple people behold not the ministerie, but the person of the Minister" (2.671).[26] In applying the idea of a "type" to the minister, Perkins found his justification less in typology than in the ahistorical concept of the living icon, "the person" of the cleric that "the simple people behold." The tendency of Perkins's thought implies that the development of Puritan typology in the late sixteenth and early seventeenth centuries owes more to sacramental concepts of images than we have previously supposed. For example, Puritan typologists were metonymic in their thinking, appropriating Old Testament names to rename themselves in a manner suggesting the paradigm of the Calvinist sacrament. The Protestant work ethic was also more closely related to sacramental theory than we have recognized. Perkins refers to the material objects of the sacrament as "signes of grace" (1.72), a phrase that became common among his successors as a general way to interpret the actions and the material property of Puritans. This development of sacramental theory probably derives from the classical characterization of occupations as *figurae negotii*, for this usage provided a precedent for understanding kinds of work as images.[27] The Puritan was thus an ordained image surrounded by images at least as much in his occupation as in his accumulation of sanctifying material goods.[28]

Although Perkins attempted to restrict the concept of living icons, making it specific to the sacrament and biblical history, his own predilections led him to extend the concept in selective ways beyond Scripture and the sacrament. By the seventeenth century, Puritans had gone far beyond Perkins in expanding the domain of relevance of the Second Commandment to include almost every aspect of cultural values and behavior. The ideology of the iconoclasts became pervasive in Puritan thought as they reconceived their culture in imagistic terms. As one author expressed it, the concept of "idols," "images," and "figures" extended to "Portraitures, Shapes, Resemblances, and Forms of things, Natural or Artificial, Real or Imaginary," and to "representations, material, aerial, real, imaginary, proper, and tropical [of tropes]."[29] Among their ideas of images were iconic art such as statuary, painting, and stained glass; altars, baptismal fonts, and architecture; clothing; the verbal rituals of the Mass book and the Book of Common Prayer; the mental images of rhetorical tropes such as metaphor; dreams; specters; masks; the imprint of a seal; and, what would become its most important and comprehensive meaning for American Puritans, people themselves as physical, material shapes. In this great variety of meanings attributed to "image," one senses the ubiquitous presence of the classical concept of *figura*. The Protestant ideology of iconoclasm recovered the whole range of visual meanings of *figura* in Latin literature, and particularly such meanings as outer appearance, material form, simulacrum, image, copy, representation, model, statue, resemblance, architectural plan, occupation, the shape of the human body, and the shape of the human face. The similarity between classical meanings of *figura* and the multifarious images perceived by the iconoclast suggests that classical thought was far more important than the Second Commandment in establishing the cultural viability of such a comprehensive idea of images.

Considering the intellectual and social importance of Protestant beliefs about icons, we might well consider why contemporary criticism has so deeply misunderstood this dimension of Protestant thought. The Puritans, its most ardent and obvious exponents in English, have long been excluded from serious consideration in literary studies, and criticism has thus deprived itself of the clearest evidence on this subject. In addition to this exclusion, and perhaps participating in its assumptions, there has also been a long-standing uncritical reliance on Erich Auerbach's interpretation of the history of the concept of *figura*.[30] In his analysis of classical thought, Auerbach is seriously misleading on two important sources, both of which were crucial to Protestant thought. As we have seen, Quintilian uses *figura* in an important way theoretically, to characterize the material shapes of spoken discourse generally. However, Auerbach gives the impression that Quintilian employs this term only in the narrow sense of specific figures of speech.[31] Auerbach also misrepresents Cicero's use of *figura* to describe the shape of the gods, arguing that Cicero does not use the word in this way when in fact he does. For example, in *De Natura Deorum* (On the Nature of the Gods), Cicero writes:

> But if the human figure [*hominis figura*] surpasses the form of all other living beings, and god is a living being, god must possess the shape [*figura*] which is the most beautiful of all; and since it is agreed that the gods are supremely happy, and no one can be happy without virtue, and virtue cannot exist without reason, and reason is only found in the human shape [*hominis figura*], it follows that the gods possess the form of man. Yet their form is not corporeal, but only resembles bodily substance; it does not contain blood, but the semblance of blood.[32]

Cicero's use of *hominis figura* in the context of a discourse on the nature of deities, together with his discussion of the noncorporeal form with its semblance of body and blood, topically suggests Calvin's preoccupations with sacramental theory. Whatever the influence of Cicero may have been, for the living icons of the Protestant Reformation the shapes of gods and men were often confused. The Protestant living image, though not precisely a god, demanded to be understood in more than human terms.

Auerbach rightly says of Cicero's use of *figura* in general that "he tried to devise what today we should call an all-embracing concept of form."[33] Perkins and his Puritan successors were engaged in a similar endeavor as Christian humanists attempting to reconcile classical and Christian thought. Although the importance of *figura* for the Protestants probably derived in part from its significance for patristic and medieval theology, Protestant beliefs about icons and the acoustic shapes of words imply the direct influence of classical sources. Here again Auerbach is misleading, for he underestimates the significance of classical ideas for Christian authors. Reductively adopting the Christian idiom of "figure" and "fulfillment" when he discusses Christian interpretation, he stresses the historicity of the medieval concept of *figura* to the point of treating it as the normative meaning in his essay. Restricting the significance of *figura* to historical prophecy, he ultimately separates the idea from symbolism altogether: "What actually makes the two forms completely different is that figural prophecy relates to an interpretation of history – indeed it is by nature a textual interpretation – while the symbol is a direct interpretation of life and originally no doubt for the most part, of nature."[34] This artificial dichotomy has been accepted by most subsequent critics, who have limited the relevance of *figura* to typological narrative and have used Auerbach's work to interpret Protestant typology as a variant of medieval typology.[35] Sacvan Bercovitch has shown that American Puritan typology defies Auerbach's distinction. Historical prophecy and narrative were fundamentally symbolist as well as figural, and the concept of nature, even where it seems ahistorical, was deeply indebted to figural interpretation well into the nineteenth century.[36] However, Bercovitch, too, begins by essentially assuming Auerbach's interpretation, and consequently his argument likewise omits consideration of the importance of classical thought for the Protestant Reformation.[37]

What this critical approach most invites us to forget is that there was no predominant sense of history in the immense variety of classical meanings of *figura,* and in most cases no sense of historicity at all. In the Protestant synthesis of classical and Christian thought, typological symbolism was only one aspect of a far more comprehensive, and for the most part ahistorical, theory of shapes – material, aerial, real, imaginary, natural and artificial, proper and figurative. For Puritan orators and iconoclasts, whose main concern was conversion through preaching and the destruction of false images, it is not surprising that a rhetorical and imagistic theory developed that had little to do with Christian interpretations of Old Testament history. In the "lively words" of the seventeenth-century preacher, Puritan iconoclasts heard the rhetorical counterpart of the "lively and natural images" they saw before them.

4

Verbal images, history, and marriage

As a seventeenth-century Puritan, John Cotton was heir to an already substantial iconoclastic tradition, and his own life and works show a firm adherence to it. For Cotton, as for other Puritans, English nonconformity was essentially an iconoclastic act. About 1615, shortly after he had become vicar of St. Botolph's church in Boston, Lincolnshire, he adopted the Puritan practice of refusing vestments, genuflection, and the use of the cross in baptism – all "images" he believed to be false.[1] An early writing defending his actions, a short tract on the need for "edification" in religious practice, shows the influence of Elizabethan Puritanism in its defense of nonconformity.[2] Cotton also seems to have advocated iconoclastic violence. In 1621 iconoclasts destroyed statuary and stained glass windows in St. Botolph's church. As one observer described it, "Pictures and statues and images, and for their sakes the windows and walls wherein they stood have been heretofore and of late pulled down and broken in pieces and defaced." Cotton disclaimed any association with this violence, but he may have done so for political reasons, since, to judge from his preaching, he was probably in favor of it.[3] His sermons on Canticles, delivered sometime after 1620 and probably about the same time as the destruction at St. Botolph's, openly expressed his aversion to "idolatry." Moreover, he specifically exhorted his hearers "to hate all abuses in Gods worship, even the very monuments of Idolatrie, and to take them away, as *Hezekiah* did the brazen Serpent."[4]

Like his predecessors, Cotton interpreted the Second Commandment both as a sanction and as a prohibition: "Though God forbid men to make themselves any Images, or likeness in his worship, yet he hath not forbidden himselfe this power to prescribe an Image or forme to us."[5] The Second Commandment requires "a distinction of Images," a differentiation of true and false images, "for the Law itselfe in con-

65

demning Images and the imaginations of mens devising, commandeth and establisheth the Images and imaginations ordained by God" (AB24). For him, as for other seventeenth-century Puritans, anything construed as "the imaginations or inventions of men" fell within the domain of the commandment: "The second *Commandement,* in forbidding Images, forbiddeth not onely bodily Images, (graven or molten, or painted) but all spirituall Images also; which are the imaginations and inventions of men" (AB17). And whatever kind of image the commandment could prohibit, it could also sanction. Cotton's emphasis on the comprehensiveness of the commandment reflects his concern to find a sanction for images that were verbal, poetic, or visionary, what we would now call literary or mental images rather than icons. His interpretation reflects the fact that his iconoclasm, aside from his nonconformity in dress and gesture, was a verbal phenomenon. Like the beliefs of the early Protestants concerning icons, his attitude toward verbal images was one of oblique reverence that often found expression in seeming repudiation.

It is difficult to underestimate the importance of verbal images in Cotton's religion. For example, in the sermons on Canticles from the 1620s, his polemic on icons presupposed a viable poetic image, the church as a "spouse" who was in danger of occupying a "harlot's bed," a building with icons (C43–44). The importance of verbal imagery that is evident in this early work was sustained throughout his career. If anything, this aspect of his thought became even more important in New England. About 1640, in America, he preached on the entire book of Revelation, and several years later he preached again on the complete text of Canticles.[6] As we will see, his beliefs about images were even the foundation of his theory of New England church polity. Far from subordinating or dismissing the imagery of prophecies, dreams, poetry, and parables in Scripture, Cotton founded his Puritanism upon them.

Seventeenth-century Puritans such as Cotton expanded the category of sanctioned rhetorical figures by relying in part on the work of William Perkins. We have already seen how Perkins developed Calvin's belief in icons, generalizing beyond the sacrament to a more comprehensive interpretation of material shapes. Perkins was equally intrigued by the possibilities he saw in the importance Calvin assigned to metonymy. Since the religious beliefs that justified iconoclasm also enshrined metonymy, Calvin's beliefs potentially granted a new importance to tropes in general. The significance of the rhetorical imagination in his theory was characteristic of the thought of most early Protestants. With the exception of Luther (an exception we will consider shortly), Reformation intellectuals self-consciously proposed some kind of figu-

rative interpretation of the sacrament's consecrating words. Calvin remarks that his adversaries denounced him as a "tropist," and this was
an epithet he shared with other Reformers.[7] From Perkins's late sixteenth-century perspective, such denunciations merely pointed to the
virtue of the early Reformers' insight into the figurative nature of religious language.[8]

Perry Miller has argued that Perkins's influence on Puritanism was
chiefly the blight of anti-rhetoric, but in fact Perkins was quite
willing to worship a rhetorical deity who communicated through
tropes and figures.[9] Moreover, in his defense of the intrinsic theological value of tropes, it is apparent that Perkins developed his ideas
by generalizing from Calvin's beliefs about metonymy. A summary
of sacramental doctrine in "A Golden Chaine" suggests the direction
of his thought:

> It commeth to passe, that the signes, as it were certaine visible words
> incurring into the external senses, do by a certaine proportionable
> resemblance draw a Christian minde to the consideration of the things
> signified, and to be applyed.
>
>   This mutuall, and, as I may say, sacramentall relation, is the cause
> of so many figurative speeches and Metonymies which are used: as
> when one thing in the Sacrament is put for another. [1.72]

Metonymy has become only one kind of figure in Scripture, and other
"figurative speeches" indicate, presumably, other sacramental relations
with the "things signified." Perkins implies that the analogies that inform the world can be conceived as tropes and reordered specifically to
the consecrating power of the "sacramentall relation." In his synthesis
of natural philosophy and sacramental theory, "proportionable resemblance" has a religious origin – or needs to be given one – in the deity's
scriptural figures, which happen to coincide with the figures of classical
rhetoric.[10]

In "The Arte of Prophecying," Perkins's belief in the privileged status
of rhetorical tropes and figures is even more obvious and more elaborate
and clearly shows the dependence of Puritan theology on rhetoric. He
delineates what he calls the "sacred tropes" of Scripture, subordinating
"sacramentall metonymy" as a particular example of a much more
broadly rhetorical approach to "the waies of expounding" the text. Perkins begins with the rhetorical figure that was frequently used to describe
the deity: "An *Anthropo-pathia* is a sacred Metaphor, whereby those
things, that are properly spoken of man, are by a similitude attributed
unto God" (2.656). Although he raises the issue of material shapes, and
the relation between the human form and the *figura* of the deity, he does
not say how one should understand the significance of this metaphor or

why he places it first. Rather, here and elsewhere he is concerned to substantiate the pervasiveness of tropes in religious thought, especially in passages of Scripture and principles of theology that had not previously been considered relevant to the use of tropes. The second of the "sacred tropes," "Sacramentall Metonymie," includes the sacrifice of the Paschal Lamb as a type among the examples (2.656). Synecdoche accounts, among other things, for the way in which the grace of Christ is communicated to those who are saved: "The communication of the properties is a *Synecdoche,* by the which by reason of the personall union, that is spoken of the whole person of Christ, which doth properly belong to one of his two natures" (2.656). The subsequent list includes a wide variety of classical figures, for example, superlatives (hyperbole), ellipsis, pleonasm, irony, and repetitions of words or sounds (2.657–59). Many of these "sacred tropes" express major theological ideas in Puritanism, and the extent to which Perkins favors a figurative interpretation of Scripture appears to be open-ended. Moreover, he does not hesitate to alter single, apparently literal, words of considerable theological import. It is sometimes necessary, he says, to substitute "many" for "all," "nothing" for "little" or "small," "none" for "few," and "often" or "long" for "alwaies" (2.657). To judge from the scriptural texts he quotes for illustration, it is by just such means that he arrives at his doctrines of limited atonement, the complete corruption of man by original sin – indeed, any of the theological statements where the expression of quantity is significant.

One might expect Perkins to privilege metonymy as Calvin does, but although he shows some preference for metonymy, it would be more accurate to say that he favors different tropes at different times. In "The Arte of Prophecying," he asserts that "all tropes are emphaticall" (2.659), that is, hyperbolic, but when he categorically defines "sacred tropes," he describes them metonymically as the "change [of] one nowne (or name) for another" (2.656). Despite this general definition, he does not make any attempt to show systematically how sacred tropes in general are ordered to a metonymic concept of figuration. In "Idolatrie," he again attempts to develop metonymy as a mode, here as a means of interpreting profane artistic images:

> Images (I graunt) are called often in Scripture gods, but for two other causes. First, because in mans intention they have a relation to God, and represent him. And therefore by a metonymie they borrow his name; as a painted man is called a man, or, as he that plaies the part of a king [in the theater], is called a king. Secondly, they are called gods, because men, though not in opinion and judgment, yet in truth made them their gods, in that they gave religious worshippe unto them. [1.661]

In "A Reformed Catholike" metaphor is implicitly invoked as a comprehensive trope, but the interpretation emphasizes a general, imagistic interpretation of verbal rituals rather than the development of metaphor as
a mode: "The right images of the new Testament which we hold and
acknowledge, are the doctrine and preaching of the Gospell, and all
things that by the word of God pertaine thereto. . . . Hence it followes,
that the preaching of the word is as a most excellent picture in which
Christ with his benefits are lively represented unto us" (1.580). In the
conceptual value he attributes to tropes, Perkins proposes an essentially
figural approach to theology, but these examples are characteristic of the
limited extent to which he is willing to develop the possibilities of any
one trope. In this respect he is a provocative thinker, but not a systematic
one. His main concern is to call attention to the wide variety of significant "figurative speeches" in Scripture, to argue that the tropes and
figures of Scripture are a compelling basis for any major tenet of Puritan
theology, and to suggest an imagistic interpretation of verbal rituals.

Cotton fully shares Perkins's beliefs about the intrinsic theological
value of tropes and figures, and some of his works suggest the direct
influence of Perkins. In an early tract on the celebration of the sabbath,
Cotton uses the trope of synecdoche as the basis for his argument.[11]
Such reasoning also appears in *The Way of Life,* where he argues from a
synecdoche that the Puritan elect within England have prevented the
deity's destruction of the country (WL71).[12] In his own rhetorical practice, Cotton's use of sound design, hyperbole, metaphor, and other
rhetorical figures implies that he also accepted Perkins's tracts as a
mandate for the use of tropes and figures in preaching. Cotton differs
from Perkins in the prominence he gives to the verbal images of concrete shapes and in the systematic claims he makes for their theological
value. His major statements on figurative meaning are less a defense of
tropes than a defense of imagery, and especially the imagery of Canticles, Revelation, and the parables of the Gospels.

Cotton's defense of figurative meaning was less obviously indebted
than Perkins's to sacramental theory, and more systematic and comprehensive in its claims for the theological value of "allegorie." Perkins's
belief that tropes and figures could be a source of theological doctrine
became in Cotton's works the belief that imagery was actually superior
in some respects to literal meaning. It was not just a case of recognizing
"allegorie" as a source of truth equivalent to literal statements, "uttering the same sense," as Perkins had claimed.[13] For Cotton, the verbal
images of Scripture expressed uniquely revelatory truths that could not
be found in other passages. Although many of Perkins's examples imply that tropes and figures could be considered privileged discourse,
Cotton's tracts – and particularly his New England tracts – were far

more self-conscious, explicit, and systematic in their defenses of verbal figures.

Cotton's most forthright defense of figurative language occurred in the context of debates about church polity during the English Civil War. In the 1640s, about ten years after his immigration to Boston, Massachusetts, he defended the New England Puritan church in several tracts written for publication in London. In his last major tract, *Of The Holinesse of Church-Members,* published in 1650 just two years before his death, Cotton responded to objections against his defense of the powers of the church as an institution. His argument for Congregationalism, the opponents charged, was nothing more than "symbolic theology," an exposition of scriptural imagery that was merely "a kinde of Ratiocination, which sollid Divinity will not admit."[14] His critics had appealed to the authority of Aquinas, specifically to the principle that symbolic theology was not argumentative. Theological truth, they argued, could not be discovered or defended through the interpretation of the symbols and parables of Scripture. In response, Cotton made no attempt whatsoever to argue that his hermeneutics were in accord with traditional scholastic principles. Indeed, he gave no hint of even wanting to be understood as anything but a figuralist.

Cotton condemned his opponents' aversion as "neither good Logick, nor good Divinity," and he did so with full awareness of the scholastic argument against symbolic theology (H68). "Great divines," he rejoined, had been "too shye of searching particularly into the interpretation of Scripture Parables. But I believe that shynesse hath sprung from that Axiome of *Aquinas,* which after him obtained too great credit in the Schooles of Divines" (H69). If "sollid Divinity" were less enthralled with scholastic delusions, he argued, it would be evident that the "parabolical" portions of Scripture were an important source of divine truth (H69). In the seventeenth-century usage of Cotton and his critics, "symbols" and "parables" had a much wider range of meaning than we give them now. "Parable" referred to the figurative passages of Scripture, including the parables of Christ, but also more generally to any similitude, comparison, or allegorical narrative. In its broadest sense, a parable was any kind of speech in which something was expressed in terms of something else. "Symbol" also meant figurative meaning in general, a term more or less interchangeable with "parable."[15] In short, Cotton defended as a viable source of religious truth what we would now call the poetic or literary portions of Scripture.

He contended that spiritual truths could not always be found, as Aquinas had claimed, in the literal statements of doctrine in Scripture. Symbols and parables were intrinsically true and irreducible to the literal passages of Scripture:

And why should Christ (as well as some Prophets before him, and *John* the Apostle after him) delight so much in Symbols and Parables, if they were not Doctrinall and Argumentative? It is true, the Legs of the lame are not equall; so is a Parable in a fools mouth, saith *Solomon.* But Christ (the wisdome of the Father) was no foole: He would never have so much accustomed himselfe to Symbols and Parables, if so much of them were to be pared off (as huskes and shells) in the interpretation thereof (as commonly is done by Expositors), or if Parables were not effectually Argumentative to all those ends of the Ministry, for which any other word of Doctrin might serve? Evident it is to any that shall observe and meditate on the Parable[s] of Christ without a forestalled prejudice taken from that Thomisticall unsound principle, That whether Christ be to teach, or convince, or reprove, or confirme, or comfort his hearers; all these ends he both intendeth, and attaineth in his Parables. [H69]

Cotton maintained that "symbols" and "parables" were "doctrinal" and "argumentative" – in short, that Aquinas was simply wrong. The poetic figures of Scripture were true and real in their own right. Moreover, parabolical meaning could sometimes reveal what ordinary literal meaning could not, for otherwise the prophets, Jesus, and John would not have used symbols and parables where "any other word of Doctrin might serve." Cotton alluded to the traditional hermeneutic cliché, that the "huskes and shells" of figurative meaning must be "pared off" to find the concealed kernel of literal meaning, but only to show that this metaphor was inadequate to describe the character of biblical truth. The scholastics had been "foole" enough to throw away what they had believed to be mere husks and shells, but symbols and parables, Cotton argued, were actually essential to religious truth.

Cotton's defense of parabolical meaning was a sweeping attack on the traditional fourfold typology, particularly as Aquinas had explained it. In the Aquinan formulation that Cotton found so inimical to his own ideas and "unsound" theologically, parabolical meaning was simply a footnote, an afterthought. Aquinas had asserted in his *Summa Theologiae:*

> Besides these four interpretations [i.e., the fourfold typology], there is the parabolical, which has been omitted [from the preceding fourfold structure]. . . . The parabolical meaning is contained in the literal [sense of Scripture], since the words indicate something properly, and also something figuratively. *The literal sense is not the figure itself, but that which is figured* [*nec est literalis sensus ipsa figura, sed id quod est figuratum*]. For when Scripture speaks of the arm of the Lord, the literal sense is not that God has such a bodily member, but that he has what such a bodily member indicates, namely active power. It is thus clear that the literal interpretation of Scripture cannot contain what is false.[16]

Employing the notion of the "literal sense" as it meant that which is true and real, Aquinas dismissed "parabolical" *figurae* as theologically fictitious in themselves. He allowed the importance and legitimacy of such figures for the illustration of doctrine, and even conceded they were "necessary and useful" in preaching, but he claimed they had no theological value.[17]

Cotton's use of metaphoric images in sermons demonstrates that the value he ascribed to imagery went well beyond the homiletic purpose Aquinas had given it. In his tracts on church polity, Cotton is explicit about the intrinsic significance of images. In contrast to the doctrines of scholastic theology, Cotton thought parabolical figures essential because they *were* uniquely revelatory of theological ideas. "Parabolicall speeches" such as Canticles, and "mysticall scriptures" such as the Revelation of John, were essential to the meaning of Scripture. Far from being cryptic images, Cotton found them especially revealing, images that "not onely pointed at, but decyphered" the world, just as metonymy had deciphered the sacrament for Calvin.[18] Where literal meaning merely represented doctrine by the conventional signification of words, such parabolical images as John's description of the apocalyptic beast revealed theological "arguments" in the "figure and resemblance" of the image itself (R2).[19] The figures that Aquinas had found merely useful to the preacher's work became theologically crucial in Cotton's Puritanism.

The theological significance of parabolical meaning was the basis of Cotton's ideas about the institutional power of the church. In his major tract on the church as an institution, *The Keyes of the Kingdom of Heaven,* he began by calling attention to the metaphor of the keys in Matt. 16.19, his central proof text, and to the need to "open the words" because they were "allegorical."[20] He meant allegory in a poetic or rhetorical sense, *not* typology, for his tract concerned the nature of power indicated by the metaphor of "the keys" and the nature of the polity determined by the metaphor of the church as "one body." These were images whose meanings he had "opened" in the Canticles sermons in the 1620s, where he had described "such congregations as do enjoy the power of the keys" (C46).[21] In 1644 in *The Keyes,* Cotton gave the justification he would repeat almost verbatim in 1650:

> If any man say, *Theologia symbolica,* or *parabolica non est argumentativa,* that arguments from such parables and mysticall resemblances in Scripture are not valid, let him enjoy his owne apprehension: and (if he can yeeld a better interpretation of the place) let him waive this collection. Nevertheless, if there were no argumentative power in parables, why did the Lord Jesus so much delight in that kind of teaching? and why did John and Daniel, and Ezekiel deliver a great

part of their prophecies in parables, if we must take them for riddles, and not for documents nor arguments? Surely if they serve not for argument they serve not for document.[22]

Parables, symbols, allegory, mystical resemblances – all these terms referred to the parabolical sense rather than typology.[23]

By claiming that scriptural imagery had a special revelatory quality, a peculiar power of decipherment, Cotton reversed the relation between parabolical meaning and fourfold typology. As he knew, his disdain for Aquinas carried the weight of Protestant intellectual tradition behind it. The writings of sixteenth-century Reformers are strewn with vituperous denunciations of the Augustinian–Aquinan fourfold interpretation, and their general import is unmistakable. "The foure-fold meaning of the Scripture must be exploded and rejected," wrote William Perkins in a Calvinistic outburst thoroughly characteristic of sixteenth-century English Protestants (1.651).[24] Cotton shared the hostility of these sixteenth-century Protestants toward Aquinas, but his manner of rejecting scholastic typology was different. Where English Protestants such as Tyndale, Whitaker, and Perkins attacked fourfold typology, leaving the corollary on parabolical meaning untouched, Cotton inverted the relative values of the parabolical sense and fourfold typology.[25] As his defenses in *The Keyes* and *The Holinesse of Church-Members* show, Cotton unabashedly placed himself on the poetic rather than the typological side of scholastic interpretation. He thus shifted the focus of his hermeneutics away from typology and greatly increased the importance of imagistic figurative language.

Although Cotton employed a wide range of tropes and figures in his rhetorical practice throughout his career, his theoretical defenses of figurative meaning and exegeses of parabolical texts do not involve the verbal sensitivity we would expect from a skilled classical rhetorician. Cotton often seems indifferent to the fact that verbal images are presented through language in Scripture, for he repeatedly treats such imagery as if it were the actual concrete shape represented. The emphatically visual quality of Cotton's most cherished figures – symbols, metaphors, allegories, and dream images – is more closely related to the nonlinguistic concept of *figura* as material shape than to any theory of tropes.[26] In this respect, Luther rather than Calvin or Perkins was probably the most influential precedent.

Luther displays a disdain for rhetorical sophistication throughout his tracts on sacramental theory. Unlike most of his fellow Protestants, Luther refused any kind of figurative interpretation of the consecrating words, denouncing "figurists," "tropists," and "representationalists" alike as "fanatics."[27] Luther believed instead in the "sacramental union" of body and bread, a union of "two diverse substances" both in "reality and in name."[28] He insisted repeatedly that tropes had nothing to do with sacramental interpretation, that one had only to understand the simple grammar of the text and accept the words literally – a stance that earned him the denunciation of "literalist" from Calvin (1383). Luther emphasized the physical presence of Christ, "that Christ's body and blood are distributed in the bread and the cup," an argument that depended on a literal interpretation of the phrase "This is my body."[29] For him, the relation between word and referent was a pure equation that did not require rhetorical analysis. It was a relation so obvious that there was nothing to debate, and Luther by and large refused to defend his own views beyond the sheer demand that he be believed.

Luther seems at first to have valued concrete shapes as little as he valued tropes. Although he believed that "the bread remains" in consecration, this aspect of the sacrament seems to have concerned him very little.[30] He opposed Catholic transubstantiation, but not strongly, and he even remarked that "it is of no great consequence whether the bread remains or not."[31] The difference between his theory and Calvin's becomes evident in his debates with Oecolampadius on the meaning of *figura* in patristic exegesis. Concerning Tertullian's paraphrase of the consecrating words *figura corporis mei* (the figure of my body), Luther argued erroneously that *figura* could not possibly mean "interpretive sign" because its only Latin meaning was material shape:

> We say that Tertullian employs the word *figura* in accordance with proper usage in the Latin language, where it means a form or figure in the mathematical sense—stating whether a thing is long, thick, broad, round, white or black, which one can see, feel, and handle, as we Germans also say about the sacrament that Christ's body is present under the form of the bread and his blood under the form of the wine. Exactly that which we call *gestalt,* "form," Tertullian calls in Latin *figura*.[32]

Unlike Calvin, whose metonymic interpretation acknowledged some kind of relation between word and material referent, Luther interpreted the words of the sacrament in a way that made the consecrated *figura* anonymous. Because he believed the word "body" was literal, and referred to something "under" the *figura* of the bread, the bread as material object was totally unacknowledged in the language of consecration. The *figura* was neither transubstantiated nor named. It was simply there and unnamed, dissociated from the interpretive signs of language altogether.

The complete separation of words and things in Luther's theory denigrated the material object more profoundly than Calvin's idea of the fetishistic empty token, because the material object was unrecognized in the consecrating words that Luther accepted as definitive of reality. The bread was so fully taken over by Christ's body that it ceased to be significant in the most fundamental sense. However, by its very exclusion the *figura* of the material object acquired a far more mysterious power than Calvin's living images. Unrecognized in language, it could not be controlled by language, made subservient to the "interpretive sign." Oddly, Luther's contempt for the material object could be, and was, transformed into its opposite: a reverence for the power of material shapes that fueled iconoclasm more strongly than any of Calvin's pronouncements.

Luther's two prefaces to Revelation demonstrate how his own doctrine inverted itself. In his first preface, published in 1522, Luther dismissed Revelation as a spurious work, "neither apostolic nor prophetic" because "Apostles do not deal with visions, but prophesy in clear, plain words."[33] By 1545, however, he had changed his views considerably, interpreting Revelation as a cryptic prophecy of the destruction of Rome. Where initially he had rejected the book because it consisted solely of images and lacked literal statements of doctrine, he was now intrigued by it for the same reason, for what he described as its oddly nonverbal quality. In his preface of 1545, Luther distinguished three kinds of "prophecy" in Scripture, of which the first two were explicit interpretations. "The first," he explained, "does it in express words, without images and figures [*Bilde und Figuren*]. So Moses, David, and more of the prophets prophesy of Christ, and Christ and the apostles prophesy of Antichrist, false teachers, etc."[34] The second kind of prophecy "does this with images [*Bilden*], but sets alongside them their interpretation in express words. So Joseph interprets dreams and Daniel both dreams and images [*Bilder*]."[35] Unlike the first two kinds, the third kind of prophecy did not depend on words at all, but simply offered "mute" images, material shapes:

> The third sort of prophecy, which is without word or interpretaion, does it with bare images and figures [*die es ohn Wort oder Auslegung, mit blossen Bilden und Figuren thut*], like this book of Revelation and like the dreams, visions and images [*Bilder*] that many holy people have from the Holy Spirit. . . . So long as this kind of prophecy remains without explanation and gets no sure interpretation, it is a concealed, mute prophecy [*eine verborgene stumme Weissagung*], and has not yet come to the profit and fruit which it is to give to Christendom.[36]

John prophesied exclusively "with bare images and figures," but what had been cause for rejection earlier was now construed as a peculiar virtue of the text.

The textuality of the text was of no interest to Luther in the "third sort" of prophecy. He took the literal meaning of the "mute prophecy" for granted, assuming the referential significance of the words. In effect, he again dissociated the material object from the interpretive sign by refusing to acknowledge the verbal presentation of the image. Language, and interpretation, belong solely to the interpreter. Oblivious of the fact that the images of Revelation were verbally composed, Luther proposed to decode this "concealed, mute prophecy," to make it speak and reveal its secrets, by discovering what images and historical events "rhyme and conjoin":

> Since it is intended as a revelation of things that are to happen in the future, and especially of tribulations and disasters for the Church, we consider that the nearest and surest grip toward finding its interpretation would be [*das sollte der näheste und gewisseste Griff sein, die Auslegung zu finden*] to take from history the events and disasters which have come upon the Church before now and hold them up alongside these images [*Bilder*], and thus place our comparison onto the Word [*und also auf die Wort vergliche*]. Where, then, they should subtly rhyme and agree with each other, we could establish our footing on that as on a sure interpretation, or at least as on an interpretation not to be overturned [*Wo sichs alsdenn würde fein mit einander reimen und eintreffen, so künnte man drauf fussen, als auf eine gewisse oder zum wenigsten als auf eine unverwerfliche Auslegung*].[37]

His rhetoric, no less than his idea, emphasized what was for him the only proper classical meaning of *figura:* material shape. His imagery of grasping and establishing a footing "on" the text, along with the acoustic metaphor of subtle rhyming that characterized the method of exposition, implied a physical engagement with the text similar to Calvin's interpretations of icons. However concealed the ultimate historical significance of the text, the words transparently displayed the "bare image," the *figura* itself, with vivid plainness. Luther's literal-minded approach to the figures of the text revered the mute image as if it were an icon rather than a verbal construct, casting exegesis as physical domination.

Cotton's intrepretations of Canticles and Revelation followed the method of exegesis that Luther outlined in his 1545 preface to Revelation. Cotton's more immediate source, however, was Thomas Brightman, an Elizabethan Protestant who composed an exegesis of Revelation very similar to what Luther had advocated. Moreover, it was Brightman, not Luther, who perceived the possibility of applying the same method to Canticles. As Brightman explained, "This Prophecie following [in Canticles] agreeth well neere in all things with that of Saint *John in the Revelation.* They fore-shew the same events in the like times. And either of them directeth his course to the same marke."[38] Brightman's extension of Luther's method opened the way to a general defense of scriptural imagery that differed significantly from Perkins's speculations about tropes and figures. Oddly, the foundation of this Lutheran theory of imagery was neither poetics nor rhetoric as such, but rather a nonlinguistic interpretation of material shapes.[39]

Cotton's English sermon notes on Canticles are his earliest extant interpretation of a parabolical book of Scripture. These notes are generally overlooked by critics and historians, but they are important because they show how Cotton initially synthesized the ideas of Luther, Calvin, Perkins, and Brightman in formulating an iconoclastic theory of verbal images. These notes are also worth detailed attention because, in one crucial respect, Cotton goes beyond his predecessors. He explicitly introduces the significance of gender for the interpretation of canonical images. Developing a theory of textual images and a theory of history simultaneously, Cotton makes both dependent on a concept of gender that extols the imaginations of men while repudiating the imaginations of women. As we will see, by interpreting the wedding feast (the social situation of the poem) as essential to Solomon's prophecy, Cotton transforms the bridegroom into a Christian visionary who spurns not only Judaic beliefs, but also his wife, in his discovery of Christianity.

Adapting Luther's method of exegesis for his basic framework, Cotton interprets the love poetry of the Song of Solomon as an allegory of history: Hidden within the cryptic, parabolical figures of the text is the narrative of past, present, and future churches. As he moves from poetic image to historical event, from verbal icon to living icon, Cotton's rhyming of poetry and history seems completely arbitrary: "*Behold, thou* art *faire* my beloved, *yea pleasant, also* our bed is *greene:* ver. 16. This is the estate of the Church in the dayes of good Josiah" (C42). A more expansive interpretation does little to mitigate the bizarre quality of this matching method of exegesis:

> Ver. 1. I am come into my garden, my sister, my *spouse, I* have gathered my *Myrrhe* with my *spice, I* have eaten my *honeycombe* with my *honey, I* have *drunke* my wine with my *milke: eate,* O *friends, yea drinke* abundantly, O beloved.
>
> *Constantine* came into the Church, enjoyed the fellowship of it, did partake in all the parts of it, yea and richly endowed it; so that the Church and all her friends did eat and *drinke,* yea and did drinke abundantly of wealth, preferments, &c., whence it was that shee fell into a deepe sleepe. [C139]

In the context of these examples, Christ loves his church according to the traditional allegory in which Solomon, as a figure of Christ, loves his bride, the church. But in addition, Christ loves his church in particular ways at particular times – in Cant. 1.16, for example, by sending Josiah to reform the "church," or in Cant. 5.1, where Christ loves his church more obliquely, by creating an afflicting surfeit of luxury in the reign of Constantine (C42–43, 139–42). What creates the effect of translated hieroglyphics is Cotton's persistent determination to show a particular historical referent for each textual image, matching ecclesiastical history and the Song of Solomon.

Cotton follows Brightman's interpretation closely at most points, and he also adopts Brightman's belief that the philosophy of resemblances governs the conjoining of verbal image and historical event, what Brightman refers to as the relation of convenience, "the correspondence of things [*convenientia rerum*]."[40] As Cotton explains it, Solomon's poetry is a hieroglyphic in which history is "not only pointed at, but deciphered" by mystical "resemblances" that have a "correspondency" to the events they describe (C223, C10). Unlike Brightman, Cotton explicitly fuses the natural philosophy of resemblance and the rhetorical concept of appropriateness to account for the "sutablenesse of the words" to "the events of each age" (C10). The resulting correspondence creates a metaphoric differentiation with poetry as one locus and history as the other. As a whole, Cotton's notes seem like two completely different books spliced together, one a pastiche of literary images and the other a quite intelligible prose history.

Cotton's exposition differs from typological narratives because he describes historical events as they fulfill poetic figures of the text, not as they fulfill Old Testament historical events. Assuming that Solomon's Song follows historical chronology, Cotton divides Canticles into sections corresponding to historical periods. Although this is purportedly a history of the collective "estate of the church," Cotton tends to define historical eras by influential individuals – Solomon, Hezekiah, Josiah, Nehemiah, and so on. He recounts Old Testament history under the kings of Israel and Judah until he reaches Cant. 3.6–11, where, he says, John the Baptist is the historical referent (C83). Chapter 4 begins with the life of Jesus and concludes with the persecutions after the deaths of the apostles. Chapter 5 and most of 6 are devoted to a synopsis of European history after Constantine. Here Cotton's sense of who was important is quite familiar from a modern perspective, disturbingly so considering the rationale for this historical narrative. For example, Cotton emphasizes the Waldensians, the Albigensians, and the reforms of Wycliffe and Huss, and he includes authors of the Italian Renaissance: "The Ministry of the Gospell should be then more powerfull; and indeed God, about that time, *Anno* 1300. stirred up *Dante, Marcillius, Potavinus, Ocham, Gregorius Ariminensis, Petrarchus, Wickliffe,* and many more, whose Ministry brought on so many, that some have counted it the first resurrection" (C158). Heroes of the Renaissance and Reformation blend together as the religious descendants of the kings of Israel and Judah.

Although Cotton implicitly privileges his own religion by attributing it to all sorts of believers over many centuries, he never proposes overtly that either Protestants or Puritans are exemplary. Luther demarcates the beginning of a historical era, but since this era follows a centuries-long account of reform in the church, neither Luther nor the Protestant Reformation in general constitutes the climactic turning point we might expect. Protestantism is portrayed as one more revival, though an important one, in the long-standing struggle to purge the church of "idolatry." England is cast as a worthy participant, but no more than that. While the churches of the English Reformation are "beautiful as Tirzah," so are the churches under the Duke of Saxony (C174–75). England does have its own line, Cant. 6.4 "Terrible as an army with banners" (a reference to the defeat of the Spanish Armada [C176]), yet Cotton's perception of the Protestant Reformation is always international in scope. The "eyes" of the bride, for example, are French and German as well as English: "What worthy Ministers did that first age of the Reformed Churches yeeld? as *Luther, Calvin, Martin Bucer, Cranmer, Hooper, Ridley,* Latymer" (C177).

Ironically, Cotton's own generation is actually diminished in this historical perspective by having so many illustrious predecessors. The greater political and military power on the Continent, and the antecedent intellectual and poetic achievements of such men as Dante in the "ministry of the gospel," make the Puritans and Cotton himself appear quite insignificant by comparison. He declines to interpret his own present time as a definitive turning point in history: Cant. 6.10, corresponding with the 1620s, is no more significant than the preceding texts/events. Cotton describes the nature of "congregations," but he makes no overt claims for institutional uniqueness, as he does later in his New England sermons. The importance of his own concept of the church remains implicit, but nevertheless substantial, in the sheer assumption that all of preceding history has been devoted to the same cause, the institution to which he himself is devoted. The turn of Cotton's own narrative from history to prophecy, from past events to imagined future, is of no consequence to him. As far as he is concerned, he is interpreting Solomon's poetic vision, not history, and since the text continues on in more or less the same manner, so does he. In the matching method of exegesis, it is the capacity of the parabolical text to continue "deciphering" events in the same way that supposedly makes the prophetic narrative of history persuasive.

The historical prophecy juxtaposed with the later chapters in Canticles is teleological, but it is not the teleology of later American Puritan histories such as Edward Johnson's *Wonder-Working Providence* or Cotton Mather's *Magnalia Christi Americana*.[41] The privileged "place" in history and geography does not belong to the Puritans. It belongs instead to the Jews and to the prophesied future "churches" of Assyria and Egypt. The address to the Shulamite at the conclusion of chapter 6 prophesies "the calling and arising of the Church of the Jewes" (C192), and chapter 7 and the first part of 8 describe them. They, not the Puritans, will be the most perfect and pure of churches: "The Jews converted shall be of much glory and authority, even as the Kings of the Earth" (C208). The Gentiles do share the glory, but only as they "resort and flock to this church of the Jewes," recognizing its beauty and purity (C227). The Puritans do not have any special significance or unique purpose in this great turning point in history. They are exhorted to be merely an appreciative audience: "Since the Church of the Jewes shall attaine to so great beauty, it ought to kindle our desire to pray earnestly for their conversion, that wee may behold the admirable fairnesse thereof, and bee delighted with her consolations" (C239–40). Cant. 8.5 describes the conversion of Assyria and Egypt (C242–48), locating the end of historical change with the Semites, not the Puritans, and the final verses are devoted to a sketch of the world converted to Christianity, awaiting the coming of the millennial Christ.

Despite its seeming arcaneness, Cotton's method of interpretation shows an anxious distrust of imagery that Robert Adolph has described as characteristic of a "modern" plain style beginning with late seventeenth-century prose. It employs isolated images whose possible significance is carefully controlled, pinned down by logical explanations that closely define and delimit the relation between "tenor" and "vehicle," between the figure and what it signifies.[42] Cotton's approach fifty years earlier is similar. He controls the significance of the images in Canticles by isolating each from its poetic context and starkly equating it with a historical referent – for example, " 'His legs are as pillars of marble, set upon sockets of fine gold' [Cant. 5.15]. These two legs seem to be *John Hus* and *Jerome* of *Prague,* who stood constantly in defence of the trueth, even unto death" (C160). Although his argument is historical rather than scientific, Cotton evinces the same desire to curb the ambiguities of the figurative imagination by carefully delimiting the signification of images. The structure of the Canticles sermons controls the signification of poetic imagery in Scripture by treating it as a hieroglyph that must be translated into historical persons and events in order to be understood.

Adolph has argued that the control of figuration in the "modern" plain style placed little value in figurative language, but Cotton's iconoclastic principles of exegesis demonstrate a more complex attitude, the Calvinist's fear of the power of visible shapes and representational images to captivate the mind. Cotton's thought is informed not by a contempt for figurative language and its capabilities but rather by the iconoclast's negative recognition of the immense power of worldly things to enthrall Protestants in "idolatry." Cotton was by no means oblivious of the celebration of sensual pleasures in Canticles, and his characterization of them suggests that he found them as compelling as Calvin had found icons:

> The first Reason why this Song is more excellent then others, is, because this Song speaketh not onely of the chiefest matter, to wit, Christ and his Church; but also more largely than any of Davids Psalmes, and with more store of more sweet and precious, exquisite and amiable Resemblances, taken from the richest Jewels, the sweetest Spices, Gardens, Orchards, Vineyards, Wine-cellars, and the chiefest beauties and all the workes of God and Man. [C9]

Just as the iconoclasts disfigured the visual art that threatened them, so Cotton proceeds to disfigure the intrinsic integrity of a poem that celebrates the temptations he fears. For example, he explicates Cant. 4.3 in the following way:

> "Thy lips are like a thread of Scarlet, and thy speech is comely." Both signify the delivery or utterance of the Doctrine of the Church at that time, which was
>
> First, as a thread slender (*tenui filo,*) not plump or swelling with humane eloquence, but savouring of Fisher-like tenuitie and simplicitie.
>
> Secondly, as a thread of Scarlet; for as Scarlet or Purple is a princely and royall weare, so their Doctrine was,
>
> First, touching the kingdom of heaven, Mat. 10.7.
>
> Secondly, though tender, yet deeply dyed in graine with royall Majesty and authority of the Spirit of God. [C106–07]

The lips "like a thread of Scarlet" that speak in the plain style do not seem to belong to any person, or to any poem, because they have been appropriated for the plain style of church authority. Cotton conveys the irrelevance of poetic context by iconoclastically separating the simile from its poetic referent and giving it another referential status, the garb of royalty. Thus love poetry becomes a defense of the "majesty" and "authority" of the deity. The context of this verse in the poem is just as irrelevant as the context of a phrase within a line. Cotton ignores the intrinsic relations within the poem, and finally it does not seem to matter whether it is the bridegroom, the bride, or the images and metaphors that provide the figures for historical events. All that Cotton requires are named material shapes, identifiable *figurae*.

Paradoxically, his overriding concern with the figurative language of parabolical meaning leads him to assume an utterly simple relation between words and things, as simplistic as Luther's notion of images in Revelation. It is this concept of referentiality that we rightly associate with the anti-rhetoric of Puritanism and that is indeed a simplistic and authoritarian literalism. Perkins's contention that Christians are the living images of Christianity, superior to any artistic image, is reproduced in Cotton's sermons through the implied equation of the poetic qualities of the figure and the material shape, an equation that eliminates the poetic figure on the pretense that there is no significant difference: Poetic figures are composed of material shapes and material shapes are live art.

To say that history is "deciphered" by parabolical texts grants an unusual power to poetic images, but in exegetical practice it severely limits the imagination. While Cotton's theory of parabolical meaning grants the sacred power of revelation to the figures of the text, his historical exegesis iconoclastically disfigures the text of Canticles, systematically destroying the validity of these figures. The iconoclastic implication that parabolical meaning is both true and fictitious is expressed in the capacity of Solomon's poetry to signify, by resembling and deciphering, something categorically other than what it is itself. Although these images reveal religious truth, they are also false in the sense of figurative-and-not-literal. Each time Cotton assigns a unique historical referent to an image in the text, in effect he declares the poetic figure obsolete in its significance. Substituting historical event for poetic image, verse by verse through the first six chapters, Cotton implies that historical knowledge replaces poetic knowledge. Thus the relevance of visionary poetry that cryptically expresses historical events is itself constrained by history. That some events have yet to occur does not change the nature of the relation between poetry and history, for Cotton establishes the principle that these poetic figures, too, will ultimately be rendered irrelevant by events. The poetic vision of Solomon is made obsolete by the exegete's iconoclastic interpretation, the disfiguring act of negative reverence that makes these images safe, controlled in their signification. Ironically, the text can remain interesting only insofar as it is powerless to reveal historical events fully, a "mute prophecy" *in*capable of fully disclosing the prophetic secrets enclosed within it.

Like Calvin and Perkins before him, Cotton preaches against idolatry to establish the deity's true icons, the living images of Christian doctrine. The poetic text is replaced, not by secular history, as Cotton often seems to say, but by figural realism, a substitution analogous to Calvin's substitution of the common bread of the Lord's Supper for the wafer of the Catholic Mass. When weighed against the poetic figuration of the scriptural text, Cotton's historical passages may seem to be in a literal sense free of all figures, but history is intelligible to Cotton in figural terms as the successive living images of the church. It is the spiritual propriety of these historical figures, their identity as members of the mystical body of Christ, that rationalizes their inclusion. Cotton takes seriously Calvin's injunction to "mark well what this word, *Christianity*, meaneth: its meaning is to be members of the Son of God."[43] What appears to us as secular history is, from Cotton's perspective, the historical succession of eminent members of the mystical body.

Cotton's figural realism ignores Calvin's distinction between the representation of the past and the living icons of the sacrament. The great individuals of history in Cotton's chronicle are, in Calvin's terms, dead images, but Cotton grants them the status of sacramental *figurae* so that history becomes the history of proper icons. Consequently, the historical narrative acquires a strangely ahistorical quality. The members of the mystical body constitute a unity that transcends space: "[Churches are] at unity, or brotherly love one with another, as one body, though scattered into many places, as *England, Scotland, Germany,* &c. In all Christendome, some Churches are more chaste, mild, unspotted than others, even of the same countrey; and yet such are but few, and though few, yet at entire unity as one body" (C191). Similarly, this unity transcends time: "The estate of many Churches, in many ages, maketh but one bodie of Christ; in every one of which Christ manifesteth himselfe, in some members more eminently than in others" (C168). The figural members of the mystical body are significant because, as living icons, they give material shape to this invisible entity. From the perspective of spiritual appropriateness, historical change is incidental, for the pervasive identity of the mystical body across space and time persists despite historical, cultural, or geographical change. "Christ is not bound to any place," Cotton warns (C61). The deity is "bound" only to the members of his mystical "body," the living icons that manifest the deity's presence.

Whereas Cotton's theory of figurative meaning overtly grants primary authority to verbal images in Scripture, his exegetical practice accomplishes an iconoclastic reversal, granting superior authority to living icons. Purportedly, it is the mystical Christ of the sacrament who is the locus of reference. However, Christ is unknowable in proportion to the grandeur of his transcendence. By contrast, his iconic "members," are knowable, and they are knowable as they enact in history the emblematic qualities of the figures of the text. For example:

"His head is as of most fine gold" [Cant. 5.11]. Christ comes now to be described in his members more particularly: This head of gold Christ shewed on the earth in the person of *Frederick,* the second, *Emperour* of *Rome,* a Prince of much purity and worth, as a head of the church of fine gold! He contended with many Popes about the headship of the church, advanced the headship of Christ and of himselfe, his Vice-gerents, above the counterfeit head of the Popes Supremacy. [C155]

Although the mystical body of Christ is the ultimate theological referent, in exegetical practice poetic figures and historical figures are referred to each other for their intelligibility. Frederick II exemplifies the properties of gold, and the golden head signifies Frederick II.[44] The organic image of the mystical body, which refers to bodily *parts,* reflects the incapacity of the mystical Christ to determine referentiality. Frederick II, *not* the mystical "body," is the intelligible person who coheres as a whole human being. As simultaneously historical and figural, Frederick II and the other "members" of the mystical body are the sacramental icons in the temporal world, the determinants of proper meaning.

Cotton's adherence to the figural realism of historical knowledge may seem arbitrarily juxtaposed to the Song of Solomon, as if the historical narrative could get along very well without the poem. However, the juxtaposition itself is an act of iconoclasm, an adaptation of sacramental metonymy that functions as negative persuasion. Representationally, it is a visual absurdity to say that the apostles and/or their doctrine are the lips of the mystical body, or that Frederick II is its head. Cotton's acutely self-conscious use of imagery continually calls attention to itself, for his image of the church as Christ's body does not finally represent to the mind's eye a mental picture, and consequently his exegesis indirectly conveys the inadequacy of representation in the poem. As nonrepresentational imagery, the visual absurdity "marks" the presence of supernatural power. For the faithful, the mental picture is a mental blank, for the mystical body remains inconceivable visually, its reality marked by figures but its integral shape unknown. Within this system of thought, the pressure to believe is intense because, for the faithless literalist who insists on his idolatrous "mental picture," the visualized mystical body is a phantasmagoric horror, a grotesque image of things and people assembled to substitute for human bodily parts. In effect, Cotton's exposition of Canticles produces a figurative interpretation of imagery itself, a nonvisual "imagery" that shifts attention away from the text and toward the history of living images whose material identity and actions are figurally intelligible in the realist terms that the paradigmatic *figura* of the sacrament requires.

Cotton's figural realism enables him to move with ease and indifference between type and poetic image – between historical things, people, and events, on the one hand, and the imagery of the text, on the other. In his search for metaphors to ornament the mystical body, poetic image and "type" tend to merge as variants of the nonverbal *figura,* the visible material shape. Since Cotton does not explicate the words of the text so much as the symbolism of the things named by the words in the text, his interpretation of "types" as such acknowledges the materiality of types but rarely gives attention to their historicity. Thus "type" conveys the idea of a static and perceptible object or person, a material shape, but rarely the sense of a historical event. For example, Solomon's temple is a "type" (C48) in which the beams of cedar (Cant. 1.17) are emblematic of the virtues of the Protestant church. Cedar, noted for "durablenesse, enduring even unto eternity," is a metaphor for Luther's "beam of cedar, the doctrine of free justification by Christ" (C48–49). Similarly, beams of fir signify the ordinances of the church and the acts of its members, "such worship and workes for the people to walke in" (C48–49). What interests Cotton is simply the attributes of the building, its structure, its ornamentation, and its ritual function – its iconic qualities as a material shape that signifies.

Since the historical succession of living images leads progressively toward its culmination in the converted Jews, they offer the teleological reference point for the history Cotton relates. Implicitly, they are the subjects of a developmental typological narrative similar to what we think of as characteristically Protestant.[45] Cotton makes analogies between past and future Jewish communities by employing Old Testament narratives to clarify the nature and means of the conversion of the Jews to Christianity. Thus their history in the Old Testament prefigures their conversion at the millennium. This is an odd typology because it relates the literal Jews of the Old Testament to the figurative Jews he imagines, composing a temporal sequence of figure and fulfillment that relates Jews to each other. The strangeness of this typology emphasizes the° cognitive transformation of conversion, for Cotton's historicized fantasy limits propriety to one social locus, the Jews. The difference that is significant is the difference between an unconverted Jew who lives within temporal constraints and the converted Jew who transcends these constraints. What would this converted Jew be like? Solomon's vision refers us back to Solomon himself: As Christian visionary, Solomon provides the archetype. Cotton ultimately locates propriety in the author of the text, whose visionary words are his confession, the requisite proof that he is a Christianized Jew.

Cotton introduces the Christian reversal of propriety by means of a contrast between Moses, representing the unconverted, and Solomon, representing the converted: "And as God led Moses to the top of mount Pisgah, to behold all the places and situations of Israel: So he lifted up Solomons spirit to the mountaine of Activitie, (that I may so speake,) where onely all times to come are present, to behold the estate of the church throughout the present, and all after ages" (C13). Cotton exploits an Old Testament event as a figural analogy to express a Christian idea, granting historical reality to Moses' experience and superiority to the spiritual sense of it, but his contrast does not concern the historical sequence from Moses to Solomon. Rather, he emphasizes the *cognitive* contrast between the materially limited vision of Moses and the spiritual vision of Solomon. Unlike Moses' view of Canaan, Solomon's poetry is a mystical vision, collapsing temporality in a single moment that encompasses all history. Moses' view from Mount Pisgah is limited to that which the eye can literally see and classical propriety can comprehend, the social and geographical "places and situations" that he understands as the future prosperity of the Israelites alone. By contrast, Cotton praises Solomon's "spirit," because he perceives with an ahistorical vision in which "all times to come are present." Cotton grants the superior perception to his Protestant Solomon, who realizes that neither land nor temple, much less nationality, can be the "places and situations" where the deity manifests itself. Rather, Solomon's perception is a vision of the elect church throughout history, of people as living images.

By itself, the contrast between Moses and Solomon lends the impression that the Christianized Solomon is free of all social constraints, free of places and situations, of the determinants of proper meaning as classical rhetoric defined them. However, Cotton places Solomon in a highly specific situation, the occasion of his wedding, emphasizing at the outset that Solomon's Christian prophecy is a vision inspired by the particular situation of the wedding feast. Thus the institution of marriage is made the social condition of Solomon's prophetic vision, the locus of his privileged discourse. The social propriety of the wedding ceremony, Cotton explains, even accounts for the parabolical figures, explaining why the "dismall passages" of ecclesiastical history are "vailed and shadowed under some sweet and amiable resemblances." Otherwise, the "marriage feast" would be "darkened by unseasonable mention of so sad occurrences" (C5). The veils and shadows of poetry, precisely what distinguish Canticles as a biblical text, are simply a matter of "Decorum," of deference to the social situation of the ceremony of marriage (C5).[46] Solomon, good convert that he is, both satisfies the demands of classical propriety and transcends the wedding as a profane occasion. Undeterred by the hindering veils and shadows of social decorum, he meets the double standard of propriety required of the Puritan convert.

Cotton attributes to Solomon a full awareness that his "worldly marriage" is the social occasion for something much grander. The Song celebrates the relation of "heavenly marriage" rather than the "worldly marriage" between Solomon and Pharaoh's daughter, for Cotton insists that Canticles is a demonstration of Solomon's "love to God" rather than Solomon's love for his new wife. He explains at length that neither Solomon's love as a bridegroom for his bride, nor their "worldly marriage," nor "the good parts of either of them," have any intrinsic value:

> Now though that marriage song [Ps. 45] was penned upon that occasion; yet it ascendeth farre above all earthly respects of worldly marriage, and by divine and heavenly workmanship sets forth a heavenly marriage song betweene Christ and his Church: Of like Argument was this song penned by Solomon himselfe, not to expresse his affections to Pharaohs daughter, or hers to him, or the good parts of either of them: no, nor the like respects to any Shunamite amongst the rest of his wives, as some have vainly conceived; for then how absurd and monstrous were some of his comparisons, likening his spouse to *A company of Horses in Pharaohs Chariot, her Head to Carmel, her Eyes to Fish pooles, her Nose to a Tower, her Teeth to a flock of Sheep, her whole Selfe to a terrible Army with Banners.* But his scope is to describe the estate of the Church towards Christ, and his respect towards her [the church], from his own time to the last judgment. [C4–5]

Applying the traditional Christian reversal of propriety, Cotton repudiates the profane reading of Canticles as a poem about worldly love. But because he does so within the context of a specific event, he defines an archetype of "worldly marriage" at the same time, thus preaching social as well as spiritual propriety.

The institution of marriage that Cotton defines indirectly suggests the influence of Calvin, for the metonymy that characterizes the marriage of Solomon and Pharaoh's daughter is similar to the paradigm of the sacrament. In Cotton's exposition, bride and bridegroom are the counterparts of the bread, but the bridegroom Solomon is also the counterpart of the cleric, the speaker of sacred tropes. Cotton emphasizes Solomon as prophetic visionary in contradistinction to the bride, who has no spiritual vision whatsoever. She is constrained within the poetic genre, for Cotton implies that she herself is unaware that the words seemingly meant for her are not addressed to her. What she unknowingly overhears is the oblique expression of the authorial bridegroom's "love for God," Solomon worshiping his deity. In Solomon's expression of "his respect towards her," "her" means the church, not Pharaoh's daughter. In Cotton's view, the author-bridegroom is aware of a double level of meaning but the bride is not, an interpretation reflected further in the interpretation of the groom, but not the bride, as a type.

Solomon is a "type of Christ" exactly because of his marriage, for "admitting the Gentiles into the fellowship of his marriage-bed" (C4). By contrast, the bride's marriage only underscores her exclusion from the prophetic vision. Cotton observes that Pharaoh's daughter is converted to "the Jewish religion" upon her marriage (C4), precisely the occasion that inspires Solomon to have his *Christian* vision of history.

The form of the poem as a dialogue is also treated as a poetic figure that must be reordered to the spiritual sense. As Solomon's prophetic vision alone, Canticles becomes a dramatic monologue, a poem delivered at the "marriage feast" in the presence of a bride who is a silent audience despite her literary appearance of speech in the poetry. In the presence of Solomon, the originator of the sacred words of the poem, the bride is similar to a loaf of bread, an object whose material presence is all that is religiously necessary. Collapsing the distinction between poetry and rhetoric, between literary art and life, Cotton's exegesis assumes that the poetic semblance of speech is the actual speech of the bride herself, for throughout his exposition, Cotton discusses the text as if the poetic image of the bride were the actual referent. In the hyperbolic fusion of the poetic bride and the historical bride, she is portrayed as living entirely within the framework of the repudiated poetic dialogue, without any transcendent vision, and consequently without any social vision except her profane one of Solomon as bridegroom and husband.

The duplicity of allegorical meaning that makes Solomon's words significant is overtly denied to the bride. Or rather, it is acknowledged only metonymically: The metonymy of marriage declares that Solomon and his bride are, and are not, two different people. Renaming the bride marks the place where the half-negation of metonymy occurs, declaring that the bride is, and is not, herself. Cotton resolves the competing claims of appropriateness in the crossing of word and referent by resorting to Luther's idea of the sacramental object. He locates propriety in Solomon alone as prophetic visionary and denies it entirely to the bride, dissociating her from the sacred interpretive signs as Luther dissociated the bread of the sacrament from the consecrating words. The bride is declared an unfit subject for the figures of Canticles herself, since she is the one for whom the poetic imagery is particularly "absurd and monstrous." Cotton imposes a naive realist's criterion on the appearance of the bride, the same necessity Calvin imposed on visual art to represent "what the eye can see." Socially, this realism is authoritarian because it suppresses the language of the object, the bride, and conceals the suppression by attributing Solomon's words to her as her own. Though the bridegroom hypothetically suffers the same fate as the bride, this is obscured by the grandeur of Solomon as prophetic visionary. Solomon as husband is lauded for his authorial vision, his wisdom, and his view of history while the bride is praised merely as an iconic object, a visible, material shape whose marriage imposes silence as religiously appropriate to her.

As Cotton describes it, the social constraints of the institution of marriage exclude women much as iconoclasm excludes Catholic art. The structure of sacramental metonymy becomes the means of repudiating and debasing the imaginations of women, creating a contrast between the sanctioned imagination of Solomon as husband and the profane imagination of Pharaoh's daughter as his wife. Like the prohibited objects of Catholic art, and like the poetry that describes her, the married woman is made the object of reinterpretation. The same institution that ascribes to men the consecrating power of tropes ascribes to women the linguistic role of a silence that cannot be heard, a silence that places her in literature and history only as a material object. Like the poetic text that yields to the living images of the temporal world, the bride's purpose is to "resemble" the truth without ever knowing it. She has no access to the parabolical figures, no poetic discourse, no sanctioned figurative meaning, and no historical vision. In effect, Cotton posits different systems of meaning for Solomon and the bride, but only one is of value, Solomon's as Christian visionary, for he alone understands the ulterior significance of Canticles as he composes it for the marriage feast. As for the bride, she and the poem receive similar treatment, the worshipful repudiation of iconoclastic exegesis.

Where Calvin's paradigm for metonymy had been the consecrating words of the sacrament, Cotton shifts the paradigm to the institution of marriage. As the social situation of Solomon's vision, marriage replaces the crucifixion as the central converting event. Declaring the "humane body" of Jesus to be irrelevant to the identity and character of the mystical body, Cotton finds an alternative ultimate locus of reference in Solomon himself as author-bridegroom.[47] The ideal religion thus depends on a social institution rather than a historical event, the metonymic ceremony of marriage. It is this institution, rather than the sacrament of the Lord's Supper, that symbolizes the prophet's relation to his deity. That the Puritans made marriage a civil ceremony, denying it status as a religious sacrament, does not contradict this interpretation. It affirms it, for it assigns the attribute of commonness to marriage, thus enabling it to become a sacramental "image" ordained by the Puritan version of the Second Commandment.

Cotton seems to have associated the sacrament and the institution of marriage through the trope of metonymy. The Song of Solomon rationalized this association because exegetical tradition had interpreted the book as an allegory of the relationship between Christ and the church. Cotton mentions this reading at the beginning and end of his exposition, describing Canticles as a "heavenly marriage-song between Christ and his church" in which the church is related to the deity as a "spouse" to a "husband" (C4, 252). However, his interpretation differs from the traditional reading because he explicitly inverts the relative values of traditional theology. Like the metaphors of his sermon rhetoric, the exegetical metaphor of marriage is interpreted to privilege the literal meaning within the trope, the social institution of marriage. By giving Solomon's marriage religious value, Cotton gives the Song of Solomon new importance as a book of Scripture. It is not just a metaphor, not just a poetic allegory of Christ's love for his church. It reveals that prophecy is a function of social conditions, and specifically of the condition of marriage.

Since the clergy of the Protestant Reformation, unlike their Catholic counterparts, were for the most part married men, it is not surprising that Cotton's exposition exalts marriage as the social condition of true mental images. The import of his exegesis was not lost on his grandson, who represents John Cotton in the *Magnalia Christi Americana* as having married and received assurance of grace on the same day:

> Settled now at Boston, his dear friend, holy Mr. Bayns, recommended unto him a pious gentlewoman, one Mrs. Elizabeth Horrocks, the sister of Mr. James Horrocks, a famous minister in Lancashire, to become his consort in a *married estate*. And it was remarkable that on the very *day* of his *wedding* to that eminently vertuous gentlewoman, he first received that assurance of God's *love* unto his own *soul,* by the *spirit* of God, effectually applying his *promise* of *eternal grace* and *life* unto him, which he happily kept with him all the rest of his days: for which cause he would afterwards often say, "God made that day, a day of double marriage to me!"[48]

Other biographies of Cotton say that he was converted many years earlier, during his years at Cambridge. Mather warps the biographical narrative, creating a coincidence between Cotton's marriage and his religious conversion, a "day of double marriage" that illustrates the ideas in Cotton's exegesis of Canticles.[49] That assurance of grace should coincide with marriage, even be reordered to it in the historical narrative, reflects the Puritan recognition of marriage as definitive, the event that makes the preacher-husband a sanctioned image, an authoritative living icon.

Cotton's synthesis of sacramental theory, traditional exegesis, Luther's reading of Revelation, and the institution of marriage created a social model of immense importance. Not only did it define the character of poetic and historical knowledge; it defined whose imagination had consecrating power, whose tropes and images would bear the sanction of canonical truth: Solomon's, but not the bride's. The privileged locus of discourse was defined above all by the relation of the bride and groom to each other, irrespective of other possible determinants of proper meaning. The namelessness of the bride is symbolic of the social status of her words, for she is excluded from the power of prophecy even as her material presence is made essential to it. With no name other than Pharaoh's daughter or Solomon's bride, she is merely a female, material object, a nonlinguistic *figura,* someone who is so completely dissociated from the interpretive signs of language that even the social fact of her silence is repudiated by the speech that Solomon attributes to her. In choosing marriage rather than Mt. Pisgah as the place and situation of historical vision, Cotton enshrines the wisdom of Solomon while reducing the bride to a human cipher, a mere physical shape in the perceptible world of figural realism.

5

1637: the Pequot War and the antinomian controversy

It has never been adequately recognized that the antinomian controversy was coincident with the first major war between Puritans and Native Americans. The antinomian controversy began in the mid-1630s when members of the First Church of Boston, where Cotton was a minister, objected to the theology of conversion preached by other ministers in Massachusetts Bay Colony. As the controversy burgeoned into a public dispute in 1636, it came to focus on the opinions of this "antinomian" faction in Cotton's congregation – a faction that included Cotton himself for awhile – and then more particularly on the opinions of one member of the Boston church, Anne Hutchinson. The crisis culminated in the double trial of Hutchinson: The judgment of the political court against her in the fall of 1637, banishing her from the colony, was echoed by the decision of the Boston congregation to excommunicate her in the spring of 1638. At the church trial, Cotton and other members of the Boston church openly shared in the repudiation of Hutchinson and her few remaining supporters, thus joining with their former opponents in the resolution of the crisis.[1]

Like the religious controversy, the Pequot War was several years in the making, and it reached its culmination at nearly the same time. The first raid on the Pequots occurred in October 1636, the month in which the first clerical conference was held on the disputes of the antinomian crisis. In the spring of 1637, when John Winthrop was elected governor of the Bay Colony, he moved decisively against the Pequots and the antinomians at once. Immediately dispatching soldiers led by Captain John Underhill to fight alongside the Connecticut soldiers of Captain John Mason, Winthrop enabled Massachusetts Bay to share in the genocidal massacre of Pequot men, women, and children at Mystic in May 1637. The remaining Pequots were pursued across Connecticut, and after a second battle in July near New Haven and the subsequent murder of those who fled to Long Island in August, the Puritans had virtually exterminated the Pequots. While the military fought the Pequots in the summer of 1637, the clergy held conferences and disputed with the antinomians, gradually closing ranks against the Hutchinson faction and finally reaching a substantial consensus in September. Winthrop and his cohorts used their powers of political office to enact punitive measures against the most outspoken members of the Hutchinson faction. The antinomians were variously fined, disenfranchised, disarmed, and banished until Winthrop and his adherents had effectively gained control. By November 1637, only a few months after the Pequot War had ended, the power of the Hutchinson faction was broken.[2]

It has long been recognized that the religious disputes of 1636–38 involved severe prejudice against Puritan women. The resolution of the antinomian controversy did much to make "women" a symbolic category of threat to Puritan authority, for though many men were also prosecuted for antinomianism, none achieved the status of Hutchinson. In the court trial, the church trial, and the subsequent narratives of these events over the next decade, Hutchinson became the symbol, the living image, of the Puritan association between antinomianism and female sexuality. In Winthrop's words, she was "the breeder and nourisher of all these distempers."[3] It is also important to recognize that the genocide of the Pequot War was an act of severe prejudice against women, far exceeding the controversy in its hostility, but likewise an event of major symbolic importance to the Puritans. As Francis Jennings has shown, the gratuitous slaughter of Pequot women at Mystic was deliberately perpetrated and carefully recorded by men such as Winthrop, Mason, and Underhill.[4]

When we consider both the war and the controversy, they appear to be distinct, separate events because only the war involved acts of violence. However, though it is true that the antinomian crisis did not result in death – no one was killed or even injured in the religious disputes – the controversy between the Hutchinson faction and their opponents nonetheless involved pervasive fears of violence. Because the antinomian controversy has mainly been considered a dispute about theology, historians have failed to see how much this crisis involved threats of violence, and how extensively antinomianism was understood by the Puritans as a threat of material harm.[5] As we will see, the connections between the violence of the war and the rhetoric of the controversy were varied and complex. A comparison of the documents shows, for example, that the violence the Puritans committed in the Pequot War was very similar to the violence they imagined and prophesied in the antinomian crisis. Such conceptual links between the two crises indicate how closely the twin victories of 1637 were related and how one kind of prejudice fostered another.

Retrospectively, it might seem that Puritans in 1637 did not in fact cast their threat of violence so widely, that their prejudice against "Indians" provided an established limit on Puritan militance. To judge from contemporaneous accounts, however, the Puritans were by no means confident that the Pequot War would be the only mass slaughter in 1637. The pervasive sense of crisis derived in part from the sheer extremity of Puritan figurative language in its religious imagery of violent death. In the uncertainty of its literal and figurative significance, the rhetoric of conversion suddenly became life-threatening. The fear that controversy over spiritual issues would produce literal warfare among the colonists is most evident in the case of John Wheelwright's fast-day sermon of January 1637 and the response to it. Wheelwright, a newly arrived preacher in the colony and a brother-in-law of Anne Hutchinson, was strongly supported by members of the Boston church when he preached this sermon. Although he claimed that he only asserted the necessity for a Christocentric theory of conversion, the response indicates that many who were present felt that he advocated violence against his enemies. Wheelwright was charged with sedition and contempt by the General Court when it met in March, and despite a petition of remonstrance from the Boston church in May, his conviction stood. When the court met again in November, Wheelwright was banished and his supporters were expressly disarmed of all "guns, pistols, swords, powder, shot, and match." As Thomas Weld later put it, Wheelwright's theological opponents feared "the extremity of danger" from the Hutchinson faction, and the fast-day sermon had done much to incite this fear.[6]

In delivering his sermon, Wheelwright was not unaware of the possibility that he might be misunderstood, and he often insisted that his language was meant only in a figurative sense. For example, he claimed that "the weapons of our warfare are not carnall but spirituall" and that he thus did not intend to take up physical combat. Nonetheless, he spent most of his sermon describing the means of "spirituall" war in imagery of excessive violence. His sermon reverberates with the figurative language of total warfare, accomplished by the "sword of the spiritt, the word of God," the "two edged sword" that "cutteth men to the hart." He repeatedly pointed out that this figurative language was intended in a "spirituall" sense, but spiritualist though he may have been, Wheelwright's imagery was exceptionally violent when he described the power of the Hutchinson faction's converting words: "We must kill them with the word of the Lord," he prophesies, for "if the Lord Jesus Christ do fall upon them, he will breake them all to powder." Although Wheelwright claimed to advocate a nonviolent method of controverting his religious opponents, it was a strategy expressed throughout by metaphors of violence.[7]

Despite his repeated attempts to differentiate literal and figurative meaning, it was still impossible to discern at several points whether his language of violence was literal or figurative. As Weld later accused, Wheelwright ambiguously observed at one point, "Moses, seeing an Egyptian striving with his brother, he came and killed him Acts 7. 24.25.26. So Christ putteth into his people a loving spiritt." His ambiguity about the Christian import of Moses' act, together with his escalation of the language in Acts (substituting "killed" for "smote"), rendered the meaning of this phrase uncertain, and apparently literal. Moreover, his failure to clarify his meaning suggested that his other language was perhaps not as "spirituall" as he claimed. Indeed, his principal idea invited misinterpretation: He warned that "if we will keepe the Lord Jesus Christ and his presence and power amongst us, we must fight," but without saying what sort of fight he meant.[8]

The suspicion that Wheelwright intended violence against his theological opponents was probably enhanced by the fact that he clearly feared violence against himself. He warned his hearers that "we must be willing to lay down our lives," for "Samson slew more at his death, then in his life, and so we may prevaile more by our deaths, then by our lives." Exhorting them "not to suffer the Lord Jesus Christ to be taken violently away from us," Wheelwright described the enemies who threatened such violence against him in terms that were commonly used for his opponents in the religious controversy, "those that go under a covenant of works, and these are enimyes to Christ," those whom the Hutchinson faction had accused of preaching a false doctrine of conversion.[9]

Wheelwright compounded the ambiguity in his specific uses of literal and figurative meaning, implicitly recasting the significance of his entire sermon, by introducing the millennial perspective of the Revelation of John. At this point he also associated cataclysmic violence with a female figure. In attributing apocalyptic significance to the cause of the Hutchinson faction, he availed himself of the imagery that Captain Mason would later use to describe the slaughter at Mystic. Wheelwright spoke of "the burning of the word of God" that would destroy the "whore" and the "Antichrist" of the apocalypse:

> Brethren, we know that the whore must be burnt, Revelation 18.8. it is not shaving of her head and paring her nayles and changing her rayment, that will serve the turne, but this whore must be burnt. Many speake of the externall burning of Rome,

5 but I am sure there must be a Spirituall burning, and that burning
   by the fire of the Gospell; This way must Antichrist be con-
   sumed. 2 Thessalonians 2. why should we not further this fire,
   who knoweth not how soone those Jewes may be converted?
   Revelation 18 and 19 chapters after the burning of the whore
10 followes, Alleluia, a praysing of the Lord in Hebrew; wee know
   not how soone the conversion of the Jewes may come, and if they
   come, they must come by the downfall of Antichrist, and if we
   take him away, we must burne him; therefore never feare com-
   bustions and burnings.

Wheelwright's words imply a figurative burning for those among the
"Antichrist" who are converted. More ominously, they imply an "externall," physical burning – associated especially with the female figure
of the whore in Revelation – for those who remain unbelievers, "enimyes to 'Christ," when the millennium arrives.[10]

In this duality, it is the female figure of the whore that is literally
burned, materially destroyed by violence. Wheelwright rejects the belief that physical modifications will be efficacious against the apocalyptic whore: Shaving her head, paring her nails, or "changing her ray-
ment" will not be enough to conquer the evil this *figura* symbolizes.
Although the male figure of the "Antichrist" is also burned in this
purification of the world, this figure is far less elaborately described. In
Wheelwright's imagined apocalypse, literal burning is primarily associated with female sexuality. Moreover, it is the difference of gender,
not race or culture, that is crucial to him, for he preaches as if the
conversion of "those Jewes" can be assumed.

Wheelwright's literal meaning is far more direct than Cotton's use of
metaphors in his English sermons on conversion. Although Wheelwright asserts a figurative significance at lines 4–6, this assertion is compromised by his insistence on the finality of the millennium as the last
chance for unbelievers to perceive the truth. Because he envisions the
literalization of his own figurative language in the apocalypse, it is an
enactment of tropes that makes the figurative language of the soul obsolete. At the apocalypse, the unconverted will simply be destroyed. There
is no ambivalence or ambiguity in the foreboding words that follow
about those who refuse to be figuratively burned, converted, by his
words: "The day shall come that shall burne like an oven and all that do
wickedly shall be stubble . . . this is a terrible day to all those that do not
obey the Gospell of Christ." Still unsure who his enemies will actually
prove to be, Wheelwright is nonetheless confident that he knows what
they deserve. When he concludes of the Antichrist that "if we take him
away, we must burne him," the context implies both a literal and a
figurative meaning for this conflagration, a doubleness that he simply

declines to clarify at this crucial moment. Because he preaches both conversion and the millennium, his rhetoric vacillates between literal and figurative meaning. Literalization of his imagery of violence depends merely on an indeterminate temporal distinction. When the millennium arrives, literal signification alone will have meaning, for the figurative language of the soul will simply be irrelevant, and literalization will no longer be perceptible as such. The apocalypse promises the certitude of signification, a purification of rhetoric as well as a purification of the church, a language of pure literal meaning.[11]

Unlike Wheelwright, Captain Mason, leader of the Connecticut militia at Mystic, expresses no ambiguity of meaning and no uncertainty about who his enemies are. With the purity of millennial signification, he recalls how the Puritan assault resulted in the total extermination of the Pequots at Mystic:

> The *Captain* [Mason, himself] also said, WE MUST BURN THEM; and immediately stepping into the *Wigwam* where he had been before, brought out a Fire Brand, and putting it into the Matts with which they were covered, set the *Wigwams* on Fire . . . and when it was thoroughly kindled, the *Indians* ran as Men most dreadfully Amazed. And indeed such a dreadful Terror did the ALMIGHTY let fall upon their Spirits, that they would fly from us and run into the very Flames, where many of them perished.

Biblical images of millennial conflagration such as those in Wheelwright's sermon were literally enacted against the Pequots at Mystic in an "externall" burning deliberately initiated by the Puritan militia. "We must burn him," Wheelwright said of the Antichrist who opposed the conversion of souls, and Mason's command, "WE MUST BURN THEM," echoes this exhortation but gives it an unmistakably literal meaning. Mason's transformation of biblical prophetic image into historical enactment receives a further commentary in his afterword, where he implies the special quality of this pure literal significance. It is an elect rhetoric for an elect militia in an elect moment in history. Perhaps alluding to tropes as turns of meaning, he explains that his deity has thus "turned" the lives of the Puritans:

> And thus when the LORD turned the Captivity of his People, and turned the Wheel upon their Enemies; we were like Men in a Dream; then was our Mouth filled with Laughter, and our Tongues with Singing; thus we may say the LORD hath done great Things for us among the Heathen, whereof we are glad. Praise ye the LORD!

Mason's eerie description, "we were like Men in a Dream," implies a grotesque inversion of referentiality, a sense of having compulsively acted out a scriptural image whose hypnotic power controlled them. He follows this assessment with an account of "special providences" in battle, implying that the Puritan soldiers were invulnerable to death, living in a special frame of reference, while enacting the biblical figure that rationalized their acts of violence. In the larger context of Puritan usage, Mason implies that the militia experienced a liminal moment in rhetoric and history, the "turn" from the rhetoric of conversion to the pure literalism of the millennium. As they experienced the former, they enacted the latter.[12]

Wheelwright's prophecy of literal vengeance was contingent on the vision of the beginning of the millennium in Revelation. Mason was far less specific about what "dream" he enacted, but he also invoked – at least in his afterword – a special frame of reference to justify his belief in the piety of mass violence. The writings of other Puritans drew on the Old Testament as a sanctioning precedent for sacred violence without any sense of needing a special frame of reference. For example, John Higginson, minister at Salem, wrote a letter to Winthrop offering several scriptural defenses of the war:

> Three places and precedents in Scripture I only make bold to present your w[orshi]p with and so I end. Judges 20, 1, 2, 8: Ezra 10, 3, 4: Hag. 2, 4. Hence may be collected this in brief, that (after serious reconciliation with the Lord of armies and Indians Himself) it belongeth firstly and chiefly to you the much honored magistrates that as you have hitherto not been wanting according as the Lord hath called, so now you will arise, be serious, be speedy, be strong, and be courageous in the Lord, etc.
>
> That also our much honored the ministers and watchmen of the Lord will not be wanting to press upon the conscience, charge as a duty, command in the name of the Lord from heaven, etc. the serious and speedy prosecution of this war.

Captain Underhill similarly defended the slaughter at Mystic by reference to the Old Testament as a precedent for holy genocide:

> It may be demanded, Why should you be so furious? (as some have said). Should not Christians have more mercy and compassion? But I would refer you to David's war. When a people is grown to such a height of blood, and sin against God and man, and all confederates in the action, there he hath no respect to persons, but harrows them, and saws them, and puts them to the sword, and the most terriblest death that may be.

In the context of appeals such as these to Scripture, Wheelwright's self-conscious attempts to distinguish a figurative "spirituall" sense may well have meant very little to many of his hearers, for other Puritans already conceived of literal violence as a spiritual act, and without any sense of tension in their determination of meaning.[13]

In the implicit referential imperative of his metaphors, his "spiritual" imagery of violent death, Wheelwright himself obliquely sanctioned the kinds of actions taken in the Pequot War. His millennial prophecy of mass slaughter described a literalization of figures for the non-elect very similar to what would soon occur at Mystic. However, Wheelwright differed from his opponents because he spoke of unidentified enemies in the present and projected the literalization of violent images into the future, into a millennium that was immanent but not yet at hand. His opponents believed they had discovered apocalyptic enemies in the present, proper objects for violence who became the means for enacting the sacred figures of the Puritan imagination.

For many of Wheelwright's opponents, the dual sense of an internal, figurative burning of the soul and an external, literal burning at the millennium shifted to a *social* concept of internal and external enemies relative to the Puritans. The phenomenon of literalization, as it linked enemies inside and outside Puritan society, is most evident in Thomas Shepard's account of the two crises. A minister of the Cambridge church and a leading opponent of Hutchinson, he overlapped his narratives of the war and the theological controversy with imagery of violence that made these crises analogous. There was, he recorded,

> a most wonderful presence of Christ's spirit in that assembly, held at Cambridge, anno 1637, about August, and continued a month together in public agitations, for the issue of this synod was this:
> (1) The Pequot Indians were fully discomfited, for as the opinions arose, wars did arise, and when these began to be crushed by the ministry of the elders and by opposing Mr. Vane and casting him and others from being magistrates, the enemies began to be crushed and were perfectly subdued by the end of the synod.[14]

To express the significance of simultaneity, he described the opponents in the war and the religious controversy with the same violent image: The ministers and magistrates "crushed" the heretical "opinions" while the military "crushed" the Pequots. Whether "the enemies" are the antinomians, the Pequots, or both is impossible to tell. Shepard intertwined both victories as different aspects of a single confrontation, one in which the Hutchinson faction became the victims of figurative violence while the Pequots became the victims of literal violence.

As Shepard's account reflects, Winthrop's bid for political power in 1637 was an attempt to establish when Puritan men's rhetoric of violence was intended literally and when it was meant only figuratively. Whereas the antinomians had failed to establish their own system of meaning while Henry Vane was governor, Winthrop proved able to impose something of his. Once in office, Winthrop and his cohorts declared their own system of meaning by denouncing their Puritan opponents as threats to social order. Despite Wheelright's fears, however, most of the punitive actions taken against the antinomians were political rather than military. The most severe punishment meted out, banishment, forced the more outspoken antinomians to become geographically external enemies, but they were never attacked by their fellow colonists, nor did they themselves attempt violence against other Puritans. Indeed, the "antinomians" – so named by their opponents – seem to have been no more of a threat to peace than other Puritans. Winthrop's successful imposition of this epithet mainly signifies who lost the struggle for political control in the colony.

The prosecution of the antinomians established social order, but only in a very limited sense. By the actions taken in 1637, Puritan men effectively agreed that, with respect to themselves, their rhetoric of violence was not to be understood literally. To put it another way, they decided not to murder each other. However, as Puritan men created this stable system of meaning among themselves, they cultivated their confusion of signification in relation to their "external" enemies. The motives for the Pequot War, the way it was fought, and the rationalizations that followed all imply that Puritan men created a consistent, coherent structure of meaning for themselves and systematically denied it to those whom they believed to be their enemies. Jennings has described the Puritan military strategy against Native Americans in New England as a policy of terrorism, "the introduction of total exterminatory war against some communities of natives in order to terrorize others."[15] The rhetoric that accompanied the actual violence was crucial to creating the threat of terrorism, for it was through the inconsistent, irrational juxtaposition of their words and their actions that the Puritans incited widespread fears outside their own society even as they established a social order within the colony.

The Puritan commitment to unstable signification is prominent in explanations of the Puritan motives for attacking the Pequots in 1637. Despite the Puritan claim of self-defense, the evidence strongly implies that the Pequots, far more than the Puritans, acted in self-defense.[16] Even the governor of the Plymouth colony observed at the time – and Winthrop recorded his comment – that the Puritans had "occasioned a war, etc., by provoking the Pequods." The Puritans' avowed motives were rendered even more disingenuous by their strange emphasis on the murders of two traders, John Stone and John Oldham, as causes of war. Stone had been murdered by the Niantics, not the Pequots, and he was considered an enemy; he had been banished from Massachusetts

Bay and threatened with death if he returned. It was the Narragansetts, not the Pequots, who had murdered Oldham, as the Narragansetts told Winthrop openly. Thus the declaration of alliance with Oldham's known murderers, the Narragansetts, to attack the Pequots made the Puritan motives for violence even more inexplicable. Winthrop did nothing to dispel this impression of irrationality. If anything, he did much to create it, enhancing the sense of threat that Puritan men could resort to excessive violence for strange, sudden, and arbitrary reasons.[17]

The confusion of Puritan motives was recapitulated in the Puritans' conduct during the war. The sense of terror they created was made pervasive by the frequent refusal of Puritan men to distinguish among "Indians," combined with their declared intent to exterminate the Pequots. At Mystic, for example, while the Puritans systematically killed all the Pequots, they also haphazardly shot some of their Narragansett allies: "Divers of the Indian friends were hurt by the English, because they had not some mark to distinguish them from the Pequods, as some of them had." The likeness of physical characteristics among Native Americans in contrast to the English required an additional physical "mark" to associate a Narragansett with the Puritans rather than the Pequots. Similarly, in his journal account of the war, Winthrop vacillated between categorically describing "Indians" and keeping a running total of the Pequot body count through the summer of 1637. This same confusion of perception was actively turned against Native Americans in their verbal exchanges with the Puritans. Captain Lion Gardener proudly narrates how the Puritans in Connecticut threatened Native Americans on Long Island (probably the Montauks). "We said we knew not the Indians one from another," he explains, recalling how he told them that if any "English" were killed, "I shall think that you of Long-Island have done it, and so we may kill all of you for the Pequits." He offered this incentive: "But if you will kill all the Pequits that come to you [fleeing the Puritan militia], and send me their heads, then I will give to you as to Weakwash, and you shall have trade with us." Yielding to the threat, the Long Islanders offered up the requisite proof of signification to demonstrate who was, and who was not, a Pequot.[18]

Not only did the Puritans commit genocide in 1637, they did it with a self-contradictory specificity and vagueness about who their enemies were. Determined to exterminate all the Pequots, as they did so they flaunted the fact that they often "knew not" which "Indians" were Pequots. After the war, Mason recounted, the few Pequots who had successfully sought refuge among the Moheags and Narragansetts were renamed to simulate their extinction: "The Pequots were then bound by COVENANT, that none should inhabit their native country, nor should

any of them be called PEQUOTS any more, but MOHEAGS and NARRAGAN-
SETTS for ever."[19] Conquest thus amounted to a permanent confusion of
tribal identities, a "covenant" that sanctioned the Puritan attitude toward Native Americans throughout the war. Like the arbitrary attribution of motives, this final verbal strategy of metonymy displayed the
Puritan appropriation of Adamic power, not now to name the world
but rather to rename the world according to the Puritan new Adam's
sacramental sense of people and things.

In the arbitrariness of their acts, their belief in their sanctity, and the
zeal with which they sought out the opportunity to commit violence,
American Puritan conduct against Native Americans adapted much of
the ideology of European iconoclasts. Now, however, the recipients of
iconoclastic violence were not merely symbolic objects, statues or
paintings representing people, but real people who had become for the
Puritans the living images of opposition to the New England Puritan
living images of grace. The connection between sacramental theory and
military practice was not lost on Captain Mason. In justification of the
genocide, he reported: "I still remember a speech of Mr. Hooker at our
going aboard [in Hartford]; THAT THEY SHOULD BE BREAD FOR US."
Thomas Hooker, minister of the Hartford congregation, appealed to
the paradigm of the sacrament to rationalize the attack on Mystic as a
sacred act of violence. The figure of sacramental metonymy exposed
who the Pequots were: not just Pequots but sacrificial victims of the
deity's elect. Moreover, by invoking the sacrament, he implied that the
war was salutary for those who engaged in it. Hooker's (or Mason's)
appeal to the sacrament did not invoke traditional Christology, the
history of Christ's sacrifice. It invoked instead the act of performing the
sacrament, and the concomitant belief that Protestants were living
icons. Where the European iconoclasts glorified themselves in the act of
destroying false idols, American Puritans similarly hallowed their destruction of the Pequots. In its implications, this extension of sacramental metonymy to justify the war resembled Underhill's sense of simultaneous effect in his intention to "save ourselves and prejudice them" by
committing genocide at Mystic.[20]

The use of metonymy in Puritan thought enhanced the sense of irrationality, both because this trope lends itself to arbitrary conjoinings
and because the sacred trope *qua* trope diminished the need for intelligible secular motives for war. For the Puritans, metonymy was its own
justification, and the varieties of metonymy they used in 1637 show a
predilection for this trope in its most iconoclastic form. Recall that
iconoclastic Protestants favored the visible material object in the conflict
of meaning created by metonymy. This pattern was duplicated in the
Puritans' New England adaptation of the paradigm when they substituted Pequots for sacramental bread. After the slaughter at Mystic, the

word "Pequot" itself became a viable sacramental threat, offering a new possibility of metonymic skewed reference to sanction violence. In their ever-expanding, metonymic chain of prejudice, the Puritans generalized from the sacrament by using the previously silent name of the material object as a trope for the next prejudicial act:

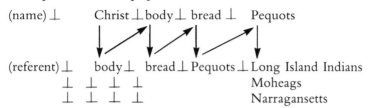

(name) ⊥   Christ ⊥ body ⊥ bread ⊥   Pequots

(referent) ⊥   body ⊥   bread ⊥ Pequots ⊥ Long Island Indians
        ⊥   ⊥   ⊥   ⊥   Moheags
        ⊥   ⊥   ⊥   ⊥   Narragansetts

This paradigm indirectly sanctioned the material object in religious rites of violence, implicitly conferring sacred significance on the *un*spoken name and its referent. Thus the metonymic chain of prejudice connecting the religious and secular motives of the war created an attenuated double bind. It asserted the sacredness of the literal meaning as well as the figurative meaning, creating a referential imperative that obliquely consecrated the unspoken name of the sacramental object and the object itself as sources of signification.

Understood iconoclastically, the paradigm fetishized the object as the source of meaning, the mystical creator of its own, hidden name. And this, apparently, was how Puritan men did understand it. The shift from European iconoclasm to American warfare, from the destruction of art to the destruction of people, suggests that the Puritans privileged themselves as the sacramental material objects that determined signification. As living icons (or as figurative "bread"), they became the privileged source of meaning, the exemplary material object. Hereafter, the counterpart false images they destroyed would have to be living or natural images like themselves. The mentality of the iconoclast is further reflected in the need to destroy the bodies of the Pequots as well as kill them, to destroy the material shape in order to destroy its power. Mason's urge for murder by conflagration is combined with scatological imagery to describe the nature of divine retribution at Mystic: The Puritans were "burning them up in the Fire of his Wrath, and dunging the ground with their Flesh: it was the LORD's doings."[21] The Pequots' punishment for their "mischief" and "violence" was to be not only murdered but destroyed totally in their material being. Their desecrated remains marked Mason's sacramental destruction of a threatening *figura*. His violence, and his interpretation of it, synthesize the physical destruction of iconoclasm and the sacred violence that the sacrament symbolized to declare his belief in the spiritual inappropriateness of the Pequots.

The decision to commit genocide, to murder women and children as well as men, follows directly from the assumptions of iconoclastic prejudice. In describing Pequot women as being murdered with children, the Puritans emphasized women specifically as childbearers, as mothers who perpetuated the offending *figurae* of an alien race. To destroy *these* bodies was an attempt to destroy the mystical, threatening power of the Pequots as material objects in the most categorical way. Although the descriptions are very brief, the larger historical context suggests that the fact of killing women and children was important to Puritan men. This practice was unusual in the seventeenth century, unconventional by either European or Native American standards, a method of warfare the English reserved for the Irish. As Jennings has shown, the Puritans actually sought out the opportunity for genocidal warfare, deliberately avoiding the more conventional strategy of attacking the Pequot men at Weinshauks to attack Mystic instead.[22] The symbolic murder of Pequot women and children was thus a specific intention of Puritan men, and they openly declared its accomplishment. Winthrop recorded in his journal:

> Our English from Connecticut, with their Indians, and many of the Naragansetts, marched in the night to a fort of the Pequods at Mistick, and, besetting the same about the break of day, after two hours' fight they took it, (by firing it,) and slew therein two chief sachems, and one hundred and fifty fighting men, and about one hundred and fifty old men, women, and children, with the loss of two English, whereof but one was killed by the enemy.

This account differs from others on the number of Pequot "fighting men," which was few or none in other reports, but Winthrop was clear on the fact that "Our English" murdered women.[23]

Captain Underhill, who led the Massachusetts forces at Mystic and whose own account was published the following year in London, including the Massachusetts Puritans among the perpetrators of the genocide:

> Captain Mason entering into a wigwam, brought out a firebrand, after he had wounded many in the house. The fires of both meeting in the centre of the fort, blazed most terribly, and burnt all in the space of half an hour . . . . Many were burnt in the fort, both men, women, and children. Others [were] forced out, and came in troops to the [Narragansett] Indians, twenty and thirty at a time, which our soldiers received and entertained with the point of the sword. Down fell men, women, and children . . . . Great and doleful was the bloody sight to the view of young soldiers that had never been in war, to see so many souls lie gasping on the ground, so thick, that you could hardly pass along.[24]

Underhill not only claimed the participation of Massachusetts Puritan men, he also repeated the fact of murdering women and children, dismissing the revulsion felt by the young men as naive. Since the Puritan militia was composed of men sent from all the towns of Massachusetts Bay, the knowledge of the genocide would have been widespread in the colony, and with the publication of Underhill's narrative, it became public knowledge in London too. The deliberateness of Puritan actions, and their concern to make this unusual violence known, imply that Puritan men felt thoroughly vindicated in their act of genocide – much as European iconoclasts had righteously proclaimed their destruction of false images in the church.

The symbolism of the slaughter of 1637 was a complex synthesis of prejudicial categories involving race, culture, and gender, and all these categories were important in the formulation of Puritan beliefs about Pequot women. Strangely, the prejudicial attitude toward Pequot women as women was not overtly stated in sexual terms in accounts of the war, despite the predilection for literalized metaphors in these narratives. In the midst of the antinomian crisis Wheelwright had envisioned the threatening whore of Revelation, a specifically sexual figure, burned by devout Christians in a millennial victory over the false church. In the Pequot War, although women literally became the objects of Christian violence and were intentionally burned to death, the Puritan narratives used no such verbal image. Rather, Pequot women were described without figurative language in terms that named familial relations. In his justification of the violence Underhill wrote, rather confusedly, "Sometimes the Scripture declareth that women and children must perish with their parents." Other narratives referred to "men, women, and children," naming family members in hierarchical order.[25]

In Cotton's sermons women and children were designated as the universal category of the renamed, as those who were "called by the name of another" (WL74). The reappearance of familial categories to describe the distinguishing feature of Puritan conduct in the war implies that the metonymy of marriage was just as important as the metonymy of the iconoclasts in the Puritan man's rationalization of the war. That is, Puritan men conceptualized both their enemies and their own family members metonymically. The shared status of metonymic objects was one of several ways in which Puritan men implicitly associated the Pequots and Puritan women in the crises of 1637. Thomas Shepard's metaphoric association of the Pequots and the antinomians as "crushed" enemies implicitly linked the Pequots and Puritan women, and Winthrop's accounts of events in 1637 also imply an association. For Winthrop, the most threatening enemies within the colony were antinomian women, and their association with the Pequots, while allusive, is continually present in his journal. For example, he records his first mention of "one Mrs. Hutchinson" and "her two dangerous errors" in his journal on the page following the "articles" of alliance between the Puritans and the Narragansetts and their joint declaration of war against the Pequots. His journal entries through the summer go back and forth between the war and the religious controversy, interweaving the accounts up to the point where he notes simultaneous "victories" celebrated by the October 12 thanksgiving day: "A day of thanksgiving kept in all the churches for our victories against the Pequods, and for the success of the [clerical] assembly." He adds, disappointedly, "But, by reason of this latter, some of Boston would not be present at the public exercises," and indeed it took several more months to suppress the "antinomians." His disappointment that the two crises did not in fact conclude simultaneously is evident at the beginning of the entry for November where he records Hutchinson's trial: "There was great hope that the late general assembly would have had some good effect in pacifying the troubles and dissensions about matters of religion; but it fell out otherwise." Only with the trial of Hutchinson did Winthrop achieve the parity of victories he desired.[26]

In his characterization of Hutchinson, Winthrop displays a fear of violence from her that is commensurate with his belief in the threat of violent destruction from the Pequots. Both his actions at the state trial in 1637 and his *Short Story* of the crisis, written soon afterward, locate the source of danger in Hutchinson. Oddly, neither ministers nor merchants are portrayed as the cause of the crisis, not even Wheelwright. Within the colony, Winthrop asserts, Hutchinson was the threat to social order, "the head of all this faction." Moreover, despite his elaborate recapitulation of the specific issues of religious controversy, he declines to explain the controversy as a conscious disagreement. Instead, he describes his enemies as having been "seduced by the meanes of a woman," who was herself an instrument of Satan's "cunning." Winthrop's allusion to the Anabaptists' takeover of the city of Münster in 1534 occurs in the context of recounting Hutchinson's speech at the state trial. Referring to Hutchinson's invocation of the book of Daniel, Winthrop sardonically remarks, "One would hardly have guessed her to have been an Antitype of *Daniel,* but rather of the Lions after they were let loose"; he continues,

> So that the Court did clearly discerne, where the fountaine was of all our distempers, and the Tragedy of *Münster* (to such as had read it) gave just occasion to feare the danger we were in, seeing (by the judgement of *Luther* writing of those troublous times) we had not to doe with so simple a Devill, as managed that businesse, and therefore he had the lesse of him.

Boston, he insinuates, faced a worse danger than Münster, because the colony's antinomians were led by a woman.[27]

The persistent and various associations between the Pequots and antinomian women implied that these were similar social categories. As the
objects of metonymy, as threatening sources of violence, as enemies of
Puritan religion, they were comparable and thus potentially interchangeable. From the perspective of Puritan women, the crystalization of the
prejudicial social categories of "Indians" and "antinomians" created a
threatening dualism, threatening because Puritan women might become
objects of literal violence as the Pequots had. Although Puritan men did
not actually resort to violence against Puritan women such as Hutchinson in 1637, they articulated the threat of interchangeability. For example, although Winthrop makes no mention of the Pequots in *A Short
Story*, a sense of shared values between Winthrop and Mason is evident in
Winthrop's final biblical allusion. He concludes his account by invoking
the narrative of Jezebel as his way of understanding what the antinomian
crisis was about: Hutchinson, he says, was an *"American Jesabel."* In
renaming her to disclose her religious significance through a biblical
parallel, Winthrop discards the content of Hutchinson's own religious
ideas as "forgeries" and portrays her as a violent, malicious opponent of
the established political and ecclesiastical order.[28] The parallel Winthrop
evokes by metonymy is not difficult to see: Hutchinson's criticism of the
Bay Colony ministers, almost all of whom she rejected as preachers of
false doctrine, was the New England analogue of Jezebel's opposition to
the prophets of Israel. Although Hutchinson's opposition never took the
form of murder, Winthrop's parallel insinuates that she might have been
as violent as Jezebel, and concomitantly that Puritan men would be
justified if they became as violent as Jehu. Because Winthrop gives no
indication at all of the limits of his analogy, he invites the transfer of the
biblical narrative's most distinctive features: unrelenting violence insti-
gated by a woman who publicly engaged in religious controversy, and
who was horribly murdered as punishment for her acts.[29] The elaborate
account of Jezebel's death shows the similarity between Winthrop's epithet and the violence of the Pequot War:

> And he [Jehu] lifted up his face to the window, and said, Who is on
> my side? who? And there looked out to him two or three eunuchs.
> And he said, Throw her [Jezebel] down. So they threw her down: and
> some of her blood was sprinkled on the wall, and on the horses: and
> he trode her under foot. And when he was come in, he did eat and
> drink, and said, Go, see now this cursed *woman,* and bury her: for she
> is a king's daughter. And they found no more of her than the skull,
> and the feet, and the palms of her hands. Wherefore they came again,
> and told him. And he said, This is the word of the LORD, which he
> spake by his servant Elijah the Tishbite, saying, In the Portion of
> Jezreel shall dogs eat the flesh of Jezebel: and the carcass of Jezebel shall

be as dung upon the face of the field in the portion of Jezreel; so that they shall not say, This is Jezebel. [2 Kings 9:30–37]

Even in the context of the lengthy Old Testament chronicles of violence and murder, this was a particularly vicious murder. But then, in the context of the early seventeenth century, the Pequot War was a particularly vicious war. Although Winthrop did not enact the biblical violence to which he alludes, his typological metonymy implies that Hutchinson could have been murdered and desecrated with divine justice just as the Pequots had been slaughtered.

When Theodore Weld wrote a preface for Winthrop's *Short Story,* he made the interchangeability of "Indians" and Hutchinson explicit. Weld, acting as agent for the colony in London, had just heard reports of the murder of Hutchinson by Native Americans on Long Island, and perhaps it was this literal act of violence that inspired him to make the conceptual substitution of Hutchinson for "Indians" in his account. Although Weld despised Wheelwright and other antinomians too, he expresses his feeling in imagery that he carefully presents as figurative. In contrast, his account of Hutchinson implies that he views her in the way the Puritans viewed the Pequots in 1637, as falling outside the boundaries of conventional restraint. Noting that she finally moved to a place called "Hell-gate" outside English jurisdiction, an important symbolic fact for Weld, he reports her murder in 1643, adding, "Some write that the Indians did burne her to death with fire, her house and all the rest [of her children]." Explaining that he has been unable to confirm her manner of death, he nonetheless includes it, portraying Hutchinson as having met the same fate as the Pequots. From his perspective, total destruction by fire, again in a familial context, seems appropriate for her: "I never heard that the Indians in those parts did ever before this, commit the like outrage upon any one family, or families, and therefore Gods hand is the more apparently seene herein, to pick out this wofull woman, to make her and those belonging to her, an unheard of heavie example of cruelty above al others." Weld attributes to his deity the judgment that Hutchinson's violent death by fire is the punishment she all along deserved, a judgment reserved for those who belong in the lower, literal category of appropriate objects of "unheard of" violence. At the same time, Weld implies that "Indians" have become more like Puritan men, wreaking the same kind of extraordinary slaughter as instruments of divine judgment. He underscores this similarity by adding a postscript on the recent conversion of some Native Americans to Christianity. By the end of Weld's narrative, Hutchinson and "Indians" have changed places in the hierarchy of prejudicial categories, with Hutchinson now the ultimate outcast.[30]

The association between the violence of war and men's attitudes toward women is most evident in the narrative written by the only Puritan leader who directly participated in both crises. Captain Underhill, a member of Cotton's church in Boston who was disenfranchised for supporting John Wheelwright, was also leader of the Massachusetts forces in the attack on Mystic and author of the first published account of the war.[31] His narrative reflects his unusual status as a participant in both crises: His account of warfare is interspersed with discussions of men's treatment of Puritan women. Underhill insinuates the substitution of one metonymic object for another by creating the sense of having substituted one narrative for another. For example, early in his account of the war, he interrupts his story of the militia's raid on Block Island to defend Puritan men's treatment of Puritan women in domestic life. Midway through his account, he describes how he received an arrow against his helmet, and this incident prompts the digression. He pauses to respond to the metaphoric "clamor" that "I daily hear in my ears, that New England men usurp over their wives, and keep them in servile subjection." He says this claim is untrue and offers the following vignette as proof: He tells us that before leaving home, he yielded to his wife's "private advice" to bring his helmet with him, casting this as a scene of seduction by comparing his wife's advice to "Delilah's flattery." He is impressed that "God useth weak means" – Underhill's wife – "to keep his purpose," but hastens to add that he does not wish to be understood to have granted any authority to women: "Yet mistake not. I say not that they [Puritan men] are bound to call their wives in council, though they are bound to take their private advice (so far as they see it make for their advantage and their good): instance Abraham. But to the matter. The arrows flying thick about us . . ." Underhill's narrative is bizarre and threatening in the freeness of its association between the ideology of Puritan domestic life and the violence of warfare. It is also threatening in his boast that his digression has "quenched" the charge of the "servile subjection" of Puritan women, since, if anything, he has substantiated the accusation.[32]

Halfway through the book, Underhill again interrupts his narrative, this time to recount a tale about two "captive English maids" whom the Pequots had taken prisoner and who were rescued by the Dutch. This second digression is both more closely related to the war and more explicitly concerned with seduction. Underhill euphemistically remarks that one maid "told us they did solicit her to uncleanness," and he then explains that this was a punishment from the deity, "God's just displeasure to them," for having "slighted" Puritan religion. Sexuality is here closely related to disdain for "the means of grace": The "captive maids" are judged to have brought on these solicitations and their captivity by their own neglect of piety. Underhill's sermonic discourse on these two women, like his earlier digression on his wife's seductive manipulativeness, insinuates that seduction is divinely sanctioned in the context of violence.[33]

Underhill's final description of women is his account of the genocide at Mystic. As we have already noted, there is nothing about seduction in this portion of the narrative. There is only the nominal recognition of gender, marriage, and parenthood in the context of a narrative of mass slaughter. One has to consider the accompanying fold-out figure to understand that this event was the culminating fusion of sexuality and violence.[34] The illustration of the Puritan men attacking the Pequot fort is also a drawing of a vagina. The circular fort with its detailed interior portrays both the Puritan men's genocidal violence and the sexual symbolism of their act. That this sexual interpretation of violence is represented only in a visual image emphasizes the way in which Pequot women were reduced to sexual material objects. In the context of Underhill's narratives about Puritan women, the portrayal of sexuality in the illustration, but not in language, implies that the image was subverbal, that the gender identity of Pequot women was completely dissociated from language.

The illustration is also iconic as images had been iconic for the first Protestant iconoclasts in Europe. The figure is art of a sort, in the sense of a created visual image. However, the exactness of the image of Calvin's seductive idols has acquired new meaning, for the drawing invokes a double sense of realism. As a graphically detailed illustration of a vagina, it represents the reductive terms in which Puritan men interpreted the *figurae* of Pequot women. At the same time, it also illustrates Puritan acts of violence at Mystic. Jennings, who says nothing about the sexual symbolism, remarks on the accuracy of the drawing in portraying how the battle at Mystic began. Most of what he describes is depicted on the inside of the symbolic vagina:

> The picture confirms textual analysis in the following particulars: (1) No Pequot or other Indian is shown with firearms; (2) Englishmen are shown shooting down unarmed Indians as well as those armed with bows and arrows; and (3), on the right, Pequots are shown trying to escape through the English line to the Narragansetts in the outer circle.[35]

As a portrayal of the Puritan man's violence, the narrative and the drawing, language and image, directly and overtly affirm each other. As a portrayal of sexuality, however, the drawing is symbolic, silent, without any counterpart in Underhill's narrative or in any other account of the war. The genocide at Mystic enacted an image, but unlike the literalization of biblical and sermonic metaphors, this image was the prohibitive and profane image of female sexuality. In a society that had come to prohibit visual art as false icons, the medium of this essentially pornographic message conformed to its meaning as a material shape in the Puritan ideology of figuralism.

Newes From America is chilling in its casual juxtaposition of topics: It is partly a sermonic narrative on the treatment of women, partly a travelogue advertising the attractions of the landscape and the land to prospective immigrants, and partly a narrative of genocidal war. Taken as a whole, it seems to include Puritan women portrayed as captives and servile wives only to imply that the distinction between the fate of the Pequot women and the fate of Puritan women depended on the willingness of Puritan men to continue making a distinction between their own wives and "maids" and the women they had killed at Mystic. But consistent distinctions were just what Puritan men claimed to be unable to accomplish. Underhill's capacity to associate casually what would seem to be radically disparate ideas, Gardener's incapacity to tell one "Indian" from another, Mason's ability to enact his dream image of horror, Wheelwright's confusion of literal and figurative meaning and the community response to it – all these were the articulation of a threat in the fragility of their signification, in their lack of a systematic relationship between signs and referents. The autocratic power to rename, as these Puritan men discovered, was the power to alter the relation between sign and referent, at any time, in any place, for any person.[36]

The shared status of metonymic object that made Puritan women and Pequot women potentially interchangeable was also expressed indirectly by the exclusion of antinomian women from the realm of language in the religious controversy within the colony. As with the captive maids of Underhill's narrative, their lack of piety was presumed to be expressed physically, through their bodies. To put it another way, the threat of punishment for heresy was the threat of literalization, the threat of the enactment of tropes of violence, monstrosity, and sexual promiscuity. The imagery of Puritan men's rhetoric about Hutchinson particularly emphasized literalization as the fitting punishment for antinomianism, for repudiating the sacred tropes of Puritan rhetoric. At the church trial Cotton told Hutchinson that her heresy – that is, her figurative, spiritual adultery – would lead inevitably to literal adultery: "And though I have not herd, nayther do I thinke, you have bine unfaythfull to your Husband in his Marriage Covenant, *yet that will follow upon it.*" Along with John Davenport and Peter Bulkeley, Cotton vituperously charged that Hutchinson's religion was that of a sexual libertine, that her beliefs advocated "that filthie Sinne of the Communitie of Woemen and all promiscuus and filthie cominge togeather of men and Woemen without Distinction or Relation of Marriage." Envisioning a disaster inherent in her "antinomian" opinions, he told Hutchinson, "you doe the uttermost to rase the very foundation of Religion to the Ground and to destroy our faith." Cotton appealed to the Revelation of John as the context of his own perspective: "I know not how to satisfye myselfe in it but accordinge to that in Revelation 22.15. If it come to this to the makinge of a Lye; than without shall be doges and such as love and makes lyes." In defending the church's sentence of excommunication, he rejected Hutchinson not only as a member of the church but as a member of human society. In these apocalyptic times the Puritan church and the human community were identical, he implied, and Hutchinson, like Jezebel, belonged "without." The priority of figurative meaning must produce a conformity in literal meaning in the referential social world. Cotton's prophecy denies the social basis of his religious rhetorical figures by asserting that life is imitative of the sacred figures. For women at least, life *must* imitate art, figuring the metaphors and images of religious rhetoric. To deviate socially from a true image is an iconoclastic act, an attack on the true figures of religion. Prophetic figure and historical referent must coincide for a proper icon.[37]

The idea that religious beliefs, or the lack of them, were inevitably given physical expression is most evident in Winthrop's and Weld's detailed accounts of the stillborn children, described as malformed, to which Hutchinson and Mary Dyer each gave birth at the time of the controversy. The belief that the malformed fetuses were proof of the horror of antinomianism associated religious heresy closely with the female gender and implied that the beliefs of the antinomians violated the natural, physical order. Winthrop referred to Dyer's premature child as "the Monster"; he was particularly fascinated with "the horns and claws" and the ears "like an Apes" and "talons like a young fowle." Weld, associating monstrosity completely with the female gender, simply reported that Mary Dyer had given birth to a headless female creature that was partly fish and partly fowl, among other things: "Mistris *Dier* brought forth her birth of a woman child, a fish, a beast, and a fowle, all woven together in one, and without an head." Weld described Hutchinson's stillborn child as "30 monstrous births or thereabouts . . . some of one shape, some of another, . . . none at all of them . . . of human shape," and he explained, "for looke as she had vented mishapen opinions, so she must bring forth deformed monsters." For these men, the monstrous births were the absolute fusion of material shape and figurative image, simultaneously phantasmagoric and real, a providential *figura* that incontrovertibly proved the religious heresy of the parents.[38]

The importance of the material shape itself is implied from the fact that, for Winthrop, descriptive words were not enough. When he heard of Hutchinson's stillborn, malformed child, he dug up the buried corpse to see for himself the material, visible *figura* of the "mishapen opinions." As he narrated it, he sent for the midwife,

> who at first confessed it was a monstrous birth, but concealed the horns and claws, and some other parts, till being straitly charged, and told it should be taken up, and viewed, then she confessed all, yet for further assurance, the childe was taken up, and though it were much corrupted, yet the horns, and claws, and holes in the back, and some scales, &c. were found and seen of above a hundred persons.[39]

The physical shape itself was the clear and incontrovertible proof of how "monstrous" were the ideas of this female heretic. In the Puritan imagination these births were the enactment of an image expressing the threat of antinomianism, the material shape of heresy. The sense of a complete collapse of the difference between literal and figurative meaning lies in the apparent unawareness of either Winthrop or Weld that their fantasies were fantasies. Unlike Mason, neither of these narrators says anything about being "like men in a dream" when they imagine monsters. Where Mason portrayed himself as operating within a special frame of reference, enacting biblical figures at the behest of his deity, Winthrop and Weld portrayed themselves as merely discovering the enactment of figures in the natural world, figures whose revelatory character was never referred to Scripture but simply accepted as self-evident proof of heresy.

By associating childbirth with antinomianism so closely, Winthrop and Weld emphasized their association of the female gender with antinomianism, implying that Puritan women were potentially a threat to the social and natural order simply because they were women. At least one of Hutchinson's supporters perceived the prejudice against women in their beliefs. John Wheelwright, whose banishment had resulted in his move to Exeter, denounced Winthrop's account of the monstrous births. Turning Winthrop's own metaphors against him, Wheelwright wrote that Winthrop's account was "a monstrous conception of his brain, a spurious issue of his intellect." Remarking on Winthrop's "certainty or rather impudence" in writing such an account, he accused Winthrop of trying "*to delude the world with untruths*."[40] Wheelwright's defense of Hutchinson and Dyer depended on restoring the difference between literal and figurative language, and on repudiating the figurative imagination of the Puritan governor as false in its literalization and false in its interpretation of gender. Wheelwright's interpretation reflects something of the difference between those who supported Hutchinson and those such as John Cotton who finally opposed her. Early in the controversy Wheelwright and Cotton had held similar views (it was Cotton who had invited Wheelwright to preach the fast-day sermon), but as the controversy developed Cotton increasingly aligned himself with Hutchinson's opponents, and at the church trial he finally condemned Hutchinson openly, resorting to literalization in his prophecy of adultery.

As Hutchinson's minister, indeed, as minister to most of the "antinomian" faction, Cotton was suspect to both clergy and magistrates in the colony, and at the time of Hutchinson's state trial he was still in some danger of being put on trial himself. Nonetheless, at the two clerical conferences in the months before the state trial, Cotton slowly but steadily closed ranks with his fellow clerics, working out a partial basis of theological agreement and joining in criticism of some of his own church in Boston. Agreement was short of complete, and in fact Cotton never did reach a consensus with his clerical opponents on all of the "sixteen questions" they debated in writing and in conferences, but Cotton did not therefore ally himself with Hutchinson. Although he defended her belief in providence, he did not in any way defend her authority in religion. Called as a witness at her state trial, Cotton was asked to confirm or deny whether Hutchinson's "revelations" were legitimate. His reply was indirect. Instead of giving an opinion about her particular case, he produced a criteria for judging true and false revelations, the one he described in *The Treatise of the Covenant of Grace.* When finally forced to apply his criteria to Hutchinson's case, Cotton said he thought she meant a "providence," not a "miracle," when she spoke of "revelations," and thus he "dare not bear witness" against her. This was the strongest defense Cotton was willing to make on her behalf, despite his own belief in a doctrine of the "revelation of the Spirit."[41]

The centrality of Hutchinson in the civil trial has tended to obscure what Cotton saw as the real question: It was not, and never had been, a matter of whether he agreed with Hutchinson. Rather, the validity of what she said was entirely a question of whether she agreed with *him.* In Cotton's own view, "she was very carefull to prevent any jealousie in me, that she should harbor any private opinions, differing from the course of my public ministry." He was willing to defend only what he perceived as her articulation of *his* doctrine, equating his own doctrine with the deity's. Cotton, no less than the other ministers, referred her ideas to his own as the test of her legitimacy. Hutchinson's disagreement, then, constituted disobedience, and by the spring of 1638, the time of her church trial, Cotton had become convinced that she did disagree with him. In between the sessions of the church trial, Cotton made one last attempt to exact doctrinal submission from her, persuading her to renounce all her "heresies" and repent her criticisms of

Massachusetts ministers. At the second session of the church trial, Hutchinson delivered a categorical repentance for her "errors" in what seemed a total capitulation to Cotton's ministerial authority – but then added that she had only begun to believe "errors" after her conviction at the state trial. This assertion brought the final round of denunciation, and Cotton advocated that she be excommunicated for "lying." In his admonition to her at the church trial, he turned against her as bitterly as her other opponents. At this point Cotton recognized Hutchinson's "selfe," her subjectivity, but only to condemn her: "I confesse I did not know that you held any of these Things nor heare of them till late. But it may be it was my sleepines and want of watchfull care over you, but you see the daynger of it and how God hath left you to your selfe to fall into thease dayngerous Evells."[42]

Cotton thus joined his fellow clergy in a categorical repudiation of Hutchinson even though he still disagreed with them on doctrine. Although he had vigorously denounced his fellow ministers in written exchanges, accusing them of preaching "unwholesome and Popish doctrine," this denunciation proved no obstacle in sharing their condemnation of her. Ten years later Cotton summarized the path he had taken from the first clerical conference in the summer of 1637 to the church trial in the spring of 1638:

> How far there arose any consent or dissent about these questions, between my Fellow-Brethren (the Elders of these churches) & my self, it is not materiall now to particularize; it is enough, that upon our clear understanding of one anothers mindes & judgments, and upon the due proceeding of our Church against convinced notorious errors and scandalls, wee have ever since (by the Grace of Christ) much amiable and comfortable Communion together in al brotherly kindness.

Agreeing to disagree on the theology of conversion, they achieved the solidarity of "brotherly kindness" by condemning Hutchinson's disagreement as disobedience to their institutional authority.[43]

Cotton's shift in attitude toward Hutchinson during the antinomian crisis has been interpreted as a substantive change of mind, but from the perspective of Cotton's English sermons it seems more likely that Hutchinson made plausible a substantive change of mind that Cotton refused. He did not so much alter his ideas during the crisis as find out what he had assumed for some time. In his English sermons on Canticles, Cotton had implicitly associated prophetic vision with men and the lack of such vision with women. Solomon was portrayed as Christian in his vision, but his bride was not, for she saw no further than profane love in the material world. The idea of a Christian woman appears in the Canticles sermons only obliquely, in the figurative discourse on the church as the figurative bride of Christ. There was no historical counterpart to the prophetic Solomon, for Pharaoh's daughter was expressly and deliberately excluded from participating in the Christic prophecy. Since Hutchinson claimed to have the prophetic vision of a Christic Solomon, not the speechless blindness of the profane bride, she was disruptive of Cotton's categories simply by speaking publicly in her own right on religious prophecy. As a married woman, she also gave the lie to the historicized fiction of the silent, ignorant bride, creating a tension between figure and referent, between poetic image and historical reality, precisely where Cotton's Canticles sermons had assumed a literalization, an absolute identity.

Cotton responded to the social reality confronting him in the antinomian crisis by becoming more explicit about the relation between religion and gender. Both religiously and politically, the physical attribute of gender became the social means of enforcing radically different linguistic roles for men and women. At the church trial Cotton explicitly warned the women of the Boston church not to believe Hutchinson on matters of doctrine because "she is but a Woman." Asserting his belief in the exclusion of Puritan women from interpretive authority exactly and only because they were women, Cotton's admonition reiterated the message of Winthrop to Hutchinson at the state trial: "We do not mean to discourse with those of your sex." At the same time Puritan women were made potentially interchangeable with the Pequots and identified with the world of literalized figures, they were also excluded from the most Puritanical forms of social authority within the colony, prophecy and magistracy. They could express their Puritanism only by their silence, especially with respect to the interpretation of figures. If they attempted to speak as the equals of men, they risked the more radical exclusion of banishment and the possibility that they might, like the Pequots, become the objects of physical violence.[44]

The sermons Cotton preached during the antinomian crisis, collected in *The Treatise of the Convenant of Grace,* express the same contempt for women as his statements at the church trial. These sermons have been praised as a model of theological acuity in their theology of conversion, but Cotton's brief digressions on the biblical Sarah indicate how much this soulful coherence was achieved at the expense of women.[45] He cites Sarah as a model of social behavior for women to imitate: "a meek and a quiet godly spirited woman, subject and obedient to her husband, and *called him Lord* whose daughters you are while you do well" (T115). Quiet, subject, and obedient, she is described as exemplifying the virtues of women who belong to the community of the elect. However, Cotton mocks his own exhortation with his two illustrations of Sarah's behavior. In the first, her silence and obedience to Abraham lead to her punishment. Cotton explicates the narrative in Gen. 12 and 20 where Sarah is represented as having lied because her husband, Abraham, has told her to. She conceals the fact that she is Abraham's wife, permitting Pharaoh, and then Abimelech, to think she is marriageable. Abraham tells her to lie because he is afraid that he will be killed, that Pharaoh and the "heathen" Abimelech would each murder him to marry Sarah. Pharaoh and Abimelech both resent Abraham's speculation and each returns Sarah to Abraham upon discovering that she is already married. Cotton then observes that *Sarah,* not Abraham, is "reproved," specifically for having "dissembled" (T113). That is, she is reproved for having *obeyed* her husband, for having lied and thereby offended the deity. Cotton never addresses the contradiction that Sarah faces within the terms of his sermon: Obedience to Abraham is just as wrong as disobedience. Sarah can do no right, not because she is plagued by original sin but because she faces a contradiction exterior to herself, the command to engage in contradictory social acts of obedience and disobedience to her husband.

The second example concerns not Sarah's silence or obedience but rather Abraham's obedience to Sarah in sleeping with Hagar. Cotton emphasizes Sarah's challenge to Abraham in Gen. 16.5, "My wrong be upon thee . . . , and the Lord judge between me and thee" (T115). Cotton finds this challenge offensive, arguing that Abraham committed "no fault" in conceiving a child by Hagar because Sarah told him to: "There was no fault in him in this matter; she had no reason to tax him upon this point; it was her own counsel . . . therefore there was no colour of any just complaint on her part" (T115–16). When Sarah attempts to reprove Abraham for having obeyed her, Abraham is vindicated by the very fact of his obedience. If Sarah has objections, Cotton argues, she has only herself to blame.

Taken together, Cotton's pair of examples demonstrates the nonreciprocal quality of men's and women's speech. Unlike Abraham's words to Sarah, Sarah's words to Abraham have no spiritual meaning, no figurative, ironic sense that will reverse their literal import. Abraham has the privilege of speaking in a contradictory sense to Sarah while needing to understand only the literal import of her words to him. Sarah's failure of "*Reverence*" consists in challenging Abraham's interpretation of her words, in demanding the reciprocity of double signification for her own speech (T115). Abraham's lordliness consists in refusing her the figurative dimension of language, insisting that his literal interpretation of her words is correct. The privilege of lordly speech is the privilege of unacknowledged self-contradiction and the exclusive possession of the figurative, spiritual sense. Cotton demonstrates the lordly status of his own rhetoric by refusing to acknowledge the contradictions in his portrayal of Sarah. In effect, he preaches that her religious task is to conceal the contradictions imposed upon her, for Cotton portrays Sarah as truly reverent only when she willingly obeys the rhetoric that makes her reproof inevitable: It is Sarah, Cotton says, who volunteers the troublesome title by which she addresses Abraham, "her Lord (as she called him)" (T116).

Although Cotton's views during the antinomian crisis often seemed ambiguous, his actions were consistent with his own values. He defended first and foremost his own sanctioned authority over the unruly "bride" in his ecclesiastical care, the Boston congregation. His defense of Hutchinson, as long as it lasted, was only an aspect of this priority. Like the Abraham of his sermon, Cotton was slow to perceive his common cause with the Abimelechs of New England, whose theological disagreements with him at first seemed the greater threat to his authority and his beliefs. However, the extent to which Cotton wished to believe that his figurative images of women were socially true, despite the obvious difference between his ideal image and the actions of Puritan women like Hutchinson, is evident in his admonition at the church trial. In his rejection of Hutchinson and his sermon on Sarah, Cotton preserved the figurative language of spiritual life, but he did so at the expense of Puritan women. While the ideas and actions of Hutchinson made Cotton realize that he needed to confront the topic of Puritan women's religious experience, his sermons and his speeches at the two trials of Hutchinson show only a refusal to consider the implications of his rhetoric for women and a desire to enforce the images portrayed in his sermons. Once he had come to believe that Hutchinson's interpretations of the figures of religious rhetoric were different from his own, he could only perceive her as dangerous, "antinomian."

The actions taken against Puritan women as a group were never so iconoclastic as the Puritan assault on Pequot women, but they were iconoclastic in an important sense. The decisions of magisterial and clerical authority in 1637 and 1638 denied the figurative imaginations of women and destroyed the material shapes of women's public speech in Puritan society. In the wake of the antinomian crisis, Cotton succeeded in establishing an ecclesiastical practice he had wanted for some time: Women's narratives of their conversions were given in private to the clergy rather than before the whole congregation. With this new practice, women were banished from public religious discourse, excluded from any public articulation of religious ideas. Cotton's account of the antinomian controversy ten years later in *The Way Cleared* reflects the same sense of confident righteousness in repudiating Puritan women, in creating a rhetorical double standard based on gender. Among the decisions made in the crises of 1637 was a guarantee that Cotton obtained for himself, the assurance of "some of our chief magistrates and others" that he could continue to preach "what I believed to be a truth." Cotton evinces no sense of contradiction in describing the place he secured for himself among the arbiters of true doctrine while simultaneously praising the banishment of Hutchinson. Although she, too, had had disagreements with the clergy about doctrine, and had said what she believed to be true, Cotton seems not to have perceived any similarity between his own dilemma and hers. While Hutchinson left for Rhode Island, Cotton was assured that he could remain in Boston with lordly status.[46]

Although Cotton did not mention the Pequot War in any of his statements or sermons about women, the Puritan attitude toward racial and cultural difference contributed substantially to prejudice based on gender within the Puritan community. The belief that the Puritans were an elect people emphasized that Puritan men and women shared a Congregationalist piety that radically set them apart from other societies. Their belief that Puritans were so much alike in contrast to all other social groups enhanced the sense that the only difference between Puritan men and women was that of gender. In the face of so much cultural likeness, the difference of gender became the accusation that gender was definitive of Puritan women as human beings, that female was all that Puritan women were because it was all that differentiated them from Puritan men. Granting religious significance to racial and cultural attributes thus increased the symbolic importance of gender differentiation within the elect community. Despite their status in relation to other cultural groups, Puritan women lived under a threat of sanctioned violence from Puritan men, a threat that they could always become objects of violence as the Pequot women had. Because figurative language could always be returned to its literal presupposition, because metonymic objects were potentially interchangeable, and because female gender was closely associated with the profane world of legitimate objects of violence, Puritan women could never belong fully to the society of the elect. Their piety was always compromised by physical characteristics that faith could not convert.

A decade after the crises of 1637, the Puritan surveyor and militia captain Edward Johnson wrote a historical narrative of the first years of the New England colony, including both the war and the controversy in his account of events. Johnson formulated the rhetorical ambiguity of Puritan authority in apocalyptic terms that echoed Wheelwright's fast-day sermon. Concerning "the Lord Christ marshalling of his invincible Army to the battell" against the "Antichrist," Johnson explained, "some suppose this onely to be mysticall, and not literall at all: assuredly the spirituall fight is chiefly to be attended, and the other not neglected, having a neer dependancy one upon the other, especially at this time."[47] If the literal sense could not be "neglected," if there was a "neer dependancy" of religious beliefs on "literall" military acts, which occasions, what people, would provoke an attack by the literal army rather than the "mysticall" one? In the Pequot War, Puritan men had demonstrated that they were capable of extreme violence, but they had also been highly arbitrary about what conditions or actions would provoke it. Thus, while Puritan men achieved a sense of security among themselves, they created, even cultivated, a sense of threat in the ambiguity of their motives for violence. The actions taken in the war and the controversy, and the narratives that followed, show that the crises of the late 1630s were less a breakdown of social order than a struggle to institute a particular kind of social order by defining acceptable forms of prejudicial violence and beliefs. The events of 1637 established the legitimacy of genocidal war against nonwhite peoples and the sanctity of prejudicial attitudes toward women, granting ecclesiastical and political sanction to the rhetoric of threat in Puritan men's speech.

6

Apocalyptic hierarchy

After the sense of immediate crisis subsided in 1638, the prejudices established by the use of state and military power were given a more abstract, systematic expression by Cotton when he preached on the whole book of Revelation in 1639–40.[1] In some respects, these sermons supporting the hegemony of institutional leaders were a delayed response to the war and the controversy. Like the advocates of the war, Cotton openly praises the virtues of violence in the "letter," similarly combining the intent of violence with an intimidating uncertainty about who the objects might be. However, by making Catholics the new categorical enemy of the Puritans, Cotton sanctions a new plurality of potential objects of violence. Not only does he revive the prejudices of the Puritans against Catholics; as we will see, what appears at first to be only an obsessive repudiation of all that is "Popish" is actually a diatribe that places many of the Puritans themselves among the potential threats to the colony. Using the imagery of catastrophic violence in Revelation, he interweaves a real and specific hatred of Catholics with a chronic vagueness about who might be considered one. The scenes of violence he depicts threaten not only Catholics but with them any Protestants or "Indians, Jews, and Pagans" who even seem Catholic (7V.12). Now it is not only Puritan women who are threatened by the violence of colonial authority. Cotton's version of anti-Catholicism invites virtually any listener to fear the hierarchical power of the colony's newly established elite.

The international scope of Cotton's prejudice is reflected in his choice of texts as well as his topic of Catholicism. There was widespread interest in apocalyptic and millennial prophecy in the seventeenth century, an interest that became a preoccupation among Puritans during the English Civil War. Traditionally, the rhetoric of the apocalypse was a religious idiom for advocating radical social change, a vehicle of protest for the most disaffected of the powerless and the poor.[2] Since Cotton and other New England leaders were forced out of the Church of England, the guise of sectarian outcast was not altogether ill fitting despite their authority within the colony. Cotton occasionally adopts this stance, but primarily he follows the precedent of Luther and Brightman, extolling the conquest over the apocalyptic beast, the Catholic church. The elect are not outcasts so much as they are the new power that casts out others, for they are portrayed as the dominant force in this world as well as the next. Moreover, the victors as Cotton describes them are Congregationalist Puritans, not just Protestants. They prove their election, and particularly their superiority over other Protestants, by the extraordinary virulence of their anti-Catholicism.

The severity of obedience to which Cotton exhorts his hearers is proportional to the splendor of the privileges accorded to the elect in the prophecies of Revelation. Because American Puritans distinguished themselves from the national (and nationalistic) Church of England, their sectarian colonization of Massachusetts was a more local enterprise and thus, ironically, one that could be imagined to have something other than – and therefore something more than – nationalist significance.[3] In Cotton's interpretation of Revelation, the domain of relevance for Puritan beliefs expands to include the space of the world and all of social reality. His 1630 farewell sermon had already announced the belief that spiritual privilege should receive territorial expression. When he preached to the departing immigrants, he described New England through the Old Testament analogy of Canaan as a place "appointed" for "Gods people," a "durable possession" where "they shall have peaceable and quiet resting," where "the sonnes of wickednesse shall afflict them no more" (G1, 3, 6). He alluded to a limited expansion of the New England Canaan when he advocated trading the "spiritualls" of conversion for the "temporalls" of the Native Americans, but in 1630 New England Puritans were still only one among many peoples, ruled by a deity perceived as being "over" them all: "This placeing of people in this or that Countrey, is from Gods soveraignty over all the earth, and the inhabitants thereof" (G6). While "Gods soveraignty" favored the Puritans, spatially conceived transcendance was still reserved exclusively for the deity. A decade later, with the interpreter himself present, the indefinite expansion of spatial domain has become the colonists' self-declared privilege. Concomitantly, where his 1630 sermon envisioned a peaceful community free of "wickednesse" through the convenience of geographical isolation, the Revelation sermons are fraught with conflict between Puritans and Catholics.

In Cotton's apocalyptic geography, the vision of a new heaven and earth in Revelation becomes a metaphoric, parabolical description of an international struggle between Puritanism and Catholicism, a parable of the universe comprehending the whole world as it justifies the "pure Church" of New England:

> For all the Vials are to be poured upon the earth, the Antichristian Church, called earth in opposition to the heavenly and pure Church mentioned Revel. 15.5. there being in it the whole Fabricke and Systeme of the world: there is an earth, and that is the lowest and basest common sort of Catholickes in that world; and there is a Sea, their corrupt Religion; there be Rivers, and fountaines of water, those that derived their corruptions into all countries (Priests and Monkes, &c.) there is a Sunne in this world, the great light thereof: the family of *Austria* in the common wealth, and the Popes supremacy in the Church. . . . Therefore this Ayre seemeth to be the Ayre of that Antichristian Church. [7V.3]

The "temporalls" of John's Revelation, the heaven, the earth, the sea, and the air, are interpreted as poetic figures with an allegorical relation to literal-historical persons and places. The "metaphoricall seas and waters," for example, signify "the Popish priests and Jesuites" (2V.22). Heaven and earth, no less than the other places named in Revelation, serve as metaphors: "If you look at the earth, as opposite to heaven, the heavenly pure Churches, so he [John] means the earthly and Antichristian Church, the Romish Popish church" (4V.2).

Cotton assiduously avoids the idea of New England as a uniquely sacred place, as the "new heaven and new earth" of conventional millenialism.[4] The new heaven and earth represent not the new life in a millennial world but the antagonism between "heaven," the Congregationalist, and "earth," the Catholic. The "new world" is not any particular place geographically but rather a present condition of the whole world. Describing the "new world," he laments, "But now when Religion is wholly corrupt, that all the whole Sea is the blood of a dead man; now the world is altered, and if you have a new world, you must have a new Sun" (4V.6). Paradoxically, now that the Protestant Reformation is at hand, the world is more corrupt than it has ever been. Cotton explicates the "new Sun" of the "new world" as the house of Austria and the pope, denouncing the domination of the world by imperial and papal power. The new earth is so "wholly corrupt" that there is no sacred place in it anywhere.[5] The place of the elect in this allegory is transcendent, "high," "among the stars of God" (4V.16). Cotton's parabolic interpretation figuratively places the Congregationalists where his 1630 sermon placed the deity, over the earth and its inhabitants. They live figuratively in the parabolical dimension of existence because, allegorically, corrupt earthly life is inappropriate to their purity. The hierarchy of figurative space symbolically reveals their superiority, contravening their apparent inferiority in the international struggle for dominion of the earth.

What most interests Cotton about the new heaven and earth is not its newness but its two-ness, the metaphoric doubling of allegory that has created a parabolical world for the Puritan to express his appropriateness as the international sacramental image of truth. Cotton uses John's prophecy of a new heaven and earth to create two heavens and earths, one for the Puritans and one for everyone else, although the Puritans seek to make this latter their own as well. The American Puritan lives in both worlds at once, maintaining his material earthly Canaan in New England while and because he allegorically transcends the earth he stands upon. The sacramental inappropriateness of the martyr who refuses to be sullied by the world's corruption is simultaneously interpreted as the temporary exile of the Congregational church to which the "new world," meaning the whole world, rightfully belongs. Though Cotton, like Winthrop, speaks of the Puritans as the focal point of vision for the rest of the world, he makes a substantial further claim.[6] The Puritans are also the potential rulers and owners of the world, entitled not only to the homage of vision but also to the very world itself. "Catholics" are everywhere, but, Cotton argues, it is Puritans who ought to be everywhere instead, for conversion includes property rights: "You have not only lawfull right unto the creatures to eat and drink, &tc. but some right and title to them by the blood of Christ" (R176). The Puritan domination of the world will occur less by the persuasiveness of converting rhetoric than by the assumption, enforced by violence, that the spiritual claim to internationally proper meaning requires literalization in the form of ownership. The earth which the pope rules, and upon which the American Congregationalist looks down from the Jerusalem of his "heavenly" perspective, is the rightful domain of the Congregationalist, who looks down with a sense of contingency as well as contempt on the "temporalls" of Catholicism. Unlike Plymouth separatists such as William Bradford, whose history is the narrative of a sect that seeks merely to maintain its presence in the world, Cotton imagines the Puritans to be saints who will one day rule the world as fully and completely as the "Catholick" Beast of the apocalypse rules it. Massachusetts Bay is merely the beginning of a literal possession of the earth, the first "appointed place" indicating the way in which the entire world will eventually become their property.

Cotton seems at first to grant elect status equally to the entire Puritan community, advocating a spatial translation of cultural privilege that parcels out the world to American Congregationalists irrespective of their status within New England society. However, belief in the validity of territorial possession depends on belief in his exegetical authority. Cotton's seeming egalitarianism depends on extending the propriety of his own system of signification throughout the world, literalizing the rhetorical concept of "place and situation" to take up the space of heaven and earth as the locus of his apocalyptic discourse. Thus the expansion of territorial privilege results in the collapse of the variants of social situation as determinants of meaning. There is, ultimately, only one locus of discourse and only one discourse, that of Puritan authority. In *Gods Promise* Cotton made the rightful ownership of property in New England dependent on conversion: "The land of *Canaan* is called a land of promise. Which they discerne, first, by discerning themselves to be in Christ, in whom all the promises are" (G7). In the Revelation sermons it is still conversion, and therefore obedience to the minister's rhetoric, that bestows the rights of property. Thus the parabolical vision of the new heaven and earth, while it portends the expansion of Puritan "temporalls," also asserts the expansion of the minister's hierarchical authority. There is no place the Puritan can go that has not already been appropriated by the rhetoric of institutional authority.

Cotton's sense of privilege expands in time as well as space to harness the power of radical change that the finality of Revelation seems to promise. Again, his exposition initially seems to grant the privilege of the elect to the Puritan community as a whole. Interpreting Revelation as a cryptic allegory of church history in much the way he interpreted Canticles, Cotton explains how the figures of the text of Revelation "resembled" and "deciphered" temporal events that, for the most part, have already occurred (R14). In this exposition, however, the living images of history are primarily English Protestants, interpreted as the predecessors of the colonists. For example, the angels who pour out the first vial are "the Martyrs of *Jesus Christ* in Queene *Maries* time, in *Edward* the sixth, and in *Henry* the eight's time" (1V.5). The angels of the second vial are "all those worthy servants of Christ, that have written either against the Trident Councell, or against *Bellarmine* . . . such hath been *Chenmitius,* and *Junius, Chamier, Whitaker,* and *Reignolds, Perkins,* and *Ames*" (2V.20). The third angel is interpreted as referring to Elizabeth and her ministers of state, who "did execute the righteous judgment of God upon the Popish Priests and Jesuites" by declaring Catholicism to be treason (3V.22).[7]

Just as in the Canticles explication, the historical personages to whom the textual images refer are significant as "members" of Christ's mystical body, again displacing Jesus as the revelatory locus of proper meaning: "And this Angell, He that first and principally hath the power of the bottomlesse pit, is the Lord Jesus: But because the Lord Jesus doth not come down in his owne presence, but in his instruments and Members, therefore they are the Angells that have these Keys" (CR4). Cotton's principles of exegesis, although similar to those used in the Canticles exposition, produce a different outcome because the successive living images of history now lead toward a figured society which is already at hand and to which he belongs. Because the American Puritans themselves now fulfill the images of the text as the iconic "instruments and Members," the New England iconoclast's claim to authority is far greater. Unlike the admiring observer of the Canticles sermons, the author of the exposition of Revelation confidently places the Puritans in the vanguard of what he believes is a worldwide transformation of "Religion." The apocalypse has arrived, and those who will rule the world in the coming millennium will be the American Puritans, conquering in an international war to establish their Congregational "ordinances" throughout the world.

In assigning pre-eminence to the American Puritans as the culmination of history, Cotton claims definitive religious authority for himself as exegete. Although he converts John into a Congregationalist visionary much as he converted Solomon, it is one thing to explain away the Old Testament love poetry of a Jewish monarch and quite another to explain away the Christian apocalyptic vision of John. Cotton's interpretation of Canticles, unusual though it was, did not directly challenge the most basic assumptions of traditional hermeneutics. Theories of Christian exegesis had always justified allegorical readings of passages in the Old Testament, and it had long been agreed that the text of Canticles was incongruous, that it did not in the "letter" express Christian truth. The same thing cannot be said of the Revelation of St. John, for it was John's special Christian insight that produced the dazzling images of the apocalypse. Because the Puritans are fulfilling a prophecy that is already Christian, they implicitly displace Christ and Scripture altogether as the locus of authority. In reading Revelation as a prophecy of Congregationalism, Cotton exploits the finality of this last book of Scripture to establish his interpretation as the last metonymic substitution. The Puritans supersede John in Christian history, but no one, he implies, will supersede the Puritans. They will not pass into history as mere shadowy types of some future fulfillment because they are themselves enacting the last images of history. The hypothetical demise of the text implied by the Canticles exegesis now acquires a potential for political reality, a potential that overtly substitutes Cotton's own rhetoric for Scripture.

Cotton indirectly asserts his hierarchial authority within Puritan society by reinterpreting the temporal closure promised in Revelation. The sense of definitive social change associated with definitive temporal change is co-opted by his belief in a "graduall" apocalypse. His sermons have wrongly been described as predicting an end to the world in 1655.[8] Here is the passage on which this reading is based, and what Cotton actually says is far more subdued than has been supposed:

> I will not be too confident, because I am not a Prophet, nor the Son of a Prophet to foretell things to come, but so far as God helps by Scripture light, about the time 1655. there will be then such a blow given to this beast, and to the head of this beast, which is *Pontifex maximus,* as that we shall see a further gradual accomplishment and fulfilling of this Prophecy here. You must not think it strange that some Prophecies receive a graduall accomplishment. [R93]

Far from predicting the dissolution of life as he knew it, Cotton interprets this "blow" to the "beast" as one more onslaught very much like the rest of the blows the beast has already received. In the admonition to become accustomed to the "graduall accomplishment" of the apocalypse, Cotton hardly predicts the end of the world. He does not even predict the end of the Catholic religion. At most, he predicts the demise of the power of the papacy, and even the significance of this end is muted by his conclusion that future events will be much like present ones: "About that time will be the expiration of the power and great authority of this Beast [i.e., not the expiration of the Beast itself]: But already we see, by the blessing of God, his power weakened, but we look for a further accomplishment" (R94). Cotton asserts the importance of the year 1655 in such a hesitant and qualified way that he vitiates any sense of immanent transformation implied by a definitive temporal closure. He insists instead that the future will be a continuation of the present, a "further" extension in a "graduall" manner of what is already taking place. In effect, then, he asserts the possibility of closure only to repudiate it.

He maintains a similar perspective in his interpretation of the seven vials. Categorically declaiming at the outset that "all things goe in a gradation," even in the disasters of the apocalypse, he evades any possibility of finality in the pouring out of the last vial by eliding apocalyptic and millennial time (1V.12). He explains, "For here's a world of businesse that is to be transacted after this [sixth] Vial is poured out: above a thousand yeers after this . . . to the last judgment" (6V.3.3). The fusion of the apocalypse and the millennium staves off any possibility of immanent change, for although "the thousand yeers are not yet begun," the "resurrection" of the church that will characterize the millennium is already in progress. It "is accomplished in some degree, unto the faithfull of it in every age" (CR20, 22). What millennial transformation or "Revelation" there will be short of the last judgment has already been disclosed and its basic contours already made known. With over half the seven vials already poured out, John's promised world catastrophe is, strangely, almost over. The apocalypse cannot lie ahead because it is virtually past already. Definitive transformation cannot occur in the future because it is already happening in the present. Since the millennial future that lies beyond is already at hand, the subsequent millennial perfection, when it comes, will be only some recognizable version of the present, a perfected Congregationalism.

In Cotton's admonition to his hearers to accept the idea of a "graduall fulfillment" of apocalyptic prophecy is the assertion of an indefinite apocalyptic present. To locate oneself in history by placing oneself in the midst of the apocalypse is to bring the possibility of definitive millennial fulfillment much closer, to make it seem immanent, hovering on the horizon, and yet place it out of reach, too, as an impossible realization for the present. By adopting the sensation of worldwide transformation through violence while simultaneously denying its actuality, he conveys not so much a historical narrative as an unchanging attitude of mind and a way of life, an indefinitely extended crisis. Unlike the martyr who refuses the temporal world, Cotton acknowledges temporal change to make time stand still, holding in suspension the present of his own discourse and thereby creating an indefinite temporal expansion for the meaning of his words. When he proudly declares that his Christology is "the Religion of the ancient Patriarks since the world began . . . and we know no other way," the effect of his interpretation is to nullify the temporal situation of his discourse as a limiting determinant of meaning (R200–01).

Cotton's denial of the social transformation associated with millennialism, implicit in his interpretation of apocalyptic space and time, is explicit in his portrayal of the orderly destruction of society in the apocalypse. The means by which the Puritans will gain the space of the world for themselves respects hierarchical order. Although the millennial rule of the saints will "most properly begin from the throwing down of Antichrist and destruction of Rome" (CR5), this overthrow does not at all mean the destruction of privileged authority. The violence of the apocalypse actually validates the status quo by respecting hierarchy in the pattern of destruction. Cotton explains that "God in his Judgements upon wicked persons, and states beginneth first with the least and lowest among them" (1V.12), because "ordinarily the first beginning of corruption is with the people, and they being first corrupted, it is meet that they should be first plagued" (4V.12). He perceives an orderly progression in the desecration wrought by the vials of wrath: "So the Lords manner is, first he breaks forth against the common people, then against the Ministers, then at last he riseth to the great Lords of the world, the Rulers of the State, they smoke for it at last" (4V.12). His apocalypse will not venture vulnerably into the un-known but will merely repeat the orderly method of an earlier era: "For by the same steps wherby antichrist came into the world, by the same steps doth the Lord undermine him and bring him downe" (1V.12). Far from overthrowing the social order, Cotton's hierarchial rationalization of violence staves off any possibility of social disorder, much less social innovation. He depicts apocalyptic warfare not as a struggle to over-throw hierarchies but rather as a struggle to substitute one autocratic authority for another, for "the Saints to Rule" instead of the "Pope" (CR5).

Throughout his explication, Cotton deflects the possibility of social transformation that the violent imagery of Revelation might seem to offer. Even the apocalyptic images of anarchic chaos and horrendous destruction do not threaten to turn the social order upside down. The unprecedented sanction of American Puritan society thus remains an abstract, unrealizable ideal for the common people in Massachusetts Bay. In social reality, the promise of international dominion and the righteous vengeance of the martyred outcast become the means for inspiring an obedience to local authority that is founded on fear. Cotton warns that the order of destruction could well be applicable to the colonists themselves, that some of the Puritans are readily expendable. The "common sort" are distinguished as the most tenuous in their privileged status as Cotton contemptuously exhorts them to "heed to your Religion . . . for if corruptions grow therein, you will be the first that will suffer by them" (1V.12). Even if their fate is starvation, the social distance between rulers and ruled is so great that it is a matter of indifference to those with authority: "Nothing more distant, from the chiefe men in a State, then the common multitude. A Judgmente upon them doth not matter much, if a famine were upon the common sort of people, Princes and Great men would not be much affected therewith" (1V.13). He concedes that rulers may ultimately "smoke for it at last," but he implies that their fate is nonetheless distinct from that of the "common sort," and he warns them to beware of the "contagion" of evil from the common people (1V.13).

Cotton explains further how the sacrifice of the common sort works: "The least of his judgments should be taken as warnings unto us, to teach us that the Lord hath taken his Sword into his hand, and will go on in judgement, untill he make the soules of men to tremble" (1V.13). The apocalyptic destruction of the common people is significant merely as a sign that the elect status of rulers may be doubtful. The judgment is "least" because the social category is least. Cotton's ready inclusion of himself among "us," the rulers, places him among the saintly elite in opposition to the common people. In *The Way of Life*, Cotton implied that the conversion of the common people would transform them into saints, but he now restricts the category of the securely saved to men who hold ecclesiastical or magisterial authority, threatening that the religion of "us" is not necessarily "your Religion."

Although Cotton subordinates the clergy to the state power of "great Lords," he also grants a special power to the ministry, the interpretive authority of the speaker over his hearers. Cotton takes upon himself an exegetical authority commensurate with his claims for Congregational polity as his own voice becomes the audible shape of authoritative speech for which he prayed at the end of the Canticles exegesis. Glossing John's words "I heard a great voice," Cotton proposes that the voice of apocalyptic revelation is "a great Voice of Christ out of the Temple," that is, "the mighty Voice of Christ, specially in Public Ordinances," and, more bluntly, "the publike Ministry" (1V.6–8). What this "great voice" first and foremost commands is obedience to itself:

> Eternall life doth he give in the Publike fellowship of his Saints, there doth hee confirme their callings to them, looke unto the Lord therefore for his blessing in this way, and so shall you be faithfull followers of these holy Angels of God, who being privately incouraged, waite for a publike voice to carry them an end in their Administrations, wherein the Lord by the mighty power of his Spirit doth confirme al his Promises, threatnings, and Commandements, and more throughly stirreth up the hearts of all his people to take hold of al that is spoken unto them. [1V.8–9]

Controverting the lingering threat of antinomian revelations, Cotton equates his institutional authority with the definitive perspective of Scripture, rebuking all "that shall despise or neglect the Publike ordinances of God in the Church, for you see here what is confirmed in the whole Church is the great voyce of God, and that without contradiction to the holy Saints and Angels" (1V.9). The social identity of his hearers as elect living images is dependent on submission to his authority.[9]

Cotton warns against any attempt to evade the interpretive powers of exegetical authority by dispersed settlement or founding a town without a church. "You have seene when some have made a beginning without Ministers," he reminds them, and the consequence for those who have "run such hazards" has been that they were "suddenly unsettled" (3V.24).[10] In the ambiguous and insinuating threat of unsettlement is the exhortation to fear the power of the natural world:

> Therefore when ever you are about such a work as this, take the Lord Jesus Christ along with you, and take rivers and fountaines of waters; that as you look for rivers and fountains for the refreshement of your

cattle, and servants, and children, you may finde a living fountaine of
the bloud of Christ, conveighed and running in the plantation where
you intend to sit downe; otherwise you wil finde the springs there,
and the fountains and rivers you sit downe by, rise up in judgment
against you. [3V.23–24]

Without the controlling language of the cleric, the colonist faces the
open rebellion of nature. The rivers that can "rise up in judgment," the
concrete shapes of nature, have something holding them in place: the
converting words of the preacher's rhetoric. The providences of nature
are thus construed as the punishment for disbelief. Where words will
not convince, the experience of being "unsettled" will. Cotton exhorts
his hearers to trust solely in his words and to believe them a priori, to
"take . . . Christ along with you, and take rivers and fountaines," the
metaphors of the converting rhetoric of the soul. Otherwise, events
will only affirm that obedience to clerical authority is essential to a
Puritan town.

In his interpretation of nature, Cotton wards off disbelief by offering
another form of his own beliefs as the definition of lack of faith. His
personified "fountaines and rivers" that may "rise up in judgment
against you" are a devout iconoclast's perception of nature as composed
of living images like himself. In terms of the sacramental paradigm,
there is no such thing as unconsecrated bread in the world of the Puritan apocalypse. Cotton says in effect that the "naturall" world is infused with the spiritual sense, asserting that consecrated bread has become the norm of appropriateness. Thus what is sacramental accrues to
itself the attributes of what is normative while retaining the qualities of
the sacramental symbol, the inadequate material object infused with the
spiritual sense and ordered to a spiritual teleology. This *figura* is opposed not to the ordinary common bread of an unconsecrated world
but to the threatening idol of iconoclasm. The idol of nature is the
referent of his own making, sacramental bread on the loose without the
taming influence of the "ordinances of Christ," the salutary, consecrating control bestowed by verbal signification. Because the "new world"
already belongs in principle to the Puritan, the only enemy he can
imagine is the idol of his own construction, a nature that does not
behave naturally, as it were, until it submits to ecclesiastical authority.

Although the "appointed place" of the Puritans seems to be the entire
world, in actuality the colonists are limited to the space the Puritan
church actually occupies. In refusing the limitations of the concept of
sacred place, and by locating the source of spiritual power and truth in
the words of ecclesiastical authority instead, the Puritan is bound to the
words of the preacher. The act of material possession, Cotton implies,

depends on the act of material rejection that hearing the "ordinances" offers. Cotton warns his hearers not to stray from the interpretive power of the institution that has promised them so much: "Let it be the wisdom of sincere hearted Christians, that come from old England for liberty and purity of Ordinances, not to leave them now for fresh medows and fountaines: and for want of planting ground, and the like, it will not be suitable to these ends for which you left your native Countrey" (3V.24). It is not that Cotton is opposed to new settlements, only that he is opposed to settlements without churches, the separation of economic and religious interests, of material objects and spiritual presence. In the direct engagement with material reality, whether it is the reality of the natural environment or the social reality of "Catholicks," the protective intervention of alienation is necessary for the "heavenly" people to possess the earth.

Describing his own words as the "natural and true meaning" of Scripture, and nature as alive with threatening icons, Cotton unites the natural world with his own authority to rationalize economic conservatism (3V.2.7). Measured against the privilege of transcendent purity, the material needs of the mortal Puritan become an embarrassment, not "suitable" for a Puritan. Cotton addresses the conditions of economic depression in the colony in 1640 by trivializing material loss.[11] It is merely a metaphor for spiritual neglect: "Doe you think a Christians outward estate shall prosper, when his inward estate growes leaner and leaner?" (4V.23). The need for meadows and planting ground cannot justify a new settlement, he warns, reversing the attitude of his 1630 sermon. These common wants are wrongly conceived and unreasonably valued, for the real causes of material loss are "worldly mindednesse," confidence, and controversy within the church: "Hath not the Lord blasted us because we grew cold-hearted, and formall in Church-fellowship, and confident, and warme, and bold-hearted in matters pertaining to our selves and to the world, and in matters that tended onely to tumult?" (4V.21). As long as the living images of the mystical body have a place to put their feet, the material purpose of Canaan is fulfilled, and any "tumult" of disagreement or economic deprivation is only evidence of bad faith.

Where Cotton's 1630 sermon interpreted the whole Puritan community as the elect, the Revelation sermons abandon this largesse to sanction only the Puritan elite. Puritan "sainthood" becomes a social category that expands or diminishes according to the judgment of men with institutional authority. In terms of the sacramental analogy, Cotton radically distinguishes between the authoritative living icons who pronounce the consecrating words and the common bread that remains silent in its iconic role. The paradigmatic relation between the authoritarian subject and the obedient object is clearest in the distribution of authority in the institution of marriage. Preaching on the importance of limiting "Prerogatives," Cotton exhorts wives to obey their husbands absolutely: "So let there be due bounds set, and I may apply it to Families; it is good for the Wife to acknowledge all power and authority to the Husband" (R73). The "due bounds" make the wife absolutely powerless, as they give the husband "all power" without bounds of any kind. Cotton thinks of setting bounds only as doing so limits the authority of the wife to nothing, granting an unlimited, authoritarian prerogative to the husband. In effect, the religious identity of the "common people," and particularly women, is made contingent on their obedience to the ecclesiastical, political, and household hierarchical order. Cotton reproduces the same paradigm of absolute obedience to autocratic authority whenever he describes social relations.[12] Thus, although the mystical body of Christ is supposedly the paradigm of communal coherence, that coherence is achieved by an interlocking system of hierarchies for which the casuistry is monotonously the same: obedience of the object to the subject. Whatever sense of organic unity or potential egalitarianism there may be in the analogy of the body is subordinated to the priority of a hierarchical power that interprets women and other "common" people as a threat.

Although the authority of the Puritan elite sanctions the secular social hierarchy, its rationalization depends on the concept of ordained images rather than the veracity of tradition. Expanding the Puritan version of the Second Commandment, Cotton extends the sanctions and prohibitions of images to include political and ecclesiastical institutional authority: The church "shall make no Images of Officers, nor Government, nor worship, but that which Christ himselfe hath set up" (R238).[13] As Winthrop put it in a speech to the General Court, the "office" of governor possesses "authority from God, in way of an ordinance, such as hath the image of God eminently stamped upon it, the contempt and violation whereof hath been vindicated with examples of divine vengeance."[14] The imagistic concept of institutional office, though highly abstract, sanctions the extreme forms of obedience that Cotton demands in the name of proper homage to divinely ordained living icons. Cotton perceives the images of state and clerical authority as mutually affirming their power over the other members of the community. The clergy, as the curators of sacred tropes and interpreters of the Second Commandment, hold the linguistic authority to sanction the prerogatives of state power. The magistrates in turn protect the clergy in their verbal freedom, not only by allowing them to preach but also by threatening the punitive sanction of violence as the means of enforcing the ordained imaginations of the clergy.

Cotton's principles of exegesis articulate a social ideal of hierarchical authority that has the force and power to control the minds of his hearers. To interpret the angels of the apocalypse as allegorical representations of eminent individuals in the English Reformation is to display the exegete's power to control the visionary images of the text. His control of apocalyptic shapes is exactly in the declaration that they definitively mean something else, some living image in history. The more absurd and forced the connection appears between scriptural image and historical referent, the greater the display of the interpreter's power. His exegesis co-opts the imaginative power of the text as the vehicle of the mind's ability to conceive of the transformation of society. His concept of hierarchical destruction is oppressive in its containment and control of the fantastical imagery of Revelation, almost a mechanical apocalypse in its rigid numerical logic, its praise of the abstractions of Congregational polity, and its arbitrary exploitation of the text as a coded allegory of historical events. That the spectacular images of Revelation should mean what Cotton declares is indeed a transforming apocalypse, but only by negation, in its attenuation of Revelation. His method of interpretation exploits its own absurdity to transform the significance of world catastrophe in John's vision into the astonishingly diminished vision of Puritan New England, thereby subduing the idea of transformation itself. The result is both an enhancement and a rejection of the figurative imagination. The appropriation of the imagination to rationalize the social structure of New England Puritanism is an oblique acknowledgment that imaginative vision is in fact compelling, so threatening in its powers that it needs to be quashed and made to serve the defense of the established social order.

Cotton's own display of power in the interpretation of the scriptural text produces an exegesis that rationalizes the use of violence in society to control the imagination. The objects of his most explicit threats of violence are Catholics, whom he believes to be the corrupting source of false imaginations. Bringing his own poetic figures into focus through his development of the prejudicial image of the Catholic, Cotton makes hatred and rejection of Catholics an essential tenet of faith (R207). The form this hatred takes is murder: "Priests and Jesuites who carried that Religion up and down the Nations, should be adjudged or condemned to a bloudy death" (3V.8). The imperative to commit violence is distinctive in the openness of the exhortations. Revelation, he says, is to be "of terrour to all Roman Catholics," to "let them know" that "blood and slaughter will be their portion one day" at the hands of Congregationalists (R23, 218). Cotton repeatedly advocates violence against "Catholicks" in terms that demand their execution. For example, he interprets the motif of bloody revenge in Rev. 16.4–6 as an imperative

to kill. Catholics deserve "a bloudy death, as bloud is expounded in the
5. and 6. verses. . . . So this is bloud which God hath given them to
drinke. And that is a usuall phrase, to give a man bloud to drinke, is to
kill him" (3V.4).

Whereas in *The Way of Life* Cotton used figurative language implicitly to articulate a referential imperative, the figures of the Revelation
sermons make this imperative explicit. Cotton overtly recognizes the
significance of literal meaning embedded in the metaphoric aphorism,
emphasizing the importance of the literal meaning of blood in the
apocalyptic image. He rejects outright the belief that converts are concerned only with "spirituall death," with figurative as opposed to literal
meaning. "The holy Ghost makes it as true in the letter," he argues,
referring to Revelation: "This Text [Rev. 16.6] is in the New Testament, not in the Old, *Thou has given them bloud to drinke, for they are
worthy*: and he speaks of the very bloud of the hearts of men: And it is
parallel with Gods justice of old; it was just then, and it is just now"
(3V.16). Insisting on a material referent, "the very bloud of the hearts
of men," he stresses the corporeal nature of the referent.[15] Ideologically,
his sanction of the "letter" of violence is less a question of literal versus
figurative meaning than an appeal to the nonverbal meaning of *figura,*
after the manner of Luther, that circumvents the concept of discourse as
a representation of referents.

The obsessive and murderous hatred of Catholics takes much of its
rationale from the iconoclast's self-declared mandate to destroy false
images. Not surprisingly, the images of Revelation reveal passim the
deity's hatred of the "Papist" Catholics as "idolaters" who worship their
false "idols" and reject the Protestant Reformation. But there is also a
new expansiveness to the Puritan crusade against false images. In this
cosmic battle, the righteousness of the iconoclast is brought in to justify
the attack on Catholicism at a new level of abstraction. It is not just that
the Catholic church has images. The institution itself has become an
"image," the counterpart to the ordained image of his own clerical authority. Cotton denounces both Anglicans and Catholics on the grounds
that their churches are the apocalyptic "image of the beast" in their
"forms" or "models" (R244). His interchangeable use of "image,"
"model," "form," and "mold" in condemning European churches as
images shows that the classical concept of *figura* informs his ideas, but it
is adapted here to describe the nonmaterial structure of an institution.
Moreover, although the old rationale of European iconoclasm is still
evident in Cotton's exhortations to assault the head of the "image," the
pope, the ideology of violence has shifted to an attack on the whole
institution.[16] Catholics not only worship idols, he charges; they are
themselves pieces of an idol.

Cotton has pretensions to an ethical justification for his exhortations to kill, but his evocation of justice turns out to be nothing more than a heuristic device. Referring to "*Moses* Morall Lawes of perpetual equity," which articulate "the unchangeable righteousness of God, he argues that Catholics must be killed because "the law of retaliation" requires it, as if revenge were one of the Ten Commandments (3V.14–16). Recalling the persecution of Lollards, Huguenots, and early English Protestants, in the fires of "*Smithfield* and elsewhere," he advocates revenge:

> It is just and right with God, *They have given thy Saints and Prophets bloud to drinke,* and therefore looke as they have measured to others, it is measured to them, by the ancient Law of God, that *is the same, and will be for ever,* Rev. 13.10. he that killeth with the sword, must be killed by the sword. So you see this point is plaine. [3V.15]

The "plaine" point of the "letter" is the apocalyptic sanctity of wanting "bloud to drinke" on the pretense that the Puritan is morally bound by Mosaic law to kill. Cotton's doctrine is ultimately imagistic rather than ethical, so dependent on imagism that the commandment "Thou shalt not kill" is converted to its opposite to justify the violent destruction of false images. The trueness or falseness of the social image, not the nature of the act, determines its acceptability. He demonstrates the principle by condemning the Catholic Queen Mary for executing Protestants and praising the Protestant Queen Elizabeth for executing Catholics. The law, no less than other aspects of a culture, is conceivable in terms of true and false images. In an iconoclastic tract written shortly after he gave the Revelation sermons, he includes "the lawes of men binding the conscience" among the false images prohibited by the Second Commandment (AB17). Such laws are like the Apocrypha, merely "the imaginations and inventions of men" and therefore without divine sanction (AB17). His willingness to include such things as the "lawes of men binding the conscience" in the category of images resonates with Quintillian's assertion that there is nothing that is not figural. In Cotton's interpolation there is nothing that is not imagistic, or potentially so, nothing that cannot be subsumed under the iconoclast's Second Commandment.

Cotton's preaching on the conversion of the soul, no less than his diatribes on the murder of Catholics, displays the iconoclast's obsession with destroying the *figura* of the human shape. For example, when he explicates Rev. 13.8, "the Lamb slain from the foundation of the world," an allusion to Christ crucified, some of the imagery recalls Old Testament ritual sacrifice, but the conceptualization is primarily that of the iconoclast. Cotton uses a generalized rhetoric of violence to reinterpret the crucifixion: The "slaughtering knife" of the priest (R200) and the "iron hammer" of the iconoclast (R198) are the new weapons of lurid destruction as the motif of blood is developed through descriptions of total bodily destruction. Christ is "slaughtered" and "crushed" as well as crucified, dismembered, and smashed, in sadistic imagery, as Cotton describes "the mighty power of the spirit applying the warm blood of Christ to our souls" (R173). Not only must Jesus die, painfully and gruesomely; he must also be "broken and crushed" (R199). Like the corpses of Jezebel and the Pequots, Christ's body is desecrated, no longer a recognizably human form.

The figurative imagery of conversion reflects the same concept of violence. The sinner "must be slaughtered in his lusts and passions," must "lay hold" on "Christs breaking and crushing" to be "conformable to him" (R200). Cotton applies his Christology to sinners who suffer "unsupportable anguishes" that "plow up the tender heart of a Christian that he lay sprawling as it were in his blood" (R175). The sensation of grotesque violence is important for children as well, he argues, rejecting the idea that one "need not use violence" with children:

> It is a vain apprehension that men have of themselves as good, to say, I thank God I have a good heart, and you shall finde me tractable, and reasonable, (though they be but naturall) and so their children are very tractable, you may lead them with a twinde theerd, and need not use violence, you may soon break them; what then are you but eggshels? what need then a iron hammer to crush all the power of the enemy? do not you and your children stand in need of the virtue of the blood of the Lamb as much as others have since the world began? . . . Christ came to crush them while they are in the shell, and unless he heal them, verily children of a span long cannot be saved. [R198–99]

He preaches the need to "crush eggshels" with an "iron hammer," to "use violence" to produce conversion. Being "tractable" is not enough, not even relevant to the condition of the soul. The elect must be figuratively crushed and slaughtered to be saved.[17]

Grossly disproportionate acts of brutality, he insinuates, are disproportionate because they are sanctifying and sanctifying because they are disproportionate. The extravagance of violence is morally symbolic, for one can understand the moral depths of original sin by the kind of "remedie" required to cure the convert of it:

> You may see by the medicine that the Lord prepares for it; it shews the depth of the depravation of the world from the beginning, it hath been corrupt and incurable, unless it were by the vertue of the death of Christ, by the sonne of God made man, taking upon him mans nature; and the greatnesse and infinitenesse of the vertue of this re-

medie doth evidently argue the bottomlesse depth of the corruption of
the world since the world began. [R196]

The "medicine" reveals the nature of the disease, the cure determines
the illness. The Protestant disdain for salvation by works becomes an
open contempt for ethics altogether as Cotton warns that the devil "had
them [the Jews of the Old Testament] fast in a golden and silken chaine,
or cord of morall vertues (so I may call them) he led the prisoners of
those days in a golden chaine" (R197). Associating moral virtue with
the devil and with Catholicism (R118–19), he implies that ethics is a
trap and a delusion, something that can only lead the hearer away from
the necessary violence of conversion.

Synthesizing the violence of the crucifixion and iconoclasm, Cotton
intensifies the pervasive sense of an urge to kill by portraying Christ as
a perpetrator of violence against both himself and others. In the figures
of conversion, it is Christ who crushes eggshells, who delivers the
blows with a "Smith's great hammer," for it requires "the strongest
iron hammer to break the Serpents head" (R196). Incorporating this
scriptural rhetoric, Cotton describes Christ as an iconoclastic savior
who is himself the weapon of physical destruction, "which is wonder-
full, this iron hammer, the Lord Jesus, that breaks all before it" (R196).
This section of the exposition culminates in a description of Christ as a
suicidal murderer, fusing the violence of the crucifixion and iconoclasm: "Christ himselfe in his soul and body must be striken, he kils
himselfe by the stroke he gives to the enemy" (R199). In his earlier
preaching, Cotton carefully described the way in which Christ the
Word, conveyed in the words of the preacher, regenerated souls. In the
Revelation sermons Cotton portrays a wordless savior who, speechless
before Pilate, submits with lamblike "silence" to state power in the
crucial moment of his self-defense (R157–58). Unlike the talkative
beast/pope, his chief apocalyptic enemy, Christ dissociates himself from
the interpretive signs of language, mutely submitting to violent death. [18]

The portrayal of Christ as one who enacts violence, as well as one
who submits to it in an act of sacrifice, has a precedent of a sort in the
figurative language of conversion. Cotton's English sermons in The
Way of Life interpret the soul as both the object and the perpetrator of
figurative violence. While the saint is figuratively crucified in regeneration, the saint also figuratively crucifies Christ with every sin: "Look at
all our sins, as so many nailes that fastned him to the Cross" (WL32).
Cotton emphasizes the simultaneity of figurative violent acts with metaphoric repetitions, such as "they were pierced with many sorrowes for
piercing of Christ" (WL127). Although these acts are figurative, mental, the paradigm of the violent saint is nonetheless present. From the

perspective of Cotton's English sermons, the depiction of the apocalyptic Christ is a verbal literalization of the figures of the soul's life, and one that reverses the traditional priorities of theology. Instead of the soul imitating Christ, Christ imitates the soul. Protestantism implied the possibility of this ideological reversal in the doctrine of the soul's privileged, unmediated relation to the deity. Cotton's apocalyptic history of living images realizes this possibility by relegating Christ to an abstract condition. By making the American Puritans the authoritative locus of sacred discourse, he privileges the internal idiom of the externally privileged material shape.

This reversal of priorities is evident in the difference between the restricted use of metaphor to depict violence in *The Way of Life* and the sanction of pervasive violence through metaphor in the Revelation sermons. In *The Way of Life* Cotton attempts to limit the implied literal meaning of metaphors of violence by restricting the domain of literal reference to the crucifixion of Christ. Preaching at length on the experience of grace as a "piercing of the heart," he stops to explain the signification of the metaphor by distinguishing literal and figurative meaning. He argues that the metaphor applies only figuratively to the hearer's life in the present:

> By the heart, you must not understand, that fleshly part of the body which is the seate of life. . . . Godly sorrow doth not kill mans bodily life, it works not death. . . . But it is meant of the *will* of a man, which lyes in the heart. . . . An heart of stone, is a stubborne and obstinate heart or will; an heart of flesh, is an heart that is tractable, and soone pierced. [WL127]

The convert is "pierced" figuratively in the experience of grace, retaining "bodily" life in the process of acquiring a "tractable" heart that is receptive to the words of conversion.

Cotton supports his intended constraints by narrating the death of Jesus in a way that sets temporal bounds to the domain of literal signification for his metaphors. His narrative emphasizes the individual humanity of Jesus and the suffering of the Passion in descriptions that focus on the specificity of this event as a single, unique death in history.[19] His metaphors of violence, grotesque though they are, refer back to his narrative for their literal base, achieving the clarity of metaphor as figurative language by giving historical bounds to its assumed literal meaning. However, when Cotton occasionally strays from this single domain of signification, blending metaphors, a sense of threat emerges in the suggestion of generalized sacrosanct violence in the present. For example, at one point he combines the imagery of nailing Christ to the cross with iconoclastic attacks on the heads of images:

"To teach Ministers not to be afraid sometimes of driving nayles to the head, nor to the consciences, but to the hearts of sinners . . . the proud, wanton, and stubborn heart [must] be pierced and wounded to the death" (WL133–34). When Cotton starts aiming at the head, the sadistic result threatens an expansion of violence by destabilizing the historical specificity of literal reference. In *The Way of Life* these blended metaphors are lapses in what is for the most part a consistent system of reference to the death of Christ. Nonetheless, such figurative language lends its oblique sanction to generalized violence, creating an unresolved tension that becomes characteristic of his rhetoric in the Revelation sermons.

Because the discourse of the soul is psychically organized by figures of murderous violence, much depends on maintaining a clear distinction between literal and figurative meaning – just the distinction that is abandoned in the crises of 1637. In the Revelation sermons Cotton exploits the semantic confusion of 1637 to sanction the belief that righteous murder can be literal as well as figurative. He conveys this belief doctrinally, in his exhortations to murder Catholics, and rhetorically, in his vivid, seemingly present-day evocations of the death of Christ. When he develops metaphors extensively to describe the regenerative slaughter of the convert in the "warme blood" of Christ, it becomes difficult to distinguish between literal and figurative meaning because the temporal frame of reference is so easily lost (R178). The theological means of differentiating the dual loci of metaphor through references to the crucifixion are of little importance when compared to the American iconoclast's general mandate for the destruction of offending corporeal shapes.

Without the restrictions of temporal bounds, Cotton attempts to restore the distinctiveness of figurative violence in conversion by reconceiving the loci of metaphor socially. He preaches a social division of labor in which the Puritan convert's life provides the figurative meaning and the dead Catholic provides the literal meaning, systematically relating the figures of the soul's life to Puritan acts of murder. In a passage on the difference between literal and figurative meaning comparable to his explanation in *The Way of Life,* he purposefully expands the domain of signification for the convert's metaphors of violence where he previously attempted to limit this meaning. Now stressing the religious value of the "letter" in his rhetoric about violent death, he directly relates the rhetoric of conversion to the Protestant need to execute Catholics. His example focuses particularly on the word "death," indicating that its literal meaning refers to "profest Catholicks and wicked enemies of the Church" while its figurative meaning, "meant of the dead Metaphorically," belongs to the rhetoric of regeneration – he cites the example of being "dead in sinne" (CR6).[20] The figurative death of Puritan conversion is accompanied by the literal death of Catholics, for the same word signifies both kinds of death (CR7). Although they share the same verbal signifier, the Puritan convert experiences, receives, only the figurative salutary violence of regeneration, while Catholics experience only the literal violence of "bloud" and "death." The death of Catholics is a sacrifice to the figurative language of the Puritan soul, providing literal meaning for the metaphors that describe the state of sin among converts.

In effect, Cotton treats the metaphors of conversion as sacred tropes, insinuating that the privileged discourse of the convert has a unique referential clarity. In contrast to the parabolical figures of Scripture, where "pillar" signifies John Huss and the angels of the third vial signify Elizabethan state power, in the rhetoric of conversion "death" signifies death already with nominal transparency. Through the assumed literal signification of his metaphors, Cotton's preaching on conversion becomes an imperative to commit murderous acts of violence. The Puritan, experiencing figurative violence and committing literal murder, preserves the metaphors of the Puritan imagination through the physical destruction of the Catholic enemy. The distinction between literal and figurative meaning, which still holds true for the Puritan convert's life, differentiates the convert's fate from the Catholic's.[21] Whereas Puritans in their material shapes remain sacred living icons, their counterparts, the Catholics, are viable objects for destruction. In the midst of his explication of the seven vials, Cotton observes:

> On the pouring out of this vial, they [Catholics] became bloud, not onely in regard that their waters themselves are bloud, the doctrine and worship which they doe hold forth to the people are corrupt, . . . but that chiefly in regard of the punishment which they [the angels] inflict on them for so doing, which is a bloudy death. [3V.4]

Whether Catholics spill the metaphorical blood of doctrine or the actual blood of Protestants they execute, they deserve death. For them, the difference between literal and figurative meaning is a distinction without a social difference.

Cotton's obsessive repetitions of "bloud" and "death" in association with "Catholicks" imply that the physical characteristics of human beings are less important than the sheer corporeality of a living thing. Where the ideology of the iconoclast takes the human *figura* as definitive of the human being, Cotton's abstraction of the concept of an image is accompanied by an increasing value attributed to human beings simply as living material objects. The particular material shape becomes less significant, for what most of all characterizes a "Catholick" is "bloud" and "death." The intensity of reification varies directly with the increasing abstraction of corporate ecclesiology. As Cotton interprets figures figuratively to describe the Catholic church as a prohibited image, his spiraling self-justification produces an increasingly reductive concept of human beings in the material world. No longer limited even by the particular qualities of human material shapes, he expands the possibilities of sacrosanct violence to fill the space of the world, prophesying a violent struggle that extends over the indefinite duration of apocalyptic time. Cotton urges a ceaseless mandate for violence, rebuking "the carnall and sinfull foolish pity that is found in any state, that shall be sparing of spilling such bloud" (3V.19). In the seemingly endless recourse to violence, the unrelenting thirst for blood, the vials of wrath seem never to be fully poured out.

Because the blood and death of objects of violence characterize the "Catholicks" in relation to the discourse of the Puritan soul, the number of possible "Catholicks" is potentially far greater than it first appears. Without relinquishing the specific ecclesiastical meaning of "Catholick," Cotton expands this social category to indefinite proportions. One can see how little it matters who is a practicing Catholic from such generalizations as Cotton's claim that "now all the world admire and worship him," the beast, the head of the false image (R61). The specific historical, geographical, and social limitations of the actual Catholic church are unimportant to the essence of the prejudicial image. When Cotton condemns "Indians, Jews, and Pagans," as well as the Church of England, because "their Religions are but so many refuges of lies," because they are "base unworthy creatures" who live in a condition of "Popish ignorance," he indicates how broad the category of "Catholick" can become (7V.12). His interpretation is undiscriminating, so generous is the category of rejection, because he abstracts an archetype of social prejudice, creating a floating sign that can arbitrarily be attached to almost any person.[22]

Exploiting the indeterminacy of the image to encompass all of human society, he argues for nothing less than a differentiation between converts and "the rest of the world." A convert

> may for a time worship the Beast in his ignorance, and do as the rest of the world do, and shew no difference between himselfe and the rest of the world: but when this electing love of God doth shed it selfe abroad into his heart, it doth make him see the counsell of God more; . . . And this is the point which the Holy Ghost tells you is of so great, and necessary, and due attention and consideration, which none but understanding eares can or will understand. [R207–08]

What the "understanding eares" hear is the rhetoric that converts them to this point of view, and because they alone "understand," by definition it persuades them alone of the religious truth of this systematic prejudice. As Cotton indicates, disbelief is viewed with contempt and branded as sinful ignorance. Since converts alone believe and understand the discourse defining them as sacramentally appropriate, the "Catholicks," who worship the beast, share the dilemma of Solomon's bride, Abraham's Sarah, and Anne Hutchinson. Deprived of the privileged discourse by the very nature of the paradigm, they are rejected for having been excluded. Cotton concludes, as well he might, that this doctrine "would be accounted great arrogance, and almost scurrility" (R208).

The indefinite social possibilities of the signifier "Catholick" ultimately include even the Puritans. Cotton greatly enhances the fear of institutional authority within the colony by undermining what seems to be his one secure social differentiation, the dualism of Catholic and Puritan that distinguishes literal and figurative meaning in his metaphors of violence. Although he dogmatically portrays Catholics and Puritans as mutually exclusive opposites throughout his exegesis, if one attempts to trace the supposed differences, many oppositions quickly dissolve. As he describes them, both Puritan and Catholic sanction the legal murder of heretics; both advocate the overthrow of a civil ruler who believes in the wrong religion; both believe that church and state should affirm each other's power; and, of course, both worship images. They also share unusual hermeneutic principles. Cotton remarks on the wisdom of the "Papists" who, like himself, believe in the literal significance of the violent imagery in Revelation: "They believe it is true in the letter. And let me say further, the holy Ghost makes it as true in the letter" (3V.16).[23] Catholics, like Puritans, also prefer "this stile" of plainness. The pope, the "head" of the apocalyptic beast, speaks "plainly and boldly, not in ambiguous or obscure phrases, but plainly in such expressions as could beare no other meaning" (R64–65). Cotton is emphatic about the style of papal rhetoric, that the beast/pope "speaks boldly, and confidently, as one that goes not behind the door, but speaks plainly" (R64).[24] The pervasive likeness extends even to similar attitudes toward mass slaughter. Among the predictable evil acts of the "Catholicks," Cotton condemns them for genocidal violence in their attacks on the Waldensians and Albigensians:

> They slew (as stands upon Record) about ten hundred thousands of them, and did burn up their Cities, and Cattell, fel'd their wood, that there might be no more Hereticks nestled in that wildernesse; and they did take a course that Midwives, and Mothers, and Infants in the womb, all should be slaughtered by fire and sword, that there might be no more continuance of that Generation. [R100]

So, in the same manner, had the Puritans overcome the Pequots at Mystic. Cotton calls it the "Authority" of a "transcendant power to violent warre" (R99).

The common qualities of Puritan and Catholic appear throughout these sermons, cultivating a sense of dual subjectivity. Especially when Cotton refers simply to the "Beast," he invites a double application of his rhetoric. At one point he even insists on it, drawing a lengthy analogy between the beast and the Puritan. He recounts how the beast, after being wounded and healed, used the power and authority of his plain speech only to "abuse" the deity who had healed him and given him power. He then applies this idea directly to the members of his congregation, including himself:

> So there is a nature in us that will abuse every mercy of God, to the corrupting of our hearts, and every judgment of God, and every deliverance from that judgement; one would not think what wofull distempers there are in our natures. If a body be stuft with choller, it will turne the whole body to feed the humour: So it is with us, we turne all the providences of God into distempers and outrageous licentiousnesse. [R76]

He considers the objection that his analogy is an exaggeration, even insulting and inappropriate to a Puritan convert: "But you will say, he [the Pope] was a Beast, and the [Catholic] Church a Beast; we hope Christians shall do better" (R76). Cotton answers with a resounding repudiation. Good Puritans are no better at all, for even "good *Hezekiah,*" champion of the iconoclasts in the Canticles sermons, shows "the depth of the body of Sinne which is not onely in wicked men . . . but in the Godly, in those that are most eminent in Grace" (R76).

Though Cotton appropriates historical events as the raw material for his prejudicial image of the "Catholick," his figure is a plausible enemy primarily because it is the projection of an altogether too familiar face: the Puritan's own. Paradoxically, this closed system of social imagery generates a corresponding openness of application because, as he admits, it so readily describes Puritans. Cotton is unrelenting in his condemnation of the regenerate Puritan: "No gift that man hath, no ordinance of God, but he will thus abuse. And therefore we have cause to sit down in dust and ashes, that we should abuse such mercies as we dayly partake in" (R76).[25] His doctrine is not a condemnation of the unregenerate "Beast" but rather a condemnation of the saved for having abused the grace of salvation with repulsive inevitability, for having made themselve indistinguishable from the unregenerate in their own use of power.[26] He even warns his congregation that they may have become altogether "counterfeit" in their "Religion" (2V.23). Insofar as they are indistinguishable from their own self-negation, the hated "Catholick," they become vulnerable to the imperative for violence in the "letter." Cotton creates the social possibility of dissociating the sign from the referent to return it to the Puritans in the form of a threat against the ungrateful regenerate in his audience.[27]

The urge to apply the "Popish" floating sign to people other than Catholics, even to Puritans, was strongly enhanced by the radical discrepancy between Cotton's exhortations to kill Catholics and the actual social situation of his hearers in Boston. The imperative for violence notwithstanding, there were no Catholics in Massachusetts Bay in 1640. Although Cotton's rhetoric conveys a sense of immanent material presence, as if Catholics were about to appear on the streets of Boston, in social reality Bostonians were being exhorted to kill an imaginary enemy, unmurderable bodies whose lack of physical proximity was quite blatant. Nonetheless, that the specified object was not there to receive the blows of the righteous iconoclast did nothing to discredit the holiness of Puritan violence, nor did it take away the epistemological necessity of maintaining the metaphors of the convert. In the absence of the most obvious referent, the demand for literal blood and death created a sense of immanent acts of violence without regard for who the objects of violence would be.[28] The discrepancy between the rhetoric of anti-Catholicism and the actual social conditions in the colony increased the sense of threat to the "common sort" among the Boston Puritans who heard these sermons. The antinomian crisis had demonstrated what was meant by the necessity of obedience to hierarchy, especially for women, and in the context of the Pequot War, the many descriptions of violence and exhortations to murder had the credence of recent example. Cotton's graphic portrayals of violence, together with his belief in the efficacy of the material shapes of speech and the sanctity of his own material shape, combined to enhance the significance of the immediate material situation of discourse as the primary determinant of meaning and therefore the most likely locus of reference. Thus, although the overt demands for violence against Catholics in the "letter" were clear, the oblique threat of violence made this preaching a rhetoric of threat against the Puritans in Cotton's audience as well.[29]

In his sermons Cotton encourages his audience to recognize the discrepancy between signs and referents, if only half consciously, by interrupting his apocalyptic drama at several points to address his audience and thereby acknowledge the local, American situation of his discourse. For example, when he broaches the possibility of a Catholic attack on Boston, the topic does not evoke an exhortation to murder, as we might expect. Instead of sustaining the sense of impending military threat that he introduces, he remarks that in New England "there is no feare of any War" with Catholics.[30] Late in the sermons on Revelation 13, he acknowledges more overtly that his sermons have no direct application in the usual sense: "We come now to the description of the second Beast, *I beheld another Beast,* etc. I do not love to be large in those Scriptures that do not so narrowly concern us, as knowing how farre, and what a vast distance by the grace of God we stand in here from them" (R223). Catholics are socially and materially "at a vast distance" from the situation of his own discourse, and yet this direct address does not signal a change in Cotton's exegesis. He continues on in more or less the same terms, and with the same sense of immediacy in his rhetoric of violence.[31]

Cotton's synthesis of historical events, social conditions, and the capabilities of rhetoric reflects his desire for power through language as a commentator on canonical texts, a power he exercised as teacher of the Church of Boston. It also reflects his appraisal of the value of state power—even in its most violent forms—to enforce his interpretations, for he clearly unites the concerns of clerical authority with those of the magistrates and military. In doing so, he institutes a more comprehensive prejudice than either their authority or his own by itself could produce. Exploiting the extremism of apocalyptic rejection to elaborate an ideology of oppressive social control, he envisions a domination of the world that will be achieved less by conversion than by violence. In his implied system of reference, the difference between the rhetoric of his earlier sermons and that of the Revelation sermons is the recognition of linguistic inaccuracy. The magistrates and military had already offered one kind of answer to the social discrepancy between signs and referents, demonstrating their willingness to resort to violence to enforce their system of signification, to suppress unsubmissive, disobedient referents. What Cotton offers in their wake is a verbal threat that depends on a different concept of the relationship between signs and referents. His sermons freely acknowledge that referents—and particularly the "common sort" of Puritans—do not necessarily have the requisite fidelity to the ordained system of signs. However, far from despairing that his discourse bears only the most oblique relation to social conditions in the colony, Cotton exploits the obvious discrepancies between sign and referent, transforming the absurdity of his diatribe against Catholics to make it the foundation of his persuasiveness.

In his rhetoric "of terrour," he subordinates his earlier belief in the literalization of imagery, the belief that sacred tropes have the power of consecration to enact what they name. Despite his apparent literalism, he ultimately depends instead on the skewed reference of the metonymic mode. His anti-Catholic sermons adapt the Calvinist belief in a sanction communicated by recognizing the inappropriateness of the consecrating signs to the referents before the eye. Availing himself of the privilege of self-contradiction, he acknowledges the absence of Catholics even as he demands the enactment of the "letter" of violence against them. Thus altering the frame of reference for his literal exhortations, he cultivates a system of skewed reference in which the threat of violence is proportional to his rhetorical capacity to evoke a social referent, the Catholic, who remains materially absent. Prophesying the destruction of "Catholicks" in an indefinite apocalyptic present, Cotton holds in suspension the paradigmatic relation of inequity: the iconoclast in the act of destroying his false idol. His paradigm still contains within it a mandate for the violence enacted by men like Mason, just as Mason found in the words of his own preacher the justification he sought for the murder of the Pequots. For Mason, however, the claim to sacred violence was constrained by the material identity of the human object he wished to destroy. Once he had murdered the whole Pequot tribe, he achieved the social closure he desired. Cotton's verbal iconoclasm contains no such material limits and therefore no such closure. His rhetoric provides a lasting consecration for the murder of "Catholicks," as if the cleric had pronounced the sacramental words before anyone had put out the loaf of bread to say them over. Because his anti-Catholic rhetoric is not, finally, an interpretation of a particular racial or cultural identity, because it transcends these categories, it can always be applied to any particular case of them, depending on what the social situation of the speaker or hearer seems to require.

In defining the aspirations of the new American colony at the end of the first decade of settlement, Cotton imagined an apocalypse that was simultaneously international and immensely provincial. In its temporal and geographical expansiveness, its undoing of closure, it claimed to take into itself both world history and the space of the world itself, but such a grandiose vision produced a concomitant local isolation. World dominion, the demise of the Catholic church, and the domination of nature remained hypothetical, a frame of mind and not a material reality. The expansiveness of this vision collapsed into an apocalyptic fear sustained by an imagined violence that defined the New England Puritan's relation to the rest of society. By exploiting the uncertainties of literal and figurative reference in Puritan rhetoric, Cotton institutionalized the apocalyptic mentality of crisis as a way of life. His preaching intensified the traditional apocalyptic need for closure, for a definitive resolution of the "literal sense" of things, but his exegesis denied, even systematically withheld, such a closure. Instead, while describing hope to the imagination, he preached hopeless obedience to a systematic prejudice. His apparently expansive prophecy of the Puritans' millennial rule narrowed to the belief that there was only a single locus of meaning, only one space and time, only one social category with the authority to determine meaning: the Puritan elite. What was sacramental was not the particular place where they lived but the institutional office they held and themselves as physical beings. Their way of speaking, the language of Canaan, was the true mode of intelligibility sheerly because they, the material vessels of apocalyptic revelation, spoke it. Appropriating the determination of meaning to themselves, they maintained their social power through their refusal to declare, and thereby limit, the significance of their own discourse, relying on the threat of violence, or the fact of it, to sustain the social conditions of their own imagining.

Appendix

Julius H. Tuttle's "Writings of the Rev. John Cotton," a bibliography of Cotton's published works, provides an authoritative list of books and tracts attributed to Cotton.[1] Useful as it is, the dates of publication it provides can be misleading as a chronology of the history of Cotton's preaching. Since Puritans were persecuted by the state in England, many of Cotton's sermons were not printed until decades after he preached them, when censorship of the press was lifted. Moreover, many of his sermon notes were not published until after his death. Sections I–III herein estimate the dates Cotton preached the first commentary on Canticles, the commentary on Ecclesiastes, and the sermons collected as *The Way of Life*.

The manner of publication of Cotton's works also raises important editorial questions, particularly when the publication was a transcript of sermons he delivered rather than something he wrote. Section IV compares different published versions of sermons Cotton preached about the time of the antinomian crisis. In this unusual instance there are two different transcripts of the same group of sermons, and the discrepancies raise questions about the concept of authorship informing the works published in Cotton's name.

Section V concerns an important iconoclastic tract that has often, but probably wrongly, been attributed to Cotton. As Tuttle indicates, the attribution of the work to Cotton in the seventeenth century was considered probable but not certain. There is reason to doubt that Cotton wrote the tract, since it is not his style of rhetoric and it expresses views somewhat different from those declared in works known to be written by him.

Section VI concerns a legendary sermon Cotton delivered to Cambridge University while he was a fellow of Emmanuel College. Stylistically, it was his most famous sermon and is often cited as an exemplary case of the Puritan plain style, but there is no extant transcript of the sermon, nor any evidence that there ever was a written version.

I

A Brief Exposition of the Whole Book of Canticles, or, Song of Solomon. London: Printed for Philip Nevil, at the signe of the Gun in Ivie-Lane, 1642

Cotton preached at least twice on the whole book of Canticles. The first series was published in 1642 and belongs to the English period of Cotton's career.[2] There are no references to New England, and there is the following reference to England as "here," that is, where Cotton was preaching:

> These things were found in *Rome,* from whence wee departed not in *England,* (blessed be the Lord) from whom the Separatists would have us to depart: But Christ still vouchsafes to be with us, converting soules, feeding his lambes, hearing our prayers; We may also worship Christ in truth without feare of lawes, yea with acceptance. When Christ goes, let all his faithfull spouses goe with him; when there are dens of Lions, and men cannot keepe the profession of Christ, but fall into their mouthes, then it is time to goe: But are there these causes now? doth not Christ dwell here in the simplicity of his ordinances? As long as Christ is here in *England,* let us not go away: but say, as Peter and John, "Lord, to whom shall we go? thou hast the words of eternal life," John vi. 68. As long as Christ is pleased to feed us, to drop milk and honey into our souls, let us not depart. [Pp. 126–27]

References to place vary between literal and figurative meanings in this passage. Cotton locates himself indirectly but literally with his reference to Christ "here in *England.*" Moreover, Cotton would not have categorically opposed emigration – "let us not go away" – if he himself had already left England.

The specific date of delivery for this commentary is difficult to determine, but there is suggestive internal evidence. Though the evidence is not conclusive, it points consistently to 1620–21 as the most likely date. The following passage offers the most specific historical reference:

> Use 3. To teach the children of the Church not to separate from the Church for corruption sake; not to looke onely at her corruptions, but to see her comelinesse also; and not adde affliction to the afflicted: Much lesse are we to think they in Bohemia, and in the Palatinate, are no Churches, for that they are now sunneburnt: The Sunne, even God, hath looked upon them; and it is not their mothers children, but the bastards of the Romane harlot have beene angry with her. Let us not then look at them with a Vultures eye, as though wee would

behold nothing but corruption and carrion; nor, with a scorching eye, make them more blacke; but with a childe-like eye, to pity them for their calamity and blacknesse which is befallen them. [P. 32]

The particular "calamity and blacknesse which is befallen" Bohemia and the Palatinate is never specified, but Cotton implies the event was quite recent and the figurative language suggests that it concerned a losing confrontation with Catholicism. In the same sermon, "Use 1" warns that "if Solomon shall set up other Gods, God will set up forraine [foreign] Princes in his kingdome" (p. 31). Cotton is probably referring to the outbreak of the Thirty Years' War. In 1619–20 the Bohemian Protestants attempted to install Frederick V, elector of the Rhenish Palatinate, as king. Their actions provoked the Spanish invasion of the Rhenish Palatinate and the defeat of the Protestants in Bohemia by the Catholic Ferdinand II. Englishmen would have been particularly concerned with these events because Frederick V was also son-in-law to James I. Moreover, the victorious Catholics dealt harshly with Protestants, and since Boston was an international port, the Bostonians may well have been in close contact with Protestant emigrants from the Continent. Cotton, for example, is reputed to have had German students living with him.[3] On the basis of this interpretation, one can infer that the sermons were delivered no earlier than 1620, and probably shortly thereafter.

Less specific evidence suggests the same date. The passage undoubtedly refers to some emigration, although the text does not disclose who the group was or where it was going. "Use 5" in the sermon concerns separatism and whether or not to "cast off England" – a reference to some separatists who "do depart from us" (p. 33). Since the phrasing implies that this was a group in the process of leaving England or one that had just left, Cotton is probably referring to the settlement of Plymouth Plantation in 1620. The topical importance of iconoclastic destruction in these sermons also suggests 1620–21. The iconoclasm at St. Botolph's occurred in 1621, and Cotton was accused of inciting the attack. Sermons such as these could easily have been interpreted as provocative because Cotton praises historical acts of iconoclasm and strongly implies the continuing virtue of violent destruction. See Chapter 4 of the text.

II

A Briefe Exposition with Practicall Observations upon the Whole Book of Ecclesiastes. Published by Anthony Tuckney, D.D. Master of St. John's Colledge in Cambridge. London: Printed by T. C. for Ralph Smith at the Bible in Cornhill, 1654

A Brief Exposition with Practicall Observations upon the Whole Book of Ecclesiastes. Published by Anthony Tuckney, D.D. Master of St. John's Colledge in Cambridge. The Second Impression, Corrected. London: Printed by W. W. for Ralph Smith at the Bible in Cornhill, 1657

The 1654 and 1657 editions are almost identical. The latter, as it says, is a "corrected" second edition of the former, but it does not appear to contain any substantial additions. Ziff has erroneously described the 1654 Ecclesiastes commentary as solely English without any reference to New England.[4] There are references to New England as well as England throughout. The commentary is apparently an interleaved set of notes from two different deliveries, one in England and one in New England. Presumably Cotton simply added to his earlier notes on Ecclesiastes when he preached on this text again in New England. It is possible to date the New England delivery from one reference to a particular incident, a detailed description of a bizarre murder:

> *Application:* I. To the prisoner, to help his conscience to sight and sense of his sins, and so to repentance. His servant was diseased with the scurvey which makes the body weak, and listlesse; and when nature is grown weak, the retentive faculty is weakned that he hath no hold of his excrements. In this case, compassion would have looked out heating Medicines, wholsome Diet, warme keeping; what compassion was there in immoderate whipping? Its Egyptian cruelty, *Exod* 5.7, 8, 14. 2[.] Striking on the head with a Cudgel, leaving wounds and bruises. 3. Diet with the Lights of a dead beast. 4. Washing his naked body in cold water, when Ice and Snow lay upon the ground, and putting on a cold and wet shirt, and kept out from fire. 5. Hanging him over the fire and smoake. 6. Binding him on horseback, and he not being able to sit[,] fell on one side till blood issued at mouth, nose, and eares, denying him a draught of water; upon this, he dyeth. *Object.* But his intention was not to hurt him, at least mortally, but to reforme him. [Pp. 76–77 in 1654 ed., pp. 72–73 in 1657 ed.]

The murder is also described at length in Winthrop's *Journal:*

> He had taken to apprentice one Nathaniel Sewell, one of those children sent over the last year for the country; the boy had the scurvey, and was withal very noisome, and otherwise ill disposed. His master used him with continual rigor and unmerciful correction, and exposed him many times to much cold and wet in the winter season, and used divers acts of rigor towards him, as hanging him in the chimney, etc., and the boy being very poor and weak, he tied him upon an horse and so brought him (sometimes sitting and sometimes hanging down) to

Boston, . . . and by the way the boy calling much for water, would give him none, though he came close by to it, so as the boy was near dead when he came to Boston, and died within a few hours after. Those who doubted whether this were murder or not, did stick upon two reasons chiefly. 1. That it did not appear that the master's intention was to hurt him, but to reform him.[5]

Winthrop's description matches Cotton's quite closely, and there is no doubt that they are talking about the same case: a man convicted of murdering his servant, claiming his intention was to reform the servant through punishment when the servant had scurvy and was too sick to work. Winthrop's description of the prisoner's crime appears in the entry for March 1644, where he also says that the prisoner, William Franklin, was executed about a week later. Since the application in Cotton's sermon speaks of the convicted murderer as present, this is probably the execution-day sermon. From this comparison of Cotton's sermon notes and Winthrop's *Journal*, one can infer that the New England commentary on Ecclesiastes was delivered in 1644.

III

The Way of Life, or, Gods Way and Course in Bringing the Soule into, keeping it in, and carrying it on, in the wayes of life and peace. London: Printed by M. F. for L. Fawne, and S. Gellibrand, at the Brasen Serpent in Pauls Church-yard, 1641

Jesper Rosenmeier has determined that *The Way of Life* sermons were preached in England sometime between 1627 and 1633.[6] Internal evidence suggests a slightly closer range, from 1628 to 1633. Within that range, 1630–32 is more likely than 1628–29.

A specific change in the doctrine of conversion indicates that these sermons were preached later than the commentary on First John, which was delivered sometime between 1628 and 1633.[7] In his notes on First John, Cotton does not distinguish between "heart" and "conscience." He proposes that the word "heart" in the Old Testament "is taken for conscience" (p. 186) and interprets Acts 2.37 ("When they heard this they were pricked in their hearts") to mean wounded in the conscience (p. 324). There is, then, no difference between the heart and the conscience, and he preaches on the conscience as the object of God's grace, interpreting conversion as a case of conscience.

In marked contrast, Cotton distinguishes carefully between the heart and the conscience in the *Way of Life* sermons, especially when he preaches on Acts 2.37, employing this distinction to argue that the natural man faces the Pauline–Augustinian dilemma of a corrupt will. This distinction, he explains, is "a Note which I never handled heretofore, but you shall find it evident in the Text [of Scripture]" (p. 126); he adds in the next sermon that to understand the difference between the heart and the conscience is "one of the hardest points in the practice of Christianity." He elaborates: "The first grace that is wrought" in the hearers at Peter's sermon in Acts 2.37 is a "pricked heart" (p. 126). Cotton takes this as a description of regeneration: "You never reade that God heales mans corrupt nature. He *heales not a stony heart, but takes it away, and gives man a new heart*" (p. 126). In the next sermon he goes into great detail on the difference between the heart and the conscience, remarking that "generally Christians confound these two, and shuffle them up together, as if they were both one, but indeed they do much differ" (p. 140). Since Cotton's own sermons on First John did "shuffle them up together," he repudiates his earlier doctrine, excusing it by remarking on the difficulty of the subject. Since Cotton continued to make the distinction between the heart and the conscience in his New England sermons, there is strong internal evidence for dating *The Way of Life* sermons at 1628 or later, after the sermons on First John.

Other evidence in the text implies a date later than 1628. One of the last sermons concerns the situation of a man being forced to "lay downe his calling" (p. 446). In the concluding sermon Cotton seems to apply this situation to himself, for there is a sentence implying that this was the last sermon he delivered at St. Botolph's: "This is the counsell of the Holy Ghost here in the text, and which though I should never speak word to you more, would be forever remembered. That a just man lives in his affliction by faith" (p. 477). A letter Cotton wrote in October 1632 indicates that he had already gone into hiding by this time to avoid persecution, so he must have preached *The Way of Life* before then. He was also seriously ill in 1632, and probably in 1631. His letter to the bishop of Lincoln written in May 1633, in which he resigned the vicarage of St. Botolph's, refers to "a long and sore sickness" that "began a year or two ago to suspend, after a sort, my ministry."[8] Whether he was alluding in his last sermon in *The Way of Life* to his illness or to the threat of persecution, this self-reference suggests sometime between 1630 and 1632 as a more likely date than 1628–29.

IV

The New Covenant, being the Substance of sundry Sermons. London: Printed by M.S. for Francis Eglesfield, & John Allen, at the Marigold, and Rising Sun in Pauls Church-yard, 1654

A Treatise of the Covenant of Grace. The second Edition, by a Copy far larger then the former; and Corrected also by the Authors own hand. This Copy was fitted for the Press, by Mr. Tho. Allen Minister in Norwich [England]. London: Printed by Ja. Cottrel, for John Allen, at the Rising-Sun in Pauls Church-yard, 1659

The 1654 and 1659 editions were probably based on two different transcripts of the same delivery. Although they match at many places, a brief comparison of the two editions indicates important discrepancies. The later, as it says, is much longer, by almost 100 pages. Moreover, there are differences in wording throughout, such as reversed adjectives, and even significant differences on major points of disputed doctrine. For example, the 1659 edition, p. 37, differs from the 1654, pp. 48–49, on the relative significance of faith and works; and the 1659, p. 42, differs from the 1654, p. 57, on the meaning of sanctification. There is no reason to assume that the 1659 edition is more authoritative than the 1654. Although longer, the later version omits some material included in the earlier. For example, several paragraphs that in 1654 occur on pp. 95–97, concerning the promise of free grace, are missing from p. 68 of the later edition. In general the 1654 version is more mystical, less precise about covenant theology, and less tolerant of those who differ on matters of doctrine. This is the only case in Cotton's published works of two different transcripts of the same sermons. The magnitude of discrepancies here may mean that other transcripts express a similar latitude taken by the transcriber. Alternatively, it is possible that Cotton not only "corrected" the second edition but also made substantive changes in the interests of ecclesiastical unity in the colony. If this was the case, then a "corrected" transcript should not be assumed to be a more accurate record of speech. It may be instead a revised version of whatever was spoken from the pulpit.

V

Some Treasure Fetched out of Rubbish or, Three short but seasonable Treatises (found in an heap of scattered Papers), which Providence hath reserved for their Service who desire to be instructed, from the Word of God, concerning the Imposition and Use of Significant Ceremonies *in the Worship of God.* viz.

I. A Discourse upon 1 Cor 14.40. Let all things be done decently and in Order. *Tending to search out the Truth in this Question,* viz. *Whether it be lawful for* Church-Governours *to command indifferent decent things in the Administration of God's Worship?* [Pp. 1–8]

II. An Enquiry, Whether the Church may not, in the Celebration of the Sacrament, use other Rites significative than those expressed in the Scripture, or add to them of her own Authority? [Pp. 9–52]

III. Three Arguments, Syllogistically propounded and prosecuted against the Surplice: *The* Cross *in Baptism: And* Kneeling *in the Act of receiving the Lord's Supper.* [Pp. 52–75]
London, Printed in the Year 1660

This work is a collection of three tracts published at the Restoration but probably written much earlier.[9] The preface is not signed, an unusual practice for Puritans, but this omission may have been due to the uncertainties of the political climate at the Restoration. The author of the preface explains, "These ensuing Treatises were found laid by the Walls, and covered with dust, in the study of an old Non-Conformist, (there being diverse Copies of each, under several unknown hands:)" (p. A2). The fact that none of the manuscripts was in the author's own hand makes attribution less certain, but in the early seventeenth century tracts were often copied and circulated among Puritans, and it was not unusual for a Puritan's writings to become known in this way. The preface identifies Cotton as the "known Author" of the first discourse and the probable author of the second, but gives no reasons for these attributions: "Mr. John Cotton, that faithful Servant of Christ, (famous in both Englands) was the known Author of the first Discourse, and (as it is verily believed) of the second also" (p. A2). Robert Nichols, a minister in Cheshire, is identified as the author of the third discourse. This one was composed for a specific occasion that makes it possible to give a date:

> Mr. Robert Nichols studiously composed the third, who was a man, though less known, yet deservedly famous for his great Abilities and profitable ministry in Cheshire, for many years, where his ministry is still very precious. When Reverend Dr. Morton was Bishop of Chester, he required in writing of those ministers in his Diocess who did not conform to the Ceremonies, the Reasons of their refusal:Thereupon these three Arguments were by Mr. Nichols presented unto him, attested by his own hand, and afterwards defended in dispute with that learned Bishop before many witnesses. The Bishop being hereby convinced of the good mans Ability and Ingenuity, was his friend to his dying day [P. A2]

Thomas Morton was bishop of Chester from July 1616 until 1618, so the third tract must have been composed during these years.[10] It is probable that the first two tracts were also written about this time, since, like the third tract, they presume that nonconformity might still be tolerated within the Church of England.

I have not found any reason to doubt Cotton's authorship of the first discourse. It is written in his style, and its topics and arguments concur with those of published works for which his own manuscript was the source. The preface is less certain in its attribution of the second discourse to Cotton, and here there is reason to question Cotton's authorship. The question is historically important as well as pertinent to a bibliography of Cotton's works, because the second tract is by far the most comprehensive of the three in its attempt to delineate a general theory of signs that would support the nonconformist cause. It ranks among the most sophisticated and thorough discourses on the Puritan figurative imagination. Considering the widespread interest in Cotton's works – both published and unpublished – by 1640, it seems unlikely that a substantial tract in "diverse Copies" on a subject of major importance would have completely escaped the notice of his devoted followers until 1660.

A brief comparison of the tracts in *Some Treasure* also casts doubt on Cotton's authorship. The style of writing in the second discourse differs from that of the first and of other published tracts known to have been composed by Cotton. Topically, argumentatively, and stylistically, the second tract has far more in common with the third, by Nichols, than with the first. Where propriety is the principal subject of the first discourse, the sign theory informing the Puritan version of the Second Commandment is the preoccupation of the second and third. In the second and third discourses, the relationship between the classical concepts of *figura* and the Puritan rationale for nonconformity is quite clear, for both acknowledge the importance of bodily shapes and treat nonconformity as a problem in the theory of signs and images. For example, the second discourse states: "A visible, corporal, material element . . . is a sign Sacramentall and mysticall, expressing some sacred mystery to the Eye, as the Word doth to the sense which receiveth the Voyce" (p. 43). Although the first tract does concern such issues as clothing and hair style, Cotton does not cast this discussion in terms of sign theory. Instead, he expounds a Pauline text on "edifying" behavior in the church, defining "decent," "indecent," "necessary," and "indifferent" as the means of developing his arguments.

The second and third discourses share a conceptual justification of nonconformity, to the point of similar, sometimes virtually identical, phrasing. For example, the second says, "The gestures of the body made, and purposely framed to shadow forth the hidden affection of the Soul, are external acts of adoration and worship" (p. 38); the third says, of genuflexion, "It is a gesture of the body, used to testify, signify, and shadow out the inward and hidden Act of the mind to some person or thing. This the learned acknowledge to be Worship" (p. 67). There is no comparable passage in the first – indeed, no comparable overt concern with the physical image of the body. What the author of the third refers to categorically as the "bodily religious Adoration of God" (p. 65) is treated only indirectly in the first. Cotton alludes negatively to the importance of the physical image when he argues that it is "undecent" for men to "pray with long haire" or for women to enter the church "bare-headed" (p. 4). However, his argument for propriety omits any discussion of ritual bodily gestures such as the second describes, whereas Nichols's argument in the third explicitly takes them into account.

An important difference between Cotton and Nichols emerges in their treatments of a topic they both discuss, the proper clothing of a cleric. The subject occasions Cotton's most elaborate description of a bodily image, the cleric in an Anglican "Gown" as opposed to a cleric in a common cloak.

> If the Church-Governours command a Minister to preach alwaies in a Gown (it being indifferent and decent so to do), he that shall now and then preach in a Cloak transgresseth the Command of the Church, but not of the Apostle. For he that preacheth in a Cloak preacheth also decently, which is all that the Rule of the Apostle requireth in this Point. [P. 4]

Both forms of dress are "decent." Cotton's argument depends exclusively on verbal directives, the "Command" of the Church of England and the words of the apostle Paul in 1 Cor. 14.40, "Let all things be done decently and in order." For a Puritan, Cotton adopts an extremely tolerant argument, contending for the propriety of the cloak without condemning the Anglican gown. Nichols is much more actively opposed to the ritual clothing of the Anglican church. Like Cotton, he believes that the surplice has not been divinely ordained, but he states his case in a different way. Where Cotton argues from the epistolary directive of Paul on decency and edification, assuming seventeenth-century standards of dress, Nichols appeals directly to a visual image of the prophets as his authority on what is proper: Their clothing "was of common and daily use, worn in Town and Field" (p. 58). He concludes against the surplice for reasons of visual imitation as much as verbal directive: "The habit of *John Baptist* was daily and common, not Ecclesiastical and Mystical. That Christ or his Apostles did use, or institute any Mystical or Ecclesiastical attire, none can shew by the holy Scriptures" (p. 59). Nichols attributes much more importance to the visual, physical image of the cleric, to the point of refusing the surplice as an improper visual image that is harmful to the church.

Of the two, Nichols seems the more probable author of the second discourse. Nichols overtly shares, as Cotton does not, its main theoretical supposition, that "a significant Ceremony is an Image, or a Representation to teach by striking the sense" (p. 19). However, although Nichols's answer to the bishop of Chester is largely a repetition and application of the more salient premises of the second discourse, this similarity does not rule out the possibility of a completely different author. It is possible that Nichols's tract resembles the second discourse merely because he copied and paraphrased heavily from it to defend himself before the bishop. In sum, the authorship of the second discourse seems to me an open question. Either Cotton or Nichols might have written it, or some other person. The evidence against Cotton's authorship, like the evidence in the preface for it, is speculative but significant.

VI
The Cambridge University sermon

Cotton is said to have adopted the plain style of rhetoric while he was a fellow at Emmanuel College, Cambridge, in the first decade of the seventeenth century. Early narratives tell us that the first time Cotton was invited to preach before the university, he surprised everyone by delivering a sermon that was more plain and more Puritan than the audience was expecting. This Cambridge sermon has become a legendary example of the Puritan plain style, but legend is all it is. Narrators of the event, including Perry Miller, refer to an oration at Cambridge, but not to a text.[11] While it seems probable that Cotton actually did preach at Cambridge before the university, I have not found any extant text of such a sermon, nor any evidence that such a text ever existed. The tale in its earliest extant form is recounted by Samuel Whiting in his biography of Cotton, written shortly before Cotton's death in 1652.[12] John Norton and Cotton Mather both narrate the event in their biographies of Cotton, appropriating substantial material from Whiting but giving it their own interpretations.[13] Thomas Allen, in his 1655 preface to Cotton's commentary on Revelation 13, also recounts the sermon delivery, claiming Cotton's own narrative of the event as his source.[14] Of these three narrators, Whiting is the only one who might actually have heard the Cambridge sermon, but he does not say he did. These narratives vary greatly in their descriptions of the legendary sermon, and each version describes, more than anything else, the biographer's *own* assumptions about the plain style.

Taken together, these biographies provide good evidence for changes in Puritan rhetoric in the second half of the seventeenth century, but they are of little use in understanding Cotton's rhetoric. Perry Miller's discussion of the plain style in *The New England Mind* might best be understood as a revival of this narrative tradition.[15] Like his predecessors, Miller describes Cotton's Cambridge sermon as emblematic of the Puritan plain style, but he merely appropriates earlier versions of the legend (primarily Thomas Allen's) as a vehicle for his own assumptions about plainness.

Notes

CHAPTER 1. INTRODUCTORY

1 David D. Hall, *The Antinomian Controversy, 1636–1638: A Documentary History* (Middletown, Conn.: Wesleyan University Press, 1968), p. 214 (for the phrase "mishapen opinions"); John Underhill, *Newes from America, or, A New and Experimentall Discoverie of New England* [London, 1638], in *History of the Pequot War*, ed. Charles Orr (Cleveland: Helman-Taylor, 1897), pp. 80–81; John Mason, *A Brief History of the Pequot War: Especially Of the memorable Taking of their Fort at Mistick in Connecticut In 1637* (Boston, 1736), pp. 20–21.

2 The main study of Puritan intellectual history has been Perry Miller, *The New England Mind*, 2 vols. (Cambridge, Mass.: Harvard University Press, 1939, 1953; rpt. Boston: Beacon Press, 1965). Miller essentially dismissed language as a possible subject of inquiry in Puritanism. Walter J. Ong adopted the same view, relentlessly, in *Ramus, Method, and the Decay of Dialogue* (Cambridge, Mass.: Harvard University Press, 1958). Although Miller addressed some social issues in the second volume of *The New England Mind*, his work contributed substantially to the separation of intellectual and social history. Sacvan Bercovitch, *The Puritan Origins of the American Self* (New Haven, Conn.: Yale University Press, 1975), is far more skeptical in its appraisal of Puritan cultural assumptions, and far more sophisticated in its treatment of rhetoric, but it does not directly address the issues of interpretation raised by the Pequot War and the Hutchinson controversy. More recent works, such as David Leverenz, *The Language of Puritan Feeling: An Exploration in Literature, Psychology, and Social History* (New Brunswick, N.J.: Rutgers University Press, 1980), implicitly raise larger social questions through a psychological analysis of Puritan sermon literature, but such works tend to limit the range of social inquiry to the characteristics of the Puritan family. In a very different vein, and one that is closer to the concerns of this study, see the sociolinguistic analyses of language and symbolism by Richard Bauman in "Aspects of Seventeenth Century Quaker Rhetoric," *Quarterly Journal of Speech* 56 (1970), pp. 67–74, and in "Speaking in the Light: The Role of the Quaker Minister," in *Explorations in the Ethnography of Speaking*, ed. Richard Bauman and Joel Sherzer (Cambridge: Cambridge University Press, 1974), pp. 144–60.

160

3 See Chapter 5.
4 Mason, *Brief History*, p. 21.
5 See the entry for "prejudice" in the *Oxford English Dictionary*.
6 Underhill, *Newes from America*, pp. 80–81.
7 "A Report of the Trial of Mrs. Anne Hutchinson before the Church in Boston," in Hall, *Antinomian Controversy*, p. 372.
8 Erich Auerbach, "Figura," in *Scenes from the Drama of European Literature: Six Essays by Erich Auerbach*, trans. Ralph Mannheim (New York: Meridian, 1959),p. 11. The essay was originally published in 1944 in *Neue Dantestudien;* all references are to the Mannheim translation.
9 On the history of the concept of *figura* in classical thought, see Auerbach, "Figura," pp. 11–28. According to Auerbach, Varro was the first author to use *figura* in a linguistic sense, to express the notion of grammatical form, but Lucretius is credited with the first use of *figura* to designate material shapes in language: *figura verborum*, a figure of words. Cicero's use of the word in rhetoric further developed the idea of acoustic shapes: *figura vocis*, the figure of the voice, and *figurae dicendi*, figures of speech in the general sense of a mode of eloquence. Both Cicero and the author of *Ad Herennium* also extended the usage of *figura* to the concept of style in the designation of the three levels of style. For example, the plain style is called *figura extenuata* in the *Ad Herennium* and *figura tenuis* in Cicero's *De Oratore*. In Quintilian's *Institutio Oratoria*, *figura* was first used to refer to rhetorical constructs such as figures of thought, *figurae sententiarum*.
10 Dell Hymes, *Foundations in Sociolinguistics: An Ethnographic Approach* (Philadelphia: University of Pennsylvania Press, 1974), p. 18.
11 The most serious challenge to the conventional assumption about Puritan meaning has been Max Weber's *The Protestant Ethic and the Spirit of Capitalism*, trans. Talcott Parsons (New York: Scribner, 1958). By demonstrating that Protestants closely associated the acquisition of material wealth and spiritual salvation, he suggests that Protestants often meant something radically different from what they seemed to say in their more pious moments. However, Weber ultimately relied on theology to explain the Puritans' association of religious virtue and acquisitiveness: Because Puritans lacked assurance of grace, they needed material signs of grace such as economic prosperity to infer that their souls were saved. To go beyond Weber, we need to be more skeptical than he was about the theological terms in which the Puritans saw themselves.
12 One of Cotton's most controversial doctrines during the controversy was his belief in the assurance of grace. Historians have often fastened on this as a reason for distinguishing Cotton's beliefs as unrepresentative of those in the early Puritan colony, but this interpretation is probably dependent on Weber's faulty analysis in *The Protestant Ethic*. Actually, despite what Weber says, belief in the assurance of grace was relatively common among Puritans. See Geoffrey F. Nuttall, *The Holy Spirit in Puritan Faith and Experience* (Oxford: Basil Blackwell, 1946), and *Visible Saints: The Congregational Way, 1640–1660* (Oxford: Basil Blackwell, 1957). Though Weber's argument has some validity for the analysis of later Protestants, his argument concerning the supposed lack of assurance of grace among Reformation Protestants is difficult to take seri-

ously. He acknowledges, for example, that Calvin believed in assurance, but dismisses this out of hand as the enthusiasm of the first years of the Reformation (*Protestant Ethic*, pp. 110–11). Many Elizabethan and Stuart Protestants believed in assurance of grace, and the idea is prevalent in Christian tradition, dating back to St. Paul's conversion in Acts and Augustine's *Confessions*. Cotton merely followed traditional Christian thought – Patristic, Calvinist, and English – in his belief in assurance. See, for example, the sermons Cotton delivered during the antinomian crisis: *A Treatise of the Covenant of Grace*, 2nd ed. (London, 1659), pp. 97–102, 199–202. (On the probable date of delivery of these sermons, see section IV of the Appendix.)

From the perspective of European Protestantism, the fact that this issue became a major point of theological debate in the antinomian crisis, 1636–38, was rather unusual. Moreover, to grant the issue as much credence as historians have done (see, e.g., Perry Miller, "Preparation for Salvation in Seventeenth-Century New England," *Journal of the History of Ideas* 4 [1943], pp. 253–86; and Norman Pettit, *The Heart Prepared: Grace and Conversion in Puritan Spiritual Life* [New Haven, Conn.: Yale University Press, 1966]) only returns us to the theological terms in which the Puritans cast themselves and depends on Weber at one of his weakest points. In fact, Cotton is interesting because he so obviously controverts the Weber thesis. According to Weber's theory, Cotton's belief that it was possible to have assurance of grace would have made him indifferent or opposed to the acquisition of material wealth. Yet as we will see, he ardently supported the Massachusetts Bay colonization as an economic enterprise and thought personal wealth was a religious virtue. As my discussion will show, assurance of grace did not obviate the chronic uncertainties of the Puritan soul that we have come to associate with lack of assurance. Nor did the belief in assurance free the Puritan from the need for worldly acquisition. Cotton shows that assurance of grace or the lack of it was not nearly so important as Weber supposed, and that we must account in some other way for the association of piety and material prosperity among the Puritans.

13 There were three biographies of Cotton written in the seventeenth century: Samuel Whiting, "Concerning the Life of the Famous Mr. Cotton," in, *Chronicles of the First Planters of the Colony of Massachusetts Bay, from 1623 to 1636*, ed. Alexander Young (Boston, 1846); John Norton, *Abel Being Dead Yet Speaketh, Or, The Life and Death of that Deservedly Famous Man of God, Mr. John Cotton* (London, 1658); and Cotton Mather [John Cotton's grandson], "The Life of Mr. John Cotton," in Mather, *Magnalia Christi Americana, or, The Ecclesiastical History of New-England*, 2 vols. (Hartford, Conn.: Silas Andrus, 1855), vol. 1, pp. 252–86. Discussions of Cotton's rhetoric have generally been concerned with the attributes of the plain style. See especially Jesper Rosenmeier, " 'Clearing the Medium': A Reevaluation of the Puritan Plain Style in Light of John Cotton's *A Practicall Commentary Upon the First Epistle Generall of John*," *William and Mary Quarterly* 37 (1980), pp. 577–91. See also Larzer Ziff, "The Literary Consequences of Puritanism," *English Literary History* 30, no. 1 (March 1963), pp. 293–305. For an introduction to Cotton's works, see Everett Emerson, *John Cotton* (New York: Twayne, 1965). For Cotton's biography, see Larzer Ziff,

The Career of John Cotton: Puritanism and the American Experience (Princeton, N.J.: Princeton University Press, 1962). For a bibliography of Cotton's published works, see Julius H. Tuttle, "Writings of the Rev. John Cotton," *Bibliographical Essays: A Tribute to Wilberforce Eames* (Cambridge, Mass.: Harvard University Press, 1924).

The history of the Puritan clergy as the history of a professional class has been treated in a variety of ways. Among the relevant studies are William Haller, *The Rise of Puritanism* (New York, 1938; rpt. New York: Harper & Bros., 1957); Irovonwy Morgan, *The Godly Preachers of the Elizabethan Church* (London: Epworth Press, 1965); Roger Manning, *Religion and Society in Elizabethan Sussex: A Study of the Enforcement of the Religious Settlement, 1558–1603* (Bristol: Leicester University Press, 1969); R. C. Richardson, *Puritanism in North-west England: A Regional Study of the Diocese of Chester to 1642* (Manchester: Manchester University Press, 1972); F. Ernest Stoeffler, *The Rise of Evangelical Pietism* (Leiden: Brill, 1965); Lawrence Stone, "The Educational Revolution in England, 1560–1640," *Past and Present* 28 (1964), pp. 41–80; Hugh Kearney, *Scholars and Gentlemen: Universities and Society in Pre-industrial Britain, 1500–1700* (Ithaca, N.Y.: Cornell University Press, 1970); Samuel Eliot Morison, *The Founding of Harvard College* (Cambridge, Mass.: Harvard University Press, 1935); and David D. Hall, *The Faithful Shepherd: A History of the New England Ministry in the Seventeenth Century* (Chapel Hill: University of North Carolina Press, 1972).

CHAPTER 2. THE REFERENTIAL IMPERATIVE

1 For examples of the ways in which anthropologists have posed these kinds of questions, see J. David Sapir and J. Christopher Crocker, eds., *The Social Use of Metaphor: Essays on the Anthropology of Rhetoric* (Philadelphia: University of Pennsylvania Press, 1977), and especially James W. Fernandez, "The Performance of Ritual Metaphors," pp. 100–31 in that collection.

2 John Cotton, *The Way of Life* (London, 1641), p. 137; all further references will be given in the text and indicated by WL. For an estimate on the date these sermons were delivered, see Section III of the Appendix.

3 Michel Foucault, *Les Mots et les choses* (Paris: Gallimard, 1966), translated by Alan Sheridan as *The Order of Things* (New York: Pantheon, 1970), p. 38; all page references are to the Sheridan translation. This is an important, highly relevant, but frustrating book from the perspective of Anglo-American studies. Foucault declines to discuss sermon literature even though he emphasizes questions about the relative values of writing and speaking, and it is just this kind of literature that offers the most counter-evidence to his thesis. Among the authors he does cite, Petrus Ramus is probably the most important for Puritan studies. However, Foucault misrepresents Ramus's ideas (pp. 35–38) when he characterizes Ramus as another example of an author who "presupposes an absolute privilege on the part of writing." In fact, Ramus is much closer to Puritans like Cotton, who value the aural qualities of language at least as much as its written form. Ramus, in the original 1562 version of his *Gramere,* undertakes the project of reforming French orthography to make one written letter stand for one

sound, and so to bring the "figures" of words more in line with the "strengths" of their sounds. See Pierre de la Ramée, *Gramere* (Paris, 1562; facsimile rpt. Menston, England: Scholar Press, 1969), esp. pp. 7 and 17–18. As Foucault notes, Ramus's "etymology" does not deal with "the original meaning of words," but neither does it deal with the inherent "virtues" of written letters, as Foucault claims (p. 35). Rather, "etymology" here and in other writers of this period (e.g., Alexander Gill, *Logonomia Anglica* [London, 1619]) is concerned not with historical origins but instead with the morphological derivation of different noun cases, verb tenses, and diverse parts of speech from the same root vocable. In Ramus's work the etymological "species" of verbs are determined by their "figures," i.e., whether they end in *-ir* or *-er,* exactly as in modern French grammar (p. 56). These "figures" then take their place in syntax as the carriers of grammatical agreement between words, what Ramus terms *convenanse* (p. 78). For Ramus, then, the meaningful links between words that determine syntactic connection are founded on the repetition of like sounds, sounds of the same "species" across the vocal space of the utterance. (I thank Dana Lloyd Spradley for his assistance in the preparation of this note.)

4   The rhetorical concept of sound design in prose is common in classical theory but has received little attention in modern criticism. The best studies of sound design are the essays on Euphuistic rhetoric and on the adaptation of the medieval Latin *cursus* to early Anglican English in *Style, Rhetoric and Rhythm: Essays by Morris W. Croll,* ed. J. Max Patrick et al. (Princeton, N.J.: Princeton University Press, 1966), pp. 241–360. The phrase "sound design" is Croll's (see, e.g., p. 242).

5   John Cotton, *A Brief Exposition with Practicall Observations upon the Whole Book of Ecclesiastes,* 2nd ed. (London, 1657), p. 1; all further references are to this edition and will be given in the text and indicated by E. Since these lectures contain many technical terms, they were probably delivered to his students.

6   Cotton's analysis of sound appeals directly to classical rather than medieval ideas. For example, Cotton enumerates "*epizeuxis,* the like sound continued in the same sentence"; "*epanalepsis,* (the same sound repeated in the beginning of the sentence, and in the end)"; "*numerus oratorius,* (the same number of syllables repeated in both sentences)"; and "*paranomasia* (the repeating of like sounds, yet somewhat differing)" (E2). He develops his defense of tropes and figures in a way that closely suggests Quintilian's concerns, and his enumeration of verbal schemes recalls Quintilian. See *Institutio Oratoria,* with an English translation by H. E. Butler, 4 vols., Loeb Classical Library (Cambridge, Mass.: Harvard University Press, 1966–79), 9.3. He may also have relied on the *Ad Herennium.* See [Cicero], *Ad C. Herennium,* with an English translation by Harry Caplan, Loeb Classical Library (Cambridge, Mass.: Harvard University Press, 1977), 4.13.19–4.30.41. Cotton's attention to sound design itself as his chosen topic of defense may owe something to Cicero's last theoretical work, *Orator.* Cicero's defense of rhetorical skill, likewise against the charge that there could and should be a nonrhetorical, nonfigural style, provoked his most elaborate and sophisticated analysis of prose rhythm, cadence, and syntax.

Cotton's display of technical devices seems at first glance an affront to any serious defense of rhetorical figures. One would suppose that a Puritan would eschew such verbal schemes, since figures of sound supposedly symbolized all that was corrupt in the art of rhetoric. However, from the larger perspective of the history of English religious rhetoric, the value Cotton attributed to sound design was neither anomalous nor unduly elaborate. English preachers in the first century of the Reformation, inheriting the rhetorical tradition of medieval Latin, tended to adapt rather than abandon the intricate sound patterns that had long characterized the public language of the church. In a general way, Cotton's conceptualization of sound design shares the sensitivity to sustained vocal patterns that informs the Anglican *Book of Common Prayer* in its adaptation of the medieval *cursus* to English prose (described by Croll in *Style, Rhetoric, and Rhythm*, pp. 303–60). Weighed against contemporaneous Anglican values, Cotton's rhetoric appears more plain and subdued than that of Anglican stylists, the style of a Puritan reformer who sought to "purify" the traditional practice of his church, but Anglicans and Puritans shared the long-standing belief that vocal patterns were an essential quality in religious rhetoric. They do not, however, seem to have held this idea for the same reasons. Seventeenth-century Anglican stylists were concerned to make sound and idea, "scheme" and "point," coincide, but they employed verbal schemes quite selectively, to enhance particular turns of wit. See George Williamson, *The Senecan Amble: A Study in Prose Form from Bacon to Collier* (Chicago: University of Chicago Press, 1951), esp. pp. 28, 48–49, 117, and 145–48. Cotton's interpretation of Ecclesiastes is informed by a much more comprehensive concept of sound design than Williamson describes.

The major histories of preaching in England relevant to the period under consideration are J. W. Blench, *Preaching in England in the Late Fifteenth and Sixteenth Centuries: A Study of English Sermons, 1450–1600* (New York: Barnes & Noble, 1964); and W. F. Mitchell, *English Pulpit Oratory from Andrewes to Tillotson* (London, 1932). The best study of prose rhetoric in early modern Europe is still Croll, *Style, Rhetoric, and Rhythm,* although he declines to discuss the implications of his ideas for Puritanism. Similarly, Wesley Trimpi, in *Ben Jonson's Poems: A Study in the Plain Style* (Stanford, Calif.: Stanford University Press, 1962), declines any comparative discussion of Jonson and his Puritan contemporaries. Wilbur S. Howell, *Logic and Rhetoric in England, 1500–1700* (Princeton, N.J.: Princeton University Press, 1956), is a useful history of rhetorical and logical theories among Cotton's contemporaries; see esp. pp. 247–52 and 282–341 on the importance of Ciceronian rhetoric and its relation to Ramism. On Ramus's theories as part of the Ciceronian controversy, see Izora Scott, *The Imitation of Cicero* (New York: Teacher's College, Columbia University, 1910), pp. 100–02. Also relevant are Jonas A. Barish, *Ben Jonson and the Language of Prose Comedy* (Cambridge, Mass.: Harvard University Press, 1960); Stanley E. Fish, *Self-Consuming Artifacts: The Experience of Seventeenth Century Literature* (Berkeley: University of California Press, 1972); and the collected essays in *Seventeenth-Century Prose: Modern Essays in Criticism,* ed. Stanley E. Fish (New York: Oxford University Press, 1971). For a study of metaphor, metonymy, and hyperbole in nineteenth-century prose that raises some of the issues I discuss, see J. Hillis Miller, "The Fiction of Realism: *Sketches by Boz, Oliver Twist, and Cruikshank's Illustrations,*" in *Charles Dickens and George Cruikshank,* papers read at a Clark Library Seminar on May 9, 1970, by J. Hillis Miller and David Borowitz, William Andrews Clark Memorial Library (Berkeley: University of California Press, 1971), pp. 1–69.

7 Quintilian, *Institutio,* 9.1.10–11. On the interchangeability of the concepts of trope and figure, see *Institutio,* 9.1.3–4. Auerbach misrepresents Quintilian's views when he says, "Basically all discourse is a forming, a figure, but the word [*figura*] is employed only for formations that are particularly developed in a poetic or rhetorical sense," that is, for figures of speech. Erich Auerbach, "Figura," in *Scenes from the Drama of European Literature: Six Essays by Erich Auerbach,* trans. Ralph Mannheim [New York: Meridian, 1959], p. 26. Moreover, Quintilian's analogies suggest that he derived his theory from the earliest usage of *figura* as a dynamic, corporeal shape, and not, as Auerbach implies, from a nonmaterial concept of form. Although it is true that Quintilian is primarily concerned to discuss rhetorical figures in the narrower sense, the general meaning of *figura,* describing the way in which all discourse is figural, is important to the rhetorical theory informing the *Institutio.* By overlooking this meaning, Auerbach considerably narrows and diminishes Quintilian's rhetoric and its importance for Christian thought.

Auerbach's analysis does not account for a preacher such as Cotton. Indeed, Cotton relies most heavily on the classical concept of *figura* just where Auerbach believes it to be least relevant to Christian thought. Cotton's development of the concept to interpret and defend his own rhetorical practice as a Puritan preacher is quite different in its suppositions from the Christian development of *figura* as Auerbach describes it. Auerbach claims that the "tropological sense" of Christian thought (which concerns the conversion of the soul) was irrelevant to the concept of *figura,* because this "sense" was allegorical and thus lacked the distinctive historicity of *figura* as it was applied to people and events in the Old Testament ("*Figura,*" p. 42). Granted that Cotton's use of *figura* in his lectures on Ecclesiastes lacks the historicity of Old Testament *figurae* (or "types"), it is also true that, as an ahistorical idea in classical rhetoric, *figura* was relevant to the tropological sense because the life of the soul was described in figures.

Cotton also differs in his interpretation of the relationship between the Old and New Testaments. Auerbach's concept of figure and fulfillment makes the implicit assumption that Old Testament *figurae* are figurative in contrast to a New Testament that, as "fulfillment" and revelation, is literal, in the sense of nonfigurative ("*Figura,*" pp. 28–49, esp. pp. 34, 41, and 44). Cotton undoes this implicit assumption of the figurative/literal relation between the two testaments by treating Scripture as a continuous history that Christ illuminates but does not disrupt or divide. He counts Solomon as among the elect of God and thus a viable model for Christian oratory: "He is said to be loved of God, and therefore by Gods own appointment to be named Jedidiah, . . . Now Gods love is the pledge, as of *Jacobs* election, Rom. 9.13. So of *Solomons*" (E4). Having Christianized Solomon, Cotton endows him with "fulfillment" status. Cotton also points out the dependence of New Testament revelation on figural meaning, even construed in a narrow sense, citing Paul's use of the image of the human body to describe the Christian church. The proof that figuration, even sound design, can be virtuous is the rhetoric of Scripture itself: "Here are many Tropes of Rhetorick used [in Eccles. 1.2]; so [also] Rom. 12.5 [So we, being many, are one body in Christ, and every one members one of another]" (E8). Thus Cotton interprets the Old and New Testaments alike as a history of elect rhetoricians, of whom Jesus is only one among many. Calvin reinterpreted Old Testament sacraments as no less efficacious than New Testament sacraments, in effect treating Scripture as a history of changing sacramental rites of the same religion; Cotton takes something of the same approach in interpreting Scripture as a continuous history of efficacious preaching. Although Cotton chooses Solomon's rhetoric for his exemplary text, his theory of rhetoric also comprehends the new dispensation of a revealed Christ, and thus it makes no difference whether the material spokesman for the Paraclete is Solomon, Paul, or Cotton himself. The revelation of Jesus Christ does not obviate the need for figures in discourse, nor does it alter the way in which all discourse is inherently figural.

For further discussion of Auerbach, see the end of Chap. 3 herein.

8 Quintilian invokes the Greek dramaturgical meaning of *schema,* the mimic gestures of actors.

9 Quintilian argues further that although a figure does something to "the simple and obvious method of expression," the use of a figure "does not necessarily involve any alteration either of the order or the strict sense of words." It is in the more narrow context of the use of patterned devices, as Auerbach rightly observes, that Quintilian says one can justifiably speak of styles as either lacking in figures, *carentem figuris,* or "adorned" with them, *figuratam.* This stylistic difference is analogous to the difference between an actor who gestures while speaking lines and an actor who plays the same part without gesturing. Measured against this more narrow criterion, Cotton, like Quintilian, is an advocate of the figured style rather than the simple style (Auerbach, *"Figura,"* p. 16). For *motus* in Quintilian, see *Institutio,* 9.1.2; *figura* and *schema* are discussed at 9.1.1–2 and 9.3.1–3; for "alteration" see 9.1.12–14 and 9.1.7.

10 *Institutio,* 9.1.12. Quintilian's concept may seem at first to share the assumptions of contemporary structuralist criticism. However, the fact that Quintilian is describing figuration in a material as well as an ideational sense is a crucial difference. Structuralist criticism tends to share more assumptions with Protestant rhetoric than with Latin rhetoric, especially the belief that tropes are true. For this idea as an aspect of Protestant thought, see especially Chapter 4.

11 Quintilian, *Institutio,* 8.4.29, 8.6.3.

12 Probably some figures lend themselves more easily to the hyperbolic mode than others, for Cotton's lecture employs many of the same figures as Quintilian's illustrations of hyperbole in the *Institutio.* Both use superlatives, figures involving repetition, comparison, metaphor, apostrophe, and personification. For Quintilian's discussion of hyperbole, see *Institutio,* 8.6.67–76.

13 In Cicero's *De Oratore,* Crassus proposes that mastery of the art of amplification is the summit of eloquence: "The highest distinction in eloquence con-

168   NOTES TO PP. 10–14

sists in amplification by means of ornament, which can be used to make one's speech not only increase the importance of a subject and raise it to a higher level, but also to diminish it and disparage it. This is requisite in all lines of argument" (Cicero, *De Oratore,* with an English translation by E. W. Sutton and H. Rackham, 2 vols., Loeb Classical Library [Cambridge, Mass.: Harvard University Press, 1976–77], 3.104). Amplification enhances the importance of some ideas while diminishing or disparaging others and is thus closely related to hyperbole. Though Quintilian lists hyperbole among the tropes, it also turns up in his discussion of amplification, unbidden but there, he apologizes, because hyperbole is viewed as a special kind of amplification as well as a trope: "I know that some may perhaps regard *hyperbole* as a species of *amplification,* since *hyperbole* can be employed to create an effect in either direction [i.e., augmentation or attenuation]. But as the name is also applied to one of the tropes, I must postpone its consideration for the present. I would proceed to an immediate discussion of this subject but for the fact that others have given separate treatment to this form of artifice" (*Institutio,* 8.4.29). In *The Way of Congregational Churches Cleared: In Two Treatises* (London, 1648), Cotton uses hyperbole in a manner that makes clear his own understanding of the trope as meaning both augmentation and diminution. Responding to the charge that New England ministers enjoy the "absolute devotion" of the magistrates, Cotton labels this hyperbole, charging that it exaggerates the truth, both "debasing" the magistrates and "advancing" the ministers falsely (pt. 1, p. 67).

14   Sibilants, in laymen's terms, are the sounds denoted by *s, z, sh,* and *sj.* Slashes, in linguistics, denote the phoneme rather than the spelling, and linguistics writes the sibilants as, respectively, /s/, /z/, /š/, and /ž/. See H. A. Gleason, Jr., *An Introduction to Descriptive Linguistics,* rev. ed. (New York: Holt, Rinehart, & Winston, 1961), p. 18. Since linguistic terminology is not widely known, I have for the most part restricted my descriptions to lay terms that will be intelligible, if not pleasing, to all readers. For a discussion of variations in early American syntax correlated with levels of formality in speaking and writing, see Merja Kytö and Matti Rissanen, "The Syntactic Study of Early American English," *Neuphilologische Mitteilungen* 84, no. 4 (1983), pp. 470–90. The transcripts of Cotton's sermons represent a mixed form in several ways, since each transcript represents both Cotton's formal speech and the transcriber's informal written version of it, and may also contain editorial revisions. I have treated Cotton as the author, although doing so oversimplifies the linguistic and social character of the document. I have also treated the transcript as if it were a complete record of speech, although it probably is not. Attempting to discern where it is incomplete, or what elements might have been added, leads only to highly speculative guesses, except where the text explicitly indicates deleted material with "etc." These are important linguistic issues, but they do not directly affect the argument I make, and even supposing these questions could be answered, it would still be the case that Cotton was primarily responsible for the words I analyze here. For a further discussion of these issues, see section IV of the Appendix.

15 In this and other illustrations of Cotton's sound design, I have assumed that visual representations of acoustic patterns will convey more to a modern reader than the technical names of figures of speech. Because *The Way of Life* is a transcript of speech, I have written the quotations in a way that preserves the importance of the sound design, adapting the method used in Croll, *Style, Rhetoric, and Rhythm,* pp. 303–60, of graphically representing the sounds. To do so, it has been necessary to modify the printed text by omitting the italics, which bear no relation to the sermons as spoken. I have also occasionally added my own italics to indicate sound repetitions. The punctuation has been retained, since it marks the sound design throughout. Where names of cited Scripture texts contribute to the sound design, I have written them out in full, for example, "Galatians" rather than "Gal." The printed text is, in some respects, a graphic misrepresentation of speech, particularly in the arbitrary length of line in the usual method of printing written prose. Consequently, I have quoted the text in a line form resembling verse to indicate graphically the lengths of phrases.

The disadvantage of this method is the impossibility of representing all the verbal patterns, and for the most part I have indicated only those I discuss. Even those are perhaps too simply illustrated. Cotton's definitions of schemes recognize a variance in phonic themes that goes beyond the graphic representations I have provided. Moreover, consonants are always pronounced together with vowel sounds. What I have, for the sake of simplicity, represented as the repetition of consonants would actually have been repetitions pronounced with variant vowel sounds – as Cotton says, repetitions of "like sounds, yet somewhat differing" (E6). An analysis of the vowels would basically strengthen my argument, because the vowel sounds provide additional patterns with variations in the phonic themes.

16 Cicero, *Orator,* with an English translation by H. M. Hubbell, Loeb Classical Library (Cambridge, Mass.: Harvard University Press, 1971), 23.77.

17 Cicero, *Orator,* 23.77–78.

18 Cicero, *Orator,* 25.83,, translation modified. Jackson Cope briefly comments on the far more obvious "incantatory" effect in the Quaker rhetoric of twenty years later. See Jackson I. Cope, "Seventeenth-Century Quaker Style," in Fish, *Seventeenth-Century Prose,* pp. 200–35, esp. p. 208.

19 Quintilian cites this as a third usage of *figura,* one which, he disdainfully remarks, was "much in vogue." He presents it as a special kind of scheme, but acknowledges that some of his contemporaries reserve the word *figura* solely for this kind of figure. He says it involves taking figure to mean "a form of expression to which a new aspect is given by art." This new aspect may be innocuous, producing only "novelty and variety," or it may be a means of evading censorship, prohibition, or some other social constraint on the speaker. Auerbach views this development of *figura* as unimportant, as symptomatic of the hairsplitting attention given to ornamentation in later classical rhetoric ("*Figura,*" p. 27). Quintilian does invite this view, but in part because he seems wary of the deeper implications of this concept, as well he might be. Not only does it raise the obvious questions about ethics and pedantry; paradoxically, the most formal and technical devices of rhetoric, the schemes, return the orator quite directly to fundamental questions about the social conditions of language use and the philosophy of rhetoric by raising questions about the relationship between the acoustic shapes of words and their referential meaning. Quintilian's concern with hidden meaning and whether it is safe to speak openly recognizes the importance of the political and social conditions of these philosophical issues. For "*controversiae figuratae*," see Quintilian, *Institutio*, 9.1.14 and 9.2.65, as well as 9.1.15. Questions of social constraint arise in 9.1.66.

20   Perhaps for the same kinds of reasons, William Tyndale had sought to discover a sacramental theory hidden in the meaning of Hebrew place names (William Tyndale, "A Brief Declaration of the Sacraments," in Tyndale, *Doctrinal Treatises and Introductions to Different Portions of the Holy Scriptures*, ed. Henry Walter [Cambridge: Cambridge University Press, for the Parker Society, 1848], p. 368).

21   For a brief, provocative discussion of this philosophy, see Foucault, "The Prose of the World," in *The Order of Things*, pp. 17–45. Although Foucault describes this as a sixteenth-century "*episteme*" (p. 32), most of his sources are from the early seventeenth century (see p. 45). That is, it was a philosophy that Cotton shared with his contemporaries. Foucault's discussion is marred by other inaccuracies. For example, he says that in this *episteme*, "words offer themselves to men as things to be deciphered" (p. 35). As we will see in Chapters 4 and 6, Cotton treats the "resemblances" he finds in Scripture as images that "decipher" the essences of referents. It is not the exegete, as Foucault says, that deciphers the resemblance, but rather the resemblance itself that deciphers the world. Foucault also misrepresents Petrus Ramus's understanding of language (p. 35). Ramus's *Gramere* does not give any evidence of relying on the mystical analogies that Foucault describes. For instance, the relation of *convenientia* in the *Gramere* simply means grammatical agreement (see n. 3 to this chapter). Foucault's analysis is nonetheless valuable, even with its omission of such relevant works as Calvin's *Institutes of the Christian Religion*, because it provides a general idea of the philosophy of analogies apart from specific beliefs about natural magic, witchcraft, or occult Renaissance philosophy. These latter topics tend to be the context of what little there is on this subject in English and American history and criticism. See, e.g., Keith Thomas, *Religion and the Decline of Magic* (New York: Scribner, 1971), pp. 223–29. Don Cameron Allen, in *Mysteriously Meant: The Rediscovery of Pagan Symbolism and Allegorical Interpretation in the Renaissance* (Baltimore: Johns Hopkins Press, 1970), pp. 238–44, perplexedly observes that Puritans evinced a persistent interest in "analogies," but he does not pursue this idea. As these works hint, the classical antecedents for this philosophy were numerous and important. The concept of convenience, for example, was closely related to the Greek *sumpatheia*. However, none of these studies contains any substantive discussion of classical sources or their relation to the philosophy of analogies as it informed the works of Puritans such as Cotton. (I thank Dana Lloyd Spradley for his assistance in the preparation of this note.)

22 Plato, *Cratylus,* trans. Benjamin Jowett, in *The Collected Dialogues including the Letters,* ed. Edith Hamilton and Huntington Cairns (Princeton, N.J.: Princeton University Press, 1961), pp. 429, 459, 465–74. Socrates also raises the issue of the influence of social convention on the meanings of words, contending that this influence is real and thus mitigates whatever true arguments might be made about the original names of things. That is, the criterion of appropriateness always limits the truth value of words no matter how "true" they may have been "originally." The influence of Augustine, widely read among Puritans, may also have been important for Cotton's beliefs about the importance and significance of acoustic figures. See Marcia C. Colish, *The Mirror of Language: A Study in the Medieval Theory of Knowledge* (New Haven, Conn.: Yale University Press, 1968); Colish comments on *De Magistro,* "Augustine believed words are acoustic signs which correspond accurately to the realities they represent. This correspondence, however, is partial, and it does not constitute identity with the things signified" (pp. 54–55).

23 Gregory Bateson, *Steps to an Ecology of the Mind* (New York: Ballantine Books, 1972), pp. 194–278. For Bateson's definition of his term "double bind," see esp. pp. 206–08. These are collected essays, of which the last, "Double Bind" (1969), is an example rather than a description of the phenomenon. Bateson offered his theory initially as an explanation of schizophrenia, but it is now considered a general psychological theory rather than an accurate description of schizophrenia. Bateson's concept includes a third dimension, the threat of punishment, which he views as necessary to a double bind situation. Puritan theology officially offers damnation as a threat of punishment, but in fact there is very little about going to hell in Cotton's sermons. The threat of violence, which I discuss in Chapter 6, was a far more frequent threat, and one that was often made indirectly. Bateson declines to discuss what happens when there is the fact of punishment, not just the threat. I discuss this dimension in Chapter 5.

24 Bateson, *Ecology of the Mind,* p. 207.

25 Milton H. Erickson, Ernest L. Rossi, and Sheila I. Rossi, *Hypnotic Realities: The Induction of Clinical Hypnosis and Forms of Indirect Suggestion* (New York: Irvington, 1976), p. 63. The authors do not clarify their differences with Bateson on the relation of primary and secondary injunctions. I have used their term, "metacommunication," but "paracommunication" might be a better name for it.

26 It is no accident that, historically, the growing interest in Puritan preaching was coincident with the growing belief in and fascination with demonic possession, for each was a version of authoritarian religious beliefs that depended on what we might now call hypnotic trances, though in varying degrees. For a discussion of the many similarities between Puritan religion and the witchcraft they claimed to despise, see Ann Kibbey, "Mutations of the Supernatural: Witchcraft, Remarkable Providences, and the Power of Puritan Men," *American Quarterly* 34 (1982), pp. 125–48.

27 The phrase "powerful illusion" is from Paul De Man, "The Resistance to Theory," *Yale French Studies* 63 (1982), p. 10. See also Gérard Genette, *Figures of*

Literary Discourse, trans. Alan Sheridan (New York: Columbia University Press, 1982), pp. 229–95.

28 Bateson mentions the possible relevance of metaphor to the double bind but does not explain its importance (*Ecology of the Mind*, p. 205).

29 See Maureen Quilligan, *The Language of Allegory: Defining the Genre* (Ithaca, N.Y.: Cornell University Press, 1979), on the importance of the pun as a way of turning meaning in allegorical narrative. As Quilligan shows, literary allegory that seeks to be redemptive is heavily concerned with "slippery slides" between literal and figurative meaning and with the reversal of literal and figurative that the allegory seeks to inspire in the reader's perception (pp. 25–86, esp. 26, 42, 49, and 84). However, Quilligan does not discuss the significance of the pun as a signifier, or the pun as an expression of the Protestant reinterpretation of traditional hermeneutics.

30 Quintilian, *Institutio*, 9.6.19.

31 Quintilian, *Institutio*, 8.6.5.

32 Quintilian, *Institutio*, 9.1.4.

33 See Butler's rendering of "*permutando aut mutando*" as "by the interchange of words and borrowing" at *Institutio*, 8.6.5. See also, e.g., William Tyndale, *The Obedience of a Christian Man*, in *Doctrinal Treatises*, pp. 303–04; Tyndale also speaks of borrowing speech.

34 The phrase "shine forth" is from Quintilian, *Institutio*, 8.6.4.

35 This example is from John Cotton, *Christ The Fountaine of Life* (London, 1651), p. 216. These sermons were delivered at about the same time as those in *The Way of Life*. See section III of the Appendix, esp. n. 7.

36 John Cotton, *A Brief Exposition with Practical Observations Upon the whole Book of Canticles* (London, 1655), p. 78.

37 Cotton, *A Brief Exposition*, p. 216.

38 For analyses of family roles that cite religious literature, see for example, David Leverenz, *The Language of Puritan Feeling: An Exploration in Literature, Psychology, and Social History* (New Brunswick, N.J.: Rutgers University Press, 1980), esp. pp. 175–85; Philip J. Greven, *The Protestant Temperament: Patterns of Child-Rearing, Religious Experience, and the Self in Early America* (New York: New American Library, 1977); Emory Elliott, *Power and the Pulpit in Puritan New England* (Princeton, N.J.: Princeton University Press, 1975); and Edmund S. Morgan, *The Puritan Family: Religion and Domestic Relations in Seventeenth-Century New England* (New York: Harper & Row, 1966). Also relevant, although it concerns a later period, is Jay Fliegelman, *Prodigals and Pilgrims: The American Revolution against Patriarchal Authority, 1750–1800* (Cambridge: Cambridge University Press, 1982).

39 Quintilian explains the discrete domains, or places, of signification by means of a proprietary concept of rhetorical appropriateness: "For metaphor should always either occupy a place already vacant, or if it fills the room of something else [*in alienum venit*], should be more impressive than that which it displaces [*plus valere eo quod expellet*]" (*Institutio*, 8.6.18). Cf. Cicero's nonproprietary concept of appropriateness in *Orator*.

40 Quintilian, *Institutio*, 8.6.1, 9.1.4.

41 Quintilian's main discussion of hyperbole occurs at *Institutio*, 8.6.67–76, and closes bk. 8. Quintilian, who makes no secret of his preference for metaphor ("it is by far the most beautiful of the tropes" [*Institutio*, 8.6.4]), has many reservations about hyperbole. Used virtuously, "it is a comely exceeding of the truth" which "does not declare positively" that there is some other truth instead (8.6.67, 8.6.75, translation modified). More disparagingly, he says that "hyperbole lies, though without any intention to deceive"; that is, it is not *mendacio* (8.6.74). Quintilian pardons hyperbole this way: "We are allowed to amplify, when the magnitude of the facts [*res*] surpasses all words" (8.6.76). It is not difficult to see what a Christian such as Cotton would have made of this excuse, for the deity of his religion by definition "surpasses all words."

42 Sacvan Bercovitch has shown that American Puritan narratives are informed by a hermeneutic theory that "transfers the source of meaning from scripture to secular history." He argues further that this transfer characterizes American, but not English, Puritan narratives. However, the same transfer occurs in the English Puritan rhetoric of the soul, for Cotton's metaphors in these sermons likewise tip the balance in favor of the civil, sensible life, locating propriety ("the source of meaning") in Puritan secular life. The fact that English sermons on the soul's life demonstrate the same hermeneutic theory as the later public histories of New England suggests where the general outlook comes from: It is the projected interior world of the Puritan convert. Bercovitch implies as much at the outset by analyzing Puritan self-confession, but his discussion omits the Puritans' most favored genre, the sermons on conversion that defined the terms of these confessions. Once we take the sermon rhetoric into account, we can understand why, as Bercovitch claims, Puritan rhetoric "blurs the difference between metaphor and experience." The privileged literal significance in the image of metaphor is the wellspring of confusion, for preaching conflates the image with experience in its mandate for the literalization of metaphor. See Sacvan Bercovitch, *The Puritan Origins of the American Self* (New Haven, Conn.: Yale University Press, 1975), esp. pp. 30 and 109–21. See also Cope, "Quaker Style," pp. 201–02; Cope observes that in George Fox's rhetoric, literal and metaphoric meaning are often indistinguishable.

43 Cicero, *Orator*, 21.70–22.74.

44 The paronomasia of "poure" and "power" was not so farfetched in the seventeenth century as it might seem in contemporary English pronunciation. In fact, the words were accounted homophones by Cotton's contemporaries, and sometimes spelled as homonyms. The evidence of contemporaneous textbooks on English pronunciation and orthography is conclusive on this point. Richard Hodges, in *Most plain Direction for True-Writing* (London, 1653; facsimile rpt. Menston, England: Scholar Press, 1968), in the section "Most Plain Directions for the True-Writing of such English words whose sounds are alike, and their significations unlike: which are heer exprest by different Letters," gives a jingle to express the homophony of "pour" and "power:" "He hath no *power* to *pour* it out" (p. 15). Similarly, Thomas Osborn, in *A Rational Way of Teaching* (London, 1688; facsimile rpt. Menston, England: Scholar Press, 1969), in "TABLE I. Of such Words which are altogether alike in Sound, but of

different Signification and Spelling," gives the following example: "*Pour* it all out, if you have so much *power*" (p. 99). The exact sound of the diphthong in "pour" and "power" in the seventeenth century is difficult to determine; there was probably a slight difference in its quality between the two words, a difference that led to their eventual divergence in pronunciation. The diphthong was probably /ou/. See Anders Orbeck, *Early New England Pronunciation* (Ann Arbor, Mich.: George Wahr, 1927), p. 52, for a rather unsophisticated and hedging affirmation; and see Alexander Gill, *Logonomia Anglica* [1619], p. 2, trans. Robin C. Alston, Stockholm Studies in English 27 (Stockholm: Almqvist & Wiksell, 1972), p. 102, for a more sophisticated confirmation, though cast in seventeenth-century terms and symbols. "Pour," "out," and "power" all shared this diphthong, giving Cotton ample material for sound repetitions in the use of "pour out" and "power." (I thank Dana Lloyd Spradley for his assistance in the preparation of this note.)

45 John Cotton, *Gods Promise to His Plantation* (London, 1630): all further references will be given in the text and indicated by G. Although some members of Cotton's audience in St. Botolph's were among the 1630 emigrants, Cotton himself did not leave England for another three years. Thus *Gods Promise* presents a sympathetic Englishman's view of colonization but not an emigrant's interpretation of the experience.

46 To put it another way, this sermon is based on a hyperbolic fusion of loci, a fusion of the convert's interior and exterior life. As such, it is an example of what Bercovitch has described as the fusion of history and allegory in American Puritan narrative (*Puritan Origins,* pp. 112–14). Cotton's sermon suggests, however, that we can also understand this phenomenon as the fusion of the literal and figurative levels of Puritan metaphor. As Bercovitch says, the American Puritans "invented a colony in the image of a saint," and consequently they also invented one with the mentality of a saint. The convert's imaged world of metaphor, with its sanction of divine truth, was not only descriptive of the soul's life; the projected metaphors of the soul were also descriptive of social and economic life in the convert's perception of the world exterior to the self. Distinguished by its literalness, not its historicity, the image in Puritan metaphor invokes the classicist, ahistorical concept of *figura* as a dynamic material shape rather than the Christian concept of biblical types that Bercovitch analyzes in Puritan narrative. For further discussion of *figura* and biblical typology, see the end of Chapter 3.

47 *The Autobiography of Benjamin Franklin,* ed. Leonard W. Labaree et al. (New Haven, Conn.: Yale University Press, 1975), p. 88.

CHAPTER 3. ICONOCLASTIC MATERIALISM

1 On iconoclasm in France see Natalie Zemon Davis, "The Rites of Violence," in Davis, *Society and Culture in Early Modern France* (Stanford, Calif.: Stanford University Press, 1975). This is a study of French Protestants in the sixteenth century, and especially useful for its comparison of Catholic and Protestant religious violence. Davis argues that Protestants sensed a "danger and defilement in the wrongful use of material objects" and thus sought to put profane things "back in the profane world where they belonged" (pp. 174, 159). On iconoclasm in the Netherlands see Phyllis Mack Crew, *Calvinist Preaching and Iconoclasm in the Netherlands, 1544–1569* (Cambridge: Cambridge University Press, 1978). Iconoclasts in the Netherlands attacked material objects almost exclusively; that is, there was almost no violence against Catholic clerics (p. 32). For a historical survey of iconoclasm in England, see John Phillips, *The Reformation of Images: Destruction of Art in England, 1535–1660* (Berkeley: University of California Press, 1973). For other descriptions of iconoclasm in continental Europe, see Carl C. Christensen, "Patterns of Iconoclasm in the Early Reformation: Strasbourg and Basel," and William S. Maltby, "Iconoclasm and Politics in the Netherlands, 1566," both in *The Image and the Word: Confrontations in Judaism Christianity, and Islam,* ed. Joseph Gutmann (Missoula, Mont.: Scholars Press, 1977), pp. 107–48, 149–64. None of these studies even broaches the possibility that Protestant theology granted power to icons, much less to "living icons."

2 Davis, *Society and Culture,* pp. 174, 159.

3 Quoted in Crew, *Preaching and Iconoclasm,* p. 23. Crew ignores the implications of this evidence.

4 Crew, *Preaching and Iconoclasm,* p. 26n.

5 See esp. Crew, *Preaching and Iconoclasm,* pp. 108–09, whose detailed analysis of the theology and social background of preachers omits discussion of sacramental symbolism and implies that the sacramental beliefs of preachers were important only to themselves.

6 John Calvin, *Institutes of the Christian Religion,* ed. John T. McNeill, trans. Ford Lewis Battles, 2 vols., Library of Christian Classics, vols. 20 and 21 (Philadelphia: Westminster Press, 1960), pp. 105, 102; all further references are to this edition and are given in the text.

7 Translation modified after Johannis Calvin, *Institutio Christianae Religionis,* ed. A. Tholuck, 2 vols. (Berlin: Gustave Eichler, 1834–35), vol. 1, p. 82. This edition is the 1559 Latin text.

8 See *iconicus* in the *Oxford Latin Dictionary.* The word is derived from the Greek *eikón* (adj., *eikonikós*). See *Liddell and Scott's Greek–English Lexicon.*

9 Phillips, in *Reformation of Images,* pp. 178, 184, oversimplifies Calvin's views, tending to attribute to him the later, even more austere, views of seventeenth-century English Puritans such as William Prynne. What Phillips describes as Laud's "misreading of Calvin" is in fact quite close to what Calvin says.

10 Although Calvin's preference for temporal images in visual art may seem to grant a special importance to historical knowledge, it does not. Considering his polemic on the severe limitations of representational visual art, it was no compliment to the subject matter to say that such art was adequate to the task of depicting "histories and events." By associating the concept of representational art with historical events, Calvin was subordinating both to living sacramental "images."

11 Analysis of iconoclasm in Ely Cathedral is based on my own observation. For further examples, see the illustrations in Phillips, *Reformation of Images.*

12 Crew, *Preaching and Iconoclasm*, p. 26.

13 Keith Thomas, *Religion and the Decline of Magic* (New York: Scribner, 1971), p. 75; Crew, *Preaching and Iconoclasm*, chap. 1.

14 John Calvin, *The Institution of Christian Religion, wrytten in Latine by maister Jhon Calvin, and translated into Englysh according to the authors last edition* (London: Reinolde Wolfe & Richard Harison, 1561), bk. 1, chap. 11, fol. 27, recto (first count). The translation identifies Thomas Norton only by his initials at the end of the work, but the book was reprinted in 1611 with a full identification of Norton as translator. The passage on living icons in the 1561 edition reads: "I consider for what use temples are ordained, me thinkes it is verie ill beseming the holinesse therof to receive any other images than these lively and natural images, which the LORDE by hys woorde hath consecrate, I mean Baptisme and the Lordes Supper, and other ceremonies werewyth our eies ought both more earnestly to be occupied and more lively to be moved, than that they should nede any other images framed by y witt of men. Loe this is the incomparable commoditie of images, whiche can by no value be recompensed, if we believe the papistes."

15 My remarks on Emmanuel College are based on F. H. Stubbings, "The Church of the Cambridge Dominican," *Proceedings of the Cambridge Antiquarian Society* 62 (1969), pp. 95–104, and "Discoveries in the Old Kitchen," *Emmanuel College Magazine* 41 (1958–59), pp. 40–43. I thank Mr. Stubbings for giving me a tour of the college and discussing the significance of the architectural changes. On Puritan practices see Horton Davies, *The Worship of the English Puritans* (Westminster: Dacre Press, 1948); and William Haller, *The Rise of Puritanism* (New York, 1938; rpt. New York: Harper & Bros., 1957), pp. 3–82.

16 On Boston practices see Mark Spurrell, *The Puritan Town of Boston*, History of Boston Series, no. 5 (Boston, Lincolnshire: Richard Kay Publications, for the Boston History Project, 1972); see p. 9 for the example of the use of the surplice as a seat cushion.

17 See Karl Marx, *Capital: A Critique of Political Economy*, vol. 1, ed. Frederick Engels, trans. from the 3rd German ed. by Samuel Moore and Edward Aveling (New York: International Publishers, 1967). On fetishism see pp. 71–83. On Protestantism and reflexiveness see p. 79. See also Marx's provocative remarks on "transubstantiation" and St. Jerome's theory of conversion, p. 103.

18 John Jewel, *An Apology of the Church of England*, ed. J. E. Booty, Folger Documents of Tudor and Stuart Civilization, vol. 5 (Charlottesville: University Press of Virginia, 1963), p. 33.

19 See esp. Cotton's first four sermons on Galatians, WL255–481.

20 On the doctrine of the mystical body of Christ, see Ernest Best, *One Body in Christ: A Study of the Relationship of the Church to Christ in the Epistles of the Apostle Paul* (London: SPCK, 1955). On the significance of this concept in Puritanism, particularly in its relation to "edification," see John S. Coolidge, *The Pauline Renaissance in England: Puritanism and the Bible* (Oxford: Oxford University Press [Clarendon Press], 1970), pp. 23–54 and 141–51.

21 Quintilian, following Greek rhetoric, defines metonymy as "the substitution of one name [*nominis*] for another" (*Institutio Oratoria*, with an English translation by H. E. Butler, 4 vols., Loeb Classical Library [Cambridge, Mass: Harvard University Press, 1966–79], 8.6.23), and Calvin uses the term in this way.

22 Although Calvin stresses that metonymy is the trope of the sacraments, his discussion of the sacraments actually begins by elaborating features of resemblance and similarity. For example, he claims that the trope indicates a similarity between the thing named and the thing renamed: "Those things ordained by God borrow the names of those things of which they bear a definite and not misleading signification, and have the reality joined with them. So great, therefore, is their similarity and closeness that transition from one to the other is easy" (1385–86). Calvin's emphasis on resemblance assumes the perspective of spiritual propriety, for the cognitive "transition" required of the communicant is to perceive the analogy, the resemblance, between the value of material "earthly" bread in ordinary life and the theological idea of the crucified and resurrected "heavenly" body of Christ as the means of sustaining spiritual life. Calvin's discussion of the consecrating words is sensitive to the classical concept of tropes in that, strictly, tropes do not name particular usages. They designate different aspects of figuration in a particular word usage. What is peculiar is Calvin's reluctance to acknowledge the metaphoric aspects of the sacramental trope. It may be that Calvin was anxious not to be confused with memorialists such as Zwingli, who interpreted the sacrament as purely metaphoric and commemorative.

23 Quintilian, *Institutio*, 8.6.23. Calvin remarks that the figure of metonymy is prevalent in Scripture, but he says very little about the characteristics of metonymy as a trope of rhetoric, leaving ambiguous how metonymy proves to be the apt indicator of the spiritual presence that he claims it is. However, perhaps he had Quintilian's definition in mind. The Calvinist deity was the omnipotent creator and possessor, and Calvin says that the deity uses metonymy "with much greater reason" than human beings have (1385).

24 *The Workes of that Famous and Worthy Minister of Christ in the Universitie of Cambridge, M. W. Perkins,* 3 vols. (Cambridge and London, 1608–31); all references are to this edition and will be given by volume and page number in the text. Perkins was one of the most influential Elizabethans for seventeenth-century Puritans such as Cotton. See Perry Miller, *The New England Mind: The Seventeenth Century* (1939; rpt. Boston: Beacon Press, 1965), esp. pp. 335–40. Although Miller discusses Perkins in an entirely different way, excluding the ideas I emphasize here and in the next chapter, he nonetheless shows that many Puritans were familiar with Perkins's works. Cotton, a generation younger than Perkins, is reputed to have heard Perkins preach. It seems likely, since Perkins was one of the best-known Puritans at Cambridge while Cotton was a student at Trinity College.

25 Like Calvin, Perkins understands Old Testament signs and the sacramental signs of his own church as equally figural and equally invested with the real spiritual presence. He was certainly familiar with the idea of a type, for he refers to the brazen serpent as a "type, sign, or image to represent Christ crucified" (1.580). Nonetheless, he implies by his interchangeable terms that type, sign, and image are all subsumed in a more comprehensive concept of *figura,* that each term names only a different aspect of his larger idea of figural significance. And he is just as likely to use "type" in a way that indicates only the idea of a living image, without any concomitant antitype. Perkins's concept of sacramental living images emphasizes the sacralization of certain persons, words, and things contemporaneous with himself. Selected *figurae* are signs of the deity's presence, but they are not especially typological. Although the idea of a "type" is certainly involved in this extension of sacramental *figurae,* Perkins relies on beliefs about true and false images rather than typology. Where scholastic typology had carefully circumscribed the notion of living *figurae* by restricting its relevance to the Old Testament, and by interpreting the Israelites as a people who only prefigured or foreshadowed – but did not participate in – Christian redemption, Perkins followed Calvin in applying the doctrine of the real spiritual presence to the Old and New Testament sacraments alike, creating a theology in which the idea of *figura* was still temporal but no longer dependent on a concept of historical progression.

26   Perkins derives the word "type" as a term appropriate to describe the minister from the Greek New Testament: "Because the doctrine of the word is hard both to be understood and to be practised, therefore the Minister ought to express that by his example, which he teacheth, as it were by a type I Pet. 5.3 *Not as though ye were Lords over Gods heritage; but that yee may be examples* (pupos [*sic* for tupos] *types) to the flocke*" (2.671). By using the literal translation "type" instead of "example," Perkins recovers the imagistic connotations in the English understanding of this passage from Peter. (I thank Dana Lloyd Spradley for his assistance in the preparation of this note.)

27   Cicero speaks of *figurae negotii,* the figures of occupations, and possibly this concept also underlies Perkins's willingness to describe the minister as a "type" in his vocation – what Perkins terms elsewhere a "particular calling." On Cicero see Erich Auerbach, *"Figura,"* in *Scenes from the Drama of European Literature: Six Essays by Erich Auerbach,* trans. Ralph Mannheim (New York: Meridian, 1959), p. 18; all references are to the Mannheim translation.

28   Cf. Max Weber, *The Protestant Ethic and the Spirit of Capitalism,* trans. Talcott Parsons (New York: Scribner, 1958), who omits consideration of the act of working as a sign of grace in its own right.

29   Robert Nichols[?], "An Enquiry," in *Some Treasure Fetched out of Rubbish* (London, 1660). This tract has often been attributed to John Cotton; see, for example, Norman Grabo, "John Cotton's Aesthetic: A Sketch," *Early American Literature* 3, no. 1 (Spring 1968), pp. 1–10. Though the tract expresses views that are similar to Cotton's in some respects, it is more likely that it was written by Nichols. See section V of the Appendix.

30   Auerbach's essay *"Figura"* was originally published in 1944.

31   Auerbach, Figura," p. 26. See Quintilian, Institutio, 9.1.10–12. See Chapter 2, n. 7, for a discussion of Auerbach's interpretation of this passage.

32   Cicero, *De Natura Deorum,* with an English translation by H. Rackham (Cambridge, Mass.: Harvard University Press, 1979), 1.18.48–49. Cf. Auerbach, "Figura," pp. 18–19. It is unclear what point Auerbach is trying to make, since he cites *De Natura Deorum,* although not the passage I quote here. He offers many qualifications about Cicero's use of *figura* concerning the gods and finally says, "In Cicero the images of the gods are usually called *signa,* never *figurae*" (p. 19). What he means is ambiguous: The example he then gives uses *signum* to mean the statue of a god (only one possible meaning of "image"), and he adds a note in which he says, "Later *figura* becomes quite frequent in the sense of 'divine image' " (p. 230), but he gives no citations. Auerbach also says, without comment, that Cicero uses *figura* frequently in *De Natura Deorum.*

33 Auerbach, *"Figura"* p. 19.

34 The quotation is from Auerbach, *"Figura,"* p. 57, but see from the beginning of sec. 2, p. 28.

35 For example, see Rosemund Tuve, *A Reading of George Herbert* (Chicago: University of Chicago Press, 1952); Barbara Lewalski, *"Samson Agonistes* and the 'Tragedy' of the Apocalypse," *PMLA* 85 (1970), pp. 1050−61, and *Donne's "Anniversaries" and the Poetry of Praise: The Creation of a Symbolic Mode* (Princeton, N.J.: Princeton University Press, 1973); Michael Murrin, *The Veil of Allegory: Some Notes toward a Theory of Allegorical Rhetoric in the English Renaissance* (Chicago: University of Chicago Press, 1969); Ursula Brumm, *American Thought and Religious Typology,* trans. John Hoaglund (New Brunswick, N.J.: Rutgers University Press, 1970); Victor Harris, "Allegory to Analogy in the Interpretation of Scriptures," *Philological Quarterly* 45 (1966), pp. 1−23; Charles K. Cannon, "William Whitaker's *Disputatio de Sacra Scriptura: A Sixteenth-Century Theory of Allegory,"* *Huntington Library Quarterly* 25 (1961), pp. 129−38; William G. Madsen, *From Shadowy Types to Truth: Studies in Milton's Symbolism* (New Haven, Conn.: Yale University Press, 1968); Jesper Rosenmeier, "The Image of Christ: The Typology of John Cotton" (Ph.D. diss., Harvard University, 1966); Sacvan Bercovitch, ed., *Typology and Early American Literature* (Amherst: University of Massachusetts Press, 1972); and Earl Miner, ed., *Literary Uses of Typology* (Princeton, N.J.: Princeton University Press, 1977). On patristic and medieval typology, see Alan C. Charity, *Events and Their Afterlife: The Dialectics of Christian Typology in the Bible and Dante* (Cambridge: Cambridge University Press, 1966); P. Synave, "La Doctrine de Saint Thomas D'Aquin: Sur le sens littéral des écritures," *Revue Biblique* 35 (1926), pp. 40−65; Jean Daniélou, *From Shadows to Reality: Studies in the Biblical Typology of the Fathers,* trans. Wulstan Hibberd (London: Burns & Oates, 1960); and John Freccero, "Medusa: The Letter and the Spirit," *Yearbook of Italian Studies,* 1972, pp. 1−18. Also relevant are Oscar Cullmann, *Christ and Time: The Primitive Christian Conception of Time and History,* trans. Floyd V. Filson (Philadelphia: Westminster Press, 1950); James S. Preus, *From Shadow to Promise: Old Testament Interpretation from Augustine to the Young Luther* (Cambridge, Mass.: Harvard University Press, 1969); and Ernst H. Kantorowicz, *The King's Two Bodies: A Study of Medieval Political Theology* (Princeton, N.J.: Princeton University Press, 1957).

36 See Sacvan Bercovitch, *The Puritan Origins of the American Self* (New Haven, Conn.: Yale University Press, 1975), esp. p. 161.

37   Bercovitch, in *Puritan Origins*, pp. 35–37, introduces the concept of *figura* through direct quotation of primary sources, but his general interpretation in chap. 2, "The Vision of History," takes Auerbach's interpretation as its point of departure, or at least shares the assumption that Augustinian typological exegesis rather than classical thought is the basis for understanding the Puritan concept of *figura*.

CHAPTER 4. VERBAL IMAGES, HISTORY, AND MARRIAGE

1   See Larzer Ziff, *The Career of John Cotton: Puritanism and the American Experience* (Princeton, N.J.: Princeton University Press, 1962), pp. 46–49. See also Samuel Whiting, "Concerning the Life of the Famous Mr. Cotton," *Chronicles of the First Planters of the Colony of Massachusetts Bay, from 1623 to 1626*, ed. Alexander Young (Boston, 1846), p. 423.

2   "A Discourse upon 1 Cor. 14.40," in *Some Treasure Fetched out of Rubbish* (London, 1660), pp. 1–8. (The preface cites Cotton as the probable author of the second tract in this collection, but this is unlikely. See section V of the Appendix.) On the importance of "edification" in Elizabethan Puritan thought, see John S. Coolidge, *The Pauline Renaissance in England: Puritanism and the Bible* (Oxford: Oxford University Press, [Clarendon Press], 1970), pp. 23–54.

3   It is difficult to draw conclusions about the social and historical conditions of his sermons in the 1620s because so little is known about the history of Boston during Cotton's years as vicar of St. Botolph's, and it is impossible to date his English sermons exactly. On iconoclasm in Boston, see Ziff, *Career of Cotton*, pp. 51–52; and Mark Spurrell, *Boston Parish Church* (n.p., n.d.), from which I quote Robert Sanderson's observation in his Visitation Sermon, 1621. Sanderson may have been exaggerating the damage, for the walls had been whited already according to the Boston Corporation records, which show that the corporation had ordered the "whytyng of the church" in 1550 (quoted in Pishey Thompson, *The History and Antiquities of Boston* [Boston: John Noble, 1856], p. 163).

4   John Cotton, *A Brief Exposition of the Whole Book of Canticles, or Song of Solomon* (London, 1642), pp. 41–42, 46–47; all further references will be given in the text and indicated by C. See section I of the Appendix for an estimate of the date the Canticles sermons were preached.

5   John Cotton, *A Modest and Cleare Answer to Mr. Balls Discourse of set formes of Prayer* (London, 1642), p. 23; all further references will be given in the text and indicated by AB.

6   Cotton's sermons began to be published after censorship of the press was lifted, so both early and later expositions of images were published at the same time. The series of Canticles sermons preached about 1620 was published in 1642. Excerpts from the Revelation sermons preached about 1640 were published as John Cotton, *The Powrring out of the Seven Vials* (London, 1642) and *The Churches Resurrection* (London, 1642). Several years after his death in 1652, two more collections were published; their appearance suggests a renewed interest in this kind of exposition: John Cotton, *An Exposition upon The Thirteenth*

Chapter of the Revelation (London, 1655), also preached about 1640 (all references will be given in the text and indicated by R); and the second series of Canticles sermons, preached in 1642 or later and published as John Cotton, *A Brief Exposition with Practical Observations Upon the whole Book of Canticles* (London, 1655). See the first page of the second Canticles commentary for a determination of the date it was preached. Expositions of Canticles in particular were a touchstone of the importance of verbal images for Protestants. For the numerous commentaries on Canticles, see Mason I. Lowance, Jr., *The Language of Canaan: Metaphor and Symbol in New England from the Puritans to the Transcendentalists* (Cambridge, Mass.: Harvard University Press, 1980), pp. 41–54; and Karen E. Rowe, "Sacred or Profane? Edward Taylor's Meditations on Canticles," *Journal of Modern Philology* 72, no. 2 (November 1974), pp. 123–38.

7 See John Calvin, *Institutes of the Christian Religion,* ed. John T. McNeill, trans. Ford Lewis Battles, 2 vols., Library of Christian Classics, vols. 20 and 21 (Philadelphia: Westminster Press, 1960), p. 1386; all further references are to this edition and will be given in the text.

8 As Barbara Lewalski has noted, in English Protestantism tropes were understood as the deity's "chosen formulations of revealed truth." Lewalski argues that this conviction amounted to an increased interest in the "poetic texture of scripture," but she does not demonstrate any systematic theory or relate this development in poetics to social values. In fact, most English Puritans followed Calvin, perceiving this as an issue in rhetoric rather than poetics. The majority of Puritans were interested in tropes principally for their argumentative value in theology, politics, and historical interpretation, and the value they placed on tropes did not necessarily extend to poetry. By focusing exclusively on poetry, Lewalski makes the unwarranted assumption that a defense of tropes was also a defense of poetry. (*Protestant Poetics and the Seventeenth Century Religious Lyric* [Princeton, N.J.: Princeton University Press, 1979], esp. pp. 76–80).

9 Perry Miller, in *The New England Mind: The Seventeenth Century* (1939; rpt. Boston: Beacon Press, 1965), pp. 335–40, discusses Perkins's *Arte of Prophecying* as a major Puritan tract, but says nothing about the section on sacred tropes and casts Perkins as a literalist and a Ramist logician. Perkins temporarily abandons Ramist dichotomies in his discussion of tropes, although at the outset he does set up a dichotomous framework that opposes "Analogicall and plaine" places to the "Crypticall and darke." He says that sacred tropes concern only the latter, and he claims further that all doctrine "necessarie unto salvation" is stated in the former. This does not turn out to be the case, however, for Perkins discusses predestination, the interpretation of the sacraments, and many other presumably "necessarie" doctrines under sacred tropes, and in ways that depend fundamentally on the interpretation of tropes. See William Perkins, *The Workes of that Famous and Worthy Minister of Christ in the Universitie of Cambridge, M. W. Perkins,* 3 vols. (Cambridge and London, 1608–31), vol. 2, p. 654; all further references are to this edition and will be given by volume and page number in the text.

10 On the natural philosophy of resemblance, see Michael Foucault, *The*

Order of Things, trans. Alan Sheridan (New York: Pantheon, 1970), pp. 17–45. See also Chapter 2 herein. Foucault's descriptive phrase "the prose of the world" seems especially apt for Perkins.

11 Concerning whether the Sabbath should begin in the morning or the evening, Cotton interprets Acts 20.7 and Gen 1.5 by arguing, "It is said by Eveninge is not here mente the night but the last parte of the daye and so by a Synechdoche the whole daye, and the morninge is not put for the daye but for the last part of the night and so by the like Synechdoche for the whole nighte" (Winton U. Solberg, ed., "John Cotton's Treatise on the Duration of the Lord's Day," *Publications of the Colonial Society of Massachusetts* 59 [1982], p. 510). Solberg identifies the date of composition as 1611, at Cambridge.

12 That is, the elect are interpreted as a part of the population that stands for the whole.

13 Although Perkins's defense of tropes and figures was all made under the aegis of the Protestant "literal sense" – the belief that there was only one theological meaning in each passage of Scripture – this one meaning did not preclude recourse to tropes and figures: "*There is only one sense, and the same is the literall. An allegorie is onely a certain manner of uttering the same sense*" (2.651). For Perkins, the "literal sense" included figurative meaning.

Perkins's stance suggests how much the terms of early Protestants derived from their self-appointed mission to "explode" the hermeneutics of Thomas Aquinas. In the first century of the Reformation in England, the belief that tropes and figures were theologically true was often expressed in such strange assertions as William Tyndale's declaration that the deity's "literal sense is spiritual." (*The Obedience of a Christian Man,* in Tyndale, *Doctrinal Treatises and Introductions to Different Portions of the Holy Scriptures,* ed. Henry Walter [Cambridge: Cambridge University Press, for the Parker Society, 1848], p. 309). See also John Donne: "In many places of Scripture the figurative sense is the literal sense" (*Devotions upon Emergent Occasions,* ed. Anthony Raspa [Montreal, 1975], p. 99, quoted in Lewalski, *Protestant Poetics,* p. 85). Perkins similarly remarked, "Christ here speaketh plainly, and by a figure also" (1.586). In their frequently confusing use of the term "literal," these authors expressed the Calvinist theory of the sacrament. "Literal" meant simultaneously the reality of the material object, the common bread, and the reality of the spiritually present mystical body of Christ expressed by metonymy. As the Protestant polemics imply, this use of "literal" challenged the metaphoric idea of figurative language as "borrowed speech," as a "transfer" of meaning, because literal and figurative no longer defined discrete loci. The bread, while literal, had also to be understood as a *figura* of Christ's body without, as it were, being moved anywhere. The bread without the spiritual presence was "the letter that kills," but the body of Christ without the bread was a mere scholastic fiction. Calvinist Protestants objected to transubstantiation because it fictionalized the bread, made it unreal as bread in the act of consecration. What they demanded instead was bread that could be simultaneously literal and figurative.

14 John Cotton, *Of the Holinesse of Church-Members* (London, 1650), p. 86; all further references will be given in the text and indicated by H.

15 For the broad definitions of "parable" see the *Oxford English Dictionary*. Cotton favors "parabolical" in his sermon and rarely speaks of "symbols." His use of "symbol" here was probably a response to the charge of "symbolic theology," which he perceived as an issue about the value of parabolical interpretations.

16 Thomas Aquinas, *Summa Theologiae*, Latin text with an English translation by Thomas Gilby (London: Blackfriars, Eyre & Spottiswoode, 1964–81), 1a.1.10, 3rd reply. I have modified the translation from *Nature and Grace: Selections from the Summa Theologiae of Thomas Aquinas*, trans. and ed. A. M. Fairweather (London: SCM Press, 1954), p. 49.

17 Aquinas, *Summa Theologiae*, 1a.1.9, 1st reply; Fairweather translation, *Nature and Grace*, p. 47.

18 For "parabolicall speeches," see WL19. For "mysticall scriptures," see R47. On the revelatory quality of figures that decipher, see esp. C10 and R2.

19 For a discussion of Cotton's interpretation of Revelation, see Chap. 6.

20 John Cotton, *The Keyes Of the Kingdom of Heaven* (London, 1644), p. 56.

21 Cotton's reliance on the metaphor of the keys merely extended in a more obvious way what Puritans had believed from the beginning. As Coolidge has shown, Puritan ecclesiology depended fundamentally on biblical metaphors (*Pauline Renaissance*, chaps. 1–2). Edwardian and Elizabethan reformers synthesized the Old Testament metaphor of the elect people as a house or temple and the New Testament Pauline metaphor of the church as "one body in Christ." The resulting composite figure defined the church's task as the "edification of the body." The church would grow through the spiritual building up of its members in doctrine and discipline. Coolidge says nothing about the rhetorical theory informing this theology, but Perkins's treatises on figural meaning and the intrinsic cognitive value of rhetorical figures indicate the self-consciousness of Elizabethan Puritan figuralism.

22 Cotton, *Keyes*, pp. 56–57.

23 See especially Sacvan Bercovitch, "Typology in Puritan New England: The Williams–Cotton Controversy Reassessed," *American Quarterly* 19 (1967), pp. 166–91. This is the most detailed treatment of Cotton and typology, written against Perry Miller's dismissal of typology as unimportant to New England thought. Bercovitch's discussion does show that typology was important for many New England Puritans, but he erroneously includes among his examples of typology such texts as Cotton's commentaries on Revelation and Canticles. It seems more likely that typology as such was revived in the mid-seventeenth century by men like Roger Williams, who were a generation younger than Cotton. This interpretation would also explain why Cotton was attacked as a symbolist and why he needed to defend himself against the fourfold interpretation in the 1640s.

    This is not to say that Cotton rejected the concept of types altogether, but types were of only minor significance to him. For example, in his dispute with Roger Williams, Cotton rejected Williams's attempt to make typology the frame of reference for their argument. Cotton narrowly circumscribed the significance of types, restricting their relevance to the exegetical exercise of interpreting Old Testament ceremonies: "*Jehosaphat* tooke faithfull care for the soules of his people in this kind, 2 *Chron.* 17.7, 8, 9. Neither did he this as a Type of Christ, but as a Servant of Christ. Those things are said to be done as Types of Christ, which being ceremoniall duties, were afterwards done by Christ in his owne Person, and so were in him accomplished, and abolished: And it would be sacriledge to performe the same after him" (*The Bloudy Tenant, Washed, and Made White in the Bloud of the Lambe* [London, 1647], p. 68). Types were of historical interest, but only in a pejorative way. They belonged to the past alone and were thus irrelevant to the present except as a way to account for ceremonial passages in Old Testament history. Whatever was important in the Old Testament, such as Jehosaphat's care for his people, was not a type.

In his debates with Williams, Cotton generally took refuge in the symbolic and parabolical texts of Scripture, appealing especially to the figures of John's Revelation. Parabolical images, not the typological interpretation of Israel's history, provided the ground for Cotton's defense of theocracy. As Cotton put it to Williams, "If *John* the Apostle have Prophecied and denounced the destruction and extirpation of Antichristian Idolaters, and their whole State, why may not a Minister and Messenger of Christ (according to the measure of light received) open those Prophecyes, and apply them with severe threatenings, against them and their State?" (*Bloudy Tenant*, p. 53). "Open those Prophecyes" Cotton did, in his lecture-sermons on Revelation in 1639–40, and he drew substantially on these lectures to compose his reply to Williams. In his lectures, as in his debates with Williams, Cotton often referred to the history of Israel as an exemplary precedent, but he did not invoke typology when he did. Moreover, his views on clerical and state power were presented, first and foremost, as explications of the images in John's Revelation. See Chapter 6 for a discussion of Cotton's interpretation of Revelation.

24 The quotation is an adaptation of Calvin, *Institutes* (pp. 507–8, 510–11).
25 See William Tyndale, *The Obedience of a Christian Man*, in *Doctrinal Treatises*, pp. 339–67; and William Whitaker, *A Disputation on Holy Scripture: Against the Papists, Especially Bellarmine and Stapleton*, trans. William Fitzgerald, Parker Society Publications 46 (Cambridge: Cambridge University Press, 1849), pp. 450ff., 627ff.
26 Perkins occasionally suggests a similar cast of mind. For example, his reference to things as "visible words" in his discussion of the "sacramentall relation" alludes to a nonverbal concept of *figura* and the iconoclastic importance of material shapes (1.72), implying a shift from abstract sign theory to a concept of language and things that emphasizes the material signifier. However, the concrete image represented in language is much more important in Cotton than in Perkins.
27 *Works of Martin Luther*, gen. ed. Helmut T. Lehmann, vol. 37, *Word and Sacrament*, III, trans. and ed. Robert H. Fischer (Philadelphia: Muhlenberg Press, 1961), e.g., pp. 326, 336.
28 *Works of Luther* (Fischer ed.) vol. 37, pp. 298–300, 296.
29 *Works of Luther*, (Fischer ed.) vol. 37, p. 329.

30 *Works of Luther* (Fischer ed.), vol. 37, p. 296.

31 *Works of Luther* (Fischer ed.), vol. 37, p. 296.

32 *Works of Luther* (Fischer ed.), vol. 37, pp. 109–10. For Tertullian's phrase, see Erich Auerbach, *"Figura,"* in *Scenes from the Drama of European Literature: Six Essays by Erich Auerbach*, trans. by Ralph Mannheim (New York: Meridian, 1959), p. 31.

33 "Preface to the Revelation of St. John (I)" [1522], trans. Charles M. Jacobs, in *Works of Martin Luther* (Philadelphia: A. J. Holman and the Castle Press, 1932), vol. 6, p. 488.

34 "Preface to the Revelation of St. John (II)" [1545], trans. Charles M. Jacobs, in *Works of Luther*, vol. 6, p. 480; translation modified after the Erlangen edition of the original German text, *Dr. Martin Luther's sämmtliche Werke*, (Frankfurt am Main: Verlag von Heyder, 1854), vol. 63, p. 159. Jacobs translates *Bilde* as "symbols." The German word for image worship is *Bilderdienst*. (I thank Dana Lloyd Spradley for his assistance in modifying the translation.)

35 "Preface to the Revelation of St. John (II)" (Jacobs trans.), p. 480; translation modified after *Werke*, vol. 63, p. 159.

36 "Preface to the Revelation of St. John (II)" (Jacobs trans.), p. 480; translation modified after *Werke*, vol. 63, p. 159.

37 "Preface to the Revelation of St. John (II)" (Jacobs trans.), p. 481; translation modified after *Werke*, vol. 63, p. 160. Cf. Ernst Lee Tuveson, *Millenium and Utopia: A Study in the Background of the Idea of Progress* (Berkeley: University of California Press, 1949), p. 26. Tuveson discusses the concepts of prophecy and progress, but not the method of interpretation as an exegesis of imagery or of parabolical meaning.

38 Thomas Brightman, *The Workes of that Famous, Reverend, and Learned Divine* (London, 1644), p. 981. Brightman does not specifically attribute his exegesis to Luther, perhaps because Luther never wrote the exposition he proposed in his preface. Brightman includes Luther in his interpretation, as the third angel of the apocalypse (pp. 480–81). Among Brightman's expositions published after his death, the exegesis of Revelation seems to have been his most popular work. It appeared in Latin in 1609 and in English in 1611 and went through many editions, including seven during the period of the Civil War. Thus, although Brightman was unusual in his interpretation, he was also well known and widely read.

For Cotton's reference to Brightman, we have only an indirect source, Anthony Tuckney, who wrote a preface for Cotton's second series of sermons on Canticles, *Exposition of Canticles* (1655), published several years after Cotton's death. Tuckney, a cousin of Cotton's and his successor at St. Botolph's, appears to have known Cotton well and is probably a reliable source. Tuckney also omits any reference to Luther. In his preface he says, "Mr. *Brightman* first fell upon this way of expounding this Book, and our *Reverend Author* [Cotton] afterwards followed him in it . . . for which they conceive they have many faire hints in the Book itself, besides the suffrage both of *Aben-Ezra*, who takes it for an history of the Church from *Abraham* to the *Messiah*, as also of some *Christian Writers*, who would have it be a Prophecie concerning the Church from *Christ* to *Constantine*."

Tuckney explains the idea of the exegesis as deriving from the interpretation of Revelation: "Sometimes I knew him [Cotton] (as to this) of another judgement, when he much approved of *Master Brightman's* Exposition of the *Revelation,* but thought somewhat strange of this way of Expounding the Canticles; & no wonder, for Mr. *Brightman* himself did not suddently fall into it; but (as he telleth you) whilst he was studying the *Revelation,* he came first to think of it." Tuckney also refers to Brightman's exposition of Daniel's vision as another exegesis of the same kind.

39 Cotton's limited indebtedness to the tropists is suggested by the obvious strain in his attempt to make Calvin a proponent of Luther's method of parabolical exegesis. Cotton ventured that Calvin actually, if obscurely, concurred on the historical significance of parabolical meaning: "Commandments in Parables are not alwayes given as an injunction of what ought to be done by way of Ordinance, but as a Prediction of what will be done by way of providence. *Calvine* giveth an hint of interpreting that parable (Mat. 22 with the parallel Parable, Luke 14.) in an historicall way, as the call of God hath been tendered to Jews and Gentiles in the course of providence" (HCM64). Cotton's willingness to see such a "hint" in Calvin suggests how little Calvin's works supported such a method of exegesis.

40 Brightman, *Workes,* p. 40. For the original Latin text, see Thomas Brightman, *Apocalypsis Apocalypseos* (Frankfurt, 1609), p. 36. Cf. Foucault, *The Order of Things,* p. 42.

41 Studies of typology have inexplicably assumed that this series of sermons follows the pattern of American historiography, despite its clear differences. See, e.g., Sacvan Bercovitch, *Puritan Origins of the American Self* (New Haven, Conn.: Yale University Press, 1975), p. 51; and Lowance, *Language of Canaan,* pp. 51–53. On the comparable English typological tradition, see William Haller, *The Elect Nation: The Meaning and Relevance of Foxe's Book of Martyrs* (New York: Harper & Row, 1938); and Bercovitch, *Puritan Origins,* pp. 72–91. Cotton was certainly aware of this kind of typological narrative, for he mentions Foxe's *Acts and Monuments* at the beginning of his exposition. Thus it seems reasonable to conclude that his departure from it was intentional.

42 Robert Adolph, *The Rise of Modern Prose Style* (Cambridge, Mass.: MIT Press, 1968), esp. chap. 6.

43 Quoted in Ronald S. Wallace, *Calvin's Doctrine of the Word and Sacrament* (London: Oliver & Boyd, 1953), p. 143.

44 Cotton's reading of the text as a coded reference to Frederick II is an adaptation of the twelfth-century pseudo-Joachite prophecy that interpreted Frederick II as the "Emperor of the Last Days." See Norman Cohn, *The Pursuit of the Millenium: Revolutionary Millenarians and Mystical Anarchists of the Middle Ages,* rev. ed. (New York: Oxford University Press, 1961; rpt. 1970), pp. 110–11.

45 See Bercovitch, *Puritan Origins,* pp. 72–108. See also Barbara Lewalski, "*Samson Agonistes* and the 'Tragedy' of the Apocalypse," *PMLA* 85 (1970), pp. 1050–61.

46 This idea is an expansion of Brightman's brief contrast between Revelation and Canticles. However, Cotton's inferences about the importance of marriage are his own. Brightman says only the following: "They [Solomon and John] also follow somewhat, a divers manner of handling it. *John* setteth forth the strifes and battells of the Church more at large, and exactly painteth out her enemies with a greater caution or heed taking. But this Propheticall Paranymph (or marriage maker) toucheth these things more sparingly, desirous onely to set forth the joyfull events of the Church, he scarcely mentioned at all any accidents, whereby this mysticall song might be disturbed: or at least so seasoning her troubles, that much pleasure may alwayes appear in them" (*Workes*, p. 981).

47 In his chronicle of Judeo-Christian history, Jesus appears as one among many virtuous historical figures, eminent of course, but not eminent enough to be an antitype, a controlling point of reference in these sermons. Cotton interprets the life of Jesus as disappointingly lacking in revelation: "Though Christ established discipline, and delivered it to the church in his time, Mat. 18.15–17, yet it was not displayed, nor shewed itself in open execution, till after his resurrection, 1 Cor. 5.1–6" (C27). That is, the church as a mystical body was more revelatory than the life of Jesus. As Jesper Rosenmeier has pointed out, in *The Way of Life* Cotton interprets Pentecost, rather than the life and death of Jesus, as the definitive religious event, and he does so in the Canticles sermons as well. See Jesper Rosenmeier, "The Image of Christ: The Typology of John Cotton" (Ph.D. diss., Harvard University, 1966).

Similarly, it is not the human *figura* of Jesus that describes the Christic mystical body, as we might expect. Cotton dismisses the *figura* of Jesus because, as a resurrected body, its perfection makes it an inappropriate analogy for the reform of the church: "Christs humane body never decayeth, and therefore needeth no repairing" (C48). Like Calvin, Cotton distinguishes radically between the body of Jesus, dead, resurrected, and absent, and the spiritually present mystical body of Christ. In effect he dismisses the former as a viable means of understanding the latter. Cotton correspondingly shifts the dramatic climax of these sermons to the conversion of the Jews. He is much more emphatic and expansive about their conversion than he is about the return of Christ at the millennium.

48 Cotton Mather, *Magnalia Christi Americana, or The Ecclesiastical History of New-England*, 2 vols. (Hartford, Conn.: Silas Andrus, 1855), vol. 1, p. 258.

49 On Cotton's biography, see Ziff, *Career of Cotton*, esp. pp. 38–58. There were two biographies before Mather's, both more reliable. See Whiting, "John Cotton," pp. 422–25, where Whiting describes Cotton's early years; and John Norton, *Abel Being Dead Yet Speaketh, Or, The Life and Death of that Deservedly Famous Man of God, Mr. John Cotton* (London, 1658). It is historically the case that Cotton became a Puritan iconoclast, refusing to perform the Anglican rituals at St. Botolph's at about the time in his life when he married Elizabeth Horrocks, but Mather does not say this. Instead, he misrepresents the known facts of his grandfather's life.

CHAPTER 5. 1637

1 "Antinomianism" means that, through grace, one believes oneself to be above the moral law. As this chapter will show, this epithet was politically but

not intellectually significant. The "antinomians" were so named by their opponents in the crisis, who might just as well have given this name to themselves.
For an account of the crisis, see Darrett B. Rutman, *Winthrop's Boston: Portrait of
a Puritan Town, 1630–1649* (Chapel Hill: University of North Carolina Press,
1965), pp. 98–134. Cotton immigrated in 1633 and was immediately made
teacher of the First Church of Boston. Hutchinson immigrated in 1634. On the
theology disputed in the crisis, see John S. Coolidge, *The Pauline Renaissance in
England: Puritanism and the Bible* (Oxford: Oxford University Press, [Clarendon
Press], 1970), pp. 137–38; and Jesper Rosenmeier, "New England's Perfection:
The Image of Adam and the Image of Christ in the Antinomian Crisis, 1634–
1638," *William and Mary Quarterly* 27, no. 3 (July 1970), pp. 435–59. The most
elaborate study to date of the antinomian crisis is Emery Battis, *Saints and
Sectaries: Anne Hutchinson and the Antinomian Controversy in the Massachusetts Bay
Colony* (Chapel Hill: University of North Carolina Press, 1962).

2 On the Pequot War, see esp. Francis Jennings, *The Invasion of America:
Indians, Colonialism, and the Cant of Conquest* (1975; rpt. New York: Norton,
1976), pp. 186–227. I have followed Jennings's analysis of the often contradictory accounts of the Pequot War, although his interpretation is marred by a
tendency to see the Pequots as innocent victims. He does, however, recount
evidence – such as the Pequot raids in the Connecticut Valley – that provides a
perspective on his interpretation. For a briefer account of the war that adopts a
similar view, see Richard Drinnon, *Facing West: The Metaphysics of Indian-Hating
and Empire-Building* (Minneapolis: University of Minnesota Press, 1980), pp.
35–61. Drinnon mentions the simultaneity of the Pequot War and the antinomian crisis (pp. 55–56), but he does not discuss the connections between racism
and sexism. He defines racism as an attitude based on physical characteristics (p.
51), yet it does not seem to occur to him that prejudice against women might
be defined in the same way. He simply describes the Puritans as "repressed"
(e.g., p. 57). Drinnon says that four hundred people were killed at Mystic (p.
43), but he does not cite his source. For Winthrop's account, see *Winthrop's
Journal: "History of New England,"* ed. James K. Hosmer, 2 vols. (New York:
Scribner, 1908; rpt. New York: Barnes & Noble, 1959), vol. 1, pp. 210–38; all
further references to *Winthrop's Journal* are to the first volume of this edition.

3 John Winthrop, *A Short Story of the Rise, reign, and ruine of the Antinomians,
Familists and Libertines* [1644], in *The Antinomian Controversy, 1636–1638: A
Documentary History*, ed. David D. Hall (Middletown, Conn.: Wesleyan Uni-
versity Press, 1968), p. 262.

4 Jennings, *Invasion*, pp. 220–25.

5 Even historians whose interpretations attempt to account for the social
significance of theological differences do not consider this aspect of the contro-
versy. See, e.g., David D. Hall, *The Faithful Shepherd: A History of the New
England Ministry in the Seventeenth Century* (Chapel Hill: University of North
Carolina Press, 1972), pp. 156–66; and Darrett B. Rutman, *American Puritanism:
Faith and Practice* (Philadelphia: Lippincott, 1970), pp. 94–107.

6 John Wheelwright, "A Fast-Day Sermon" [1637], in Hall, *Antinomian Controversy*, pp. 152–72, esp. pp. 152–53; David Hall, Introduction to Hall, *Antino-*

mian Controversy, pp. 3–23, esp. p. 10; Thomas Weld, Preface to Winthrop, *A Short Story*, pp. 201–19, esp. p. 210.

7 Wheelwright, "Fast-Day Sermon," pp. 163, 163, 170.

8 Wheelwright, "Fast-Day Sermon," pp. 168, 159.

9 Wheelwright, "Fast-Day Sermon," pp. 166, 166, 167.

10 Wheelwright, "Fast-Day Sermon," pp. 165–66, 165.

11 Wheelwright, "Fast-Day Sermon," p. 168.

12 John Mason, *A Brief History of the Pequot War: Especially Of the memorable Taking of their Fort at Mistick in Connecticut In 1637* (Boston, 1736), p. 8; Jennings, *Invasion*, pp. 202–27; Mason, *Brief History*, p. 22. Concerning the first publication of Mason's history by Thomas Prince in 1736, see Richard Slotkin, *Regeneration through Violence: The Mythology of the American Frontier, 1600–1860* (Middletown, Conn.: Wesleyan University Press, 1973), pp. 183–86.

13 John Higginson to Winthrop, ca. May 1637, printed in Charles M. Segal and David C. Stineback, *Puritans, Indians, and Manifest Destiny* (New York: Putnam, 1977), pp. 125–29 (quotation from p. 128); John Underhill, *Newes from America, or, A New and Experimentall Discoverie of New England* [London, 1638], in *History of the Pequot War*, ed. Charles Orr (Cleveland: Helman-Taylor, 1897), pp. 80–81.

14 Michael McGiffert, ed., *God's Plot: The Paradoxes of Puritan Piety, Being the Autobiography and Journal of Thomas Shepard* ([Amherst]: University of Massachusetts Press, 1972), pp. 66–67.

15 Jennings, *Invasion*, p. 213.

16 Jennings shows that it was the Puritans, not the Pequots, who refused to honor their own negotiations for a treaty (*Invasion*, pp. 191–98).

17 Jennings, *Invasion*, pp. 202–15; *Winthrop's Journal*, pp. 189–90, 194.

18 *Winthrop's Journal* (pp. 220, 227); *Leift Lion Gardener his relation to the Pequot Warres* [n.d.], in Orr, *History*, pp. 112–49 (quotations from pp. 132, 137, 137).

19 Mason, *Brief History*, p. 18.

20 Mason, *Brief History*, p. 22; Underhill, *Newes from America*, p. 80.

21 Mason, *Brief History*, p. 14.

22 The gratuitous murder of Pequot women at Mystic was an act that Puritan historians in the latter seventeenth century concealed (Jennings, *Invasion*, p. 212). Jennings briefly compares the English perception of the Irish and the Native Americans (pp. 7–8, 46, 212–13). For a more expansive discussion of the English experience in Ireland, see Nicholas P. Canny, "The Ideology of English Colonization: From Ireland to America," *William and Mary Quarterly* 30 (1973), pp. 575–98.

23 *Winthrop's Journal*, p. 220. As Jennings points out, Winthrop also omitted direct mention of the Massachusetts forces. Winthrop added, "The story is more fully described in the next leaf," which is now lost, if indeed it was written.

24 Underhill, *Newes From America*, pp. 80–81.

25 Underhill, *Newes From America*, p. 81. His phrasing implied that women were children in relation to Pequot men, that Pequot husbands were fathers to their wives. See also, e.g., *Winthrop's Journal*, p. 200.

26 *Winthrop's Journal*, pp. 193–95, 238–39.

27 Winthrop, *A Short Story*, pp. 262, 275–76.

28 Winthrop, *A Short Story*, p. 310.

29 In the biblical narrative, Jezebel retains her own religion, the worship of Baalim, when she marries Ahab. Ahab, instead of converting her to the worship of Yahweh, is instead enthralled by the possibilities of her religion. Having seduced Ahab to belief in her religion, Jezebel has the prophets of Yahweh killed and establishes in their place the prophets of Baal, who in turn are killed by Elijah. Jezebel then threatens Elijah with death, and he returns the threat in the form of a prophecy of Jezebel's awful death, a prophecy that is repeated several times in the Bible before it is fulfilled. The narration of her murder by Jehu, already fantasized several times in prophecy, is the single most lengthy description of her in Scripture, and supposedly the event that revealed the deity's judgment of her. Jehu considers the murder a kingly act, one that will rid the country of the worship of Baalim, a religion he arbitrarily dismisses as Jezebel's "whoredoms" and "witchcrafts."

30 Weld, Preface to Winthrop, *A Short Story*, pp. 209, 215, 218.

31 Underhill, *Newes From America*. *Winthrop's Journal*, p. 240, records Underhill's disenfranchisement.

32 Underhill, *Newes From America*, pp. 52–53.

33 Underhill, *Newes From America*, pp. 70–71.

34 Copies of the original publication of Underhill's book are extremely rare, and the drawing was omitted from the nineteenth-century Helman-Taylor edition. For a reprint of the drawing, see Jennings, *Invasion*, p. 224. For "figure," see the upper left corner. The drawing is signed "R.H." in the lower left corner.

35 Jennings, *Invasion*, p. 224.

36 Underhill's association of the topic of land and the topic of women was probably not fortuitous. On the use of women as a metaphor for the land in American culture, see Annette Kolodny, *The Lay of the Land: Metaphor as Experience and History in American Life and Letters* (Chapel Hill: University of North Carolina Press, 1975). Slotkin, in *Regeneration through Violence,* discusses Underhill's interpretation at some length (pp. 69–78). Although he acknowledges that sexuality is a topic in the narrative, by which he means simply the section on the captive maids, it receives only a cursory mention in his analysis. Slotkin concludes of Underhill's narrative that it "posits a theory of order but his [Underhill's] concept [of order] relies more on a belief in personal self-restraint than on imposed discipline" (p. 78). Slotkin also implies that the significance of Underhill's narrative is minor because he was among those disenfranchised in the antinomian crisis. Yet elsewhere Slotkin observes that "the experience of Underhill at the Pequot fort was repeated numerous times during King Philip's War," characterizing this experience as a "hideous lapse from civilized self-restraint" in which "white troops would become hysterical with rage and massacre the Indian wounded, women, and children with a fury unmatched even by the Indians themselves" (p. 143).

37 Hall, *Antinomian Controversy*, p. 372. Hutchinson was condemned, finally, for lying about when she had first believed her supposedly heretical ideas.

38   Winthrop, *A Short Story*, pp. 281, 282; Weld, Preface to Winthrop, *A Short Story*, p. 214.

39   Winthrop, *A Short Story*, pp. 281–82.

40   *John Wheelwright: His Writings*, ed. Charles H. Bell (Boston, 1876), pp. 195–96, quoted in Lyle Koehler, "The Case of the American Jezebels: Anne Hutchinson and Female Agitation during the Years of Antinomian Turmoil, 1636–1640," *William and Mary Quarterly* 31 (1974), p. 73. Although Koehler advances some interesting evidence overlooked by earlier historians, his analysis remains quite conventional. For a more insightful interpretation, though based on more conventional sources, see Ben Barker-Benfield, "Anne Hutchinson and the Puritan Attitude toward Women," *Feminist Studies* 1, no. 2 (Fall 1972), pp. 65–96.

41   On the criteria for judging true and false revelations, see T199ff. These same criteria appear in the trial (Hall, *Antinomian Controversy*, pp. 340, 342).

42   For Cotton's admonition of Hutchinson at the trial, see Hall, *Antinomian Controversy*, pp. 372, 385. For an account of Hutchinson's submission at the trial, see John Cotton, *The Way of Congregational Churches Cleared: In two Treatises* (London, 1648), pt. 1, pp. 85–86; the passage on Hutchinson's care "to prevent any jealousie in mee," is from pt. 1, p. 88.

43   For the other ministers' "Popish doctrine," see Hall, *Antinomian Controversy*, p. 134. Cotton's summary is from *The Way Cleared*, pt. 1, p. 47.

44   Hall, *Antinomian Controversy*, pp. 370, 314.

45   John Coolidge has argued that *The Treatise of the Covenant of Grace* displays a masterful theology, a synthesis of Christology and Puritan covenant theology that he views as the high point of the Pauline renaissance in Anglo-American Protestant thought. See Coolidge, *Pauline Renaissance*, pp. 132–38, 143–44. As an assessment of Cotton's achievement from the perspective of theology, Coolidge's argument is persuasive. However, he considers Cotton's works only from a theological point of view.

46   On the institution of the new practice, see Rutman, *Winthrop's Boston*, p. 130. For the guarantee that Cotton obtained for himself, see Cotton, *The Way Cleared*, pt. 1, pp. 53–54. The theology of the resurrection, an important issue of dispute at the church trial, is perhaps the best example of an inevitable conflict between men's and women's theology in a religion where the gender identity of the deity is an essential tenet of faith. The so-called heresy that provoked Cotton's prediction of adultery was Hutchinson's "denying the Resurrection of these very Bodies," as Cotton put it (Hall, *Antinomian Controversy*, p. 371). It was not that Hutchinson disbelieved in the resurrection. As she explained it, "I scruple not the Resurrection but what Body shall rise," and the reason for her scruple was, "I cannot yet see Christ is united to thease fleshly bodies" (Hall, *Antinomian Controversy*, pp. 363–64). She believed that in conversion the soul was united to Christ, but the natural body was not. This was the theologically correct answer for a *woman* who believed she was united to a *male* mystical body, who believed in the virtue of marital fidelity, and who believed that female sexuality belonged to the realm of the natural world and the ordinary literal sense. In sum, she believed that her womanliness was a quality of her natural life but not of her spiritual life – the orthodox Puritan view. That the theologically correct answer for her was not the theologically correct answer for men is evident from the outrage of all the clerics at her theology of the resurrection. The clergy believed their theology was objective, and Hutchinson's statements imply that she thought her theology was objective, too.

47   Edward Johnson, *The Wonder-Working Providence of Sion's Saviour in New England* [1653], ed. J. Franklin Jameson (New York: Scribner, 1910; rpt. New York: Barnes & Noble, 1959), p. 270.

CHAPTER 6. APOCALYPTIC HIERARCHY

1   Transcripts of three portions of this series were published in London. *The Powrring out of the Seven Vials* appeared in 1642, with a second edition in 1645; all references are to the first edition and will be given in the text and indicated by V. Since the text is paginated by vial, and occasionally by sermon within each of the seven sections, quotations are cited by vial, sermon where necessary, and pagination within the sequence for each vial (e.g., a quotation from the sixth vial, third sermon, ninth page would be cited as 6V.3.9). *The Churches Resurrection* appeared in 1642; all references will be given in the text and indicated by CR. *An Exposition upon The Thirteenth Chapter of the Revelation* was published in 1655, with a second edition in 1656; as before, references are to the first edition and are indicated in the text by R.

The date the sermons were delivered is based on Thomas Allen's preface to the collection published in 1655. Allen, minister of Charlestown when Cotton preached these sermons, says Cotton gave weekly lectures that he attended. Allen writes, "I say I do here declare and testifie unto the world that these Sermons upon the 13th Chapter of the *Revelation*, for the substance of them (giving allowance for such defects of the Amanuensis, which cannot but be expected ordinarily, and yet I confesse are but very few in this Treatise) were published [i.e., preached] by that faithful servant of the Lord, Mr. *John Cotton*, about the 11. and 12 moneths (if I mistake not) of the year 1639. and the first and second of the yeare 1640. upon his weekly Lecture at Boston in *New-England*, where he went over the other Chapters of the *Revelation*, as he did this thirteenth Chapter."

2   Treatises on the apocalypse deserve more systematic analysis than they have yet received. On the political history of millenarianism, see Norman Cohn, *The Pursuit of the Millennium: Revolutionary Millenarians and Mystical Anarchists of the Middle Ages*, rev. ed. (New York: Oxford University Press, 1961; rpt. 1970). On the period of the English Civil War, see the works of Christopher Hill, especially *Puritanism and Revolution: Studies in the Interpretation of the English Revolution of the Seventeenth Century* (New York: Schocken Books, 1958; rpt. 1967), and *The World Turned Upside Down: Radical Ideas during the English Revolution* (New York: Viking Press, 1972). Cohn's analysis is generally more informed than Hill's concerning the intellectual tradition of apocalyptic interpretation, and more careful in its attribution of populism. Hill wrongly assumes that historical exegeses of Revelation were a populist invention of the "naive" and "untrained"; see, for example, his remarks on Arise Evans and

Mary Cary in *The World Turned Upside Down*, pp. 76, 259. See also Chap. 4, n. 38, herein, on Brightman's expositions and their popularity. For a different view of radicalism in the English Civil War, see Michael Walzer, *The Revolution of the Saints: A Study in the Origins of Radical Politics* (Cambridge, Mass.: Harvard University Press, 1965). Also helpful is William Haller, *Liberty and Reformation in the Puritan Revolution* (New York: Columbia University Press, 1955). On contemporaneous attitudes in America, see Cecilia Tichi, *New World, New Earth: Environmental Reform in American Literature from the Puritans through Whitman* (New Haven, Conn.: Yale University Press, 1979), pp. 1–66; James P. Maclear, "New England and the Fifth Monarchy: The Quest for the Millennium in Early American Puritanism," *William and Mary Quarterly* 32 (1975), pp. 223–60; and Ernest Lee Tuveson, *Millennium and Utopia: A Study in the Background of the Idea of Progress* (Berkeley: University of California Press, 1949). Although the sermons of 1639–40 were Cotton's first systematic and lengthy exposition of the apocalypse, there are hints that he adhered to the general themes of this interpretation as early as 1630 and as late as 1650. In WL150, he alludes to this interpretation: "Notable is that place, *Revel.* 9.1 to 6. It is a lively description of the Friers & Priests of the Church of Rome, being let out of the bottomlesse pit of ignorance and darknesse, in which their Religion was hatched." In a thanksgiving day sermon in 1650, Cotton preached on Rev. 15.3 The sermon concerns regicide and the condition of England. For the text and a useful introduction to it, see Francis J. Bremer, "In Defense of Regicide: John Cotton on the Execution of Charles I," *William and Mary Quarterly* 37 (1980), pp. 103–24. Although Cotton urged peace and cooperation between Presbyterians and Independents, he still found a place for the text that is emblematic of his 1640 sermons, "Thou hast given them Blood to Drinke" (p. 116).

3   Francis Jennings, in *The Invasion of America: Indians, Colonialism, and the Cant of Conquest* (New York: Norton, 1976), pp. 3–42, discusses nationalist conquests in the Americas in comparative terms but does not fully consider the difference between the Puritans and other New World colonists in this respect. The Puritans' antagonistic relation to the Church of England and the Stuart monarchy required that they distinguish themselves from much of the English nationalist ideology.

4   Cotton's use of the metaphors of later American millenialist rhetoric is symptomatic of the difference in his apocalyptic geography. For example, he speaks not of a church *in* the wilderness but of the way in which a church may metaphorically "become a wildernesse" (4V.14); he prophesies about "plantations," but they are in England, not New England (5V.11). Although Cotton's interpretation seems more antiquarian than later Puritan narratives and the literature of "manifest destiny" in general, it is actually much closer to twentieth-century thought. In its international dimensions, its fixation on a single international enemy, and its fearful visions of world-wide holocaust, it states many of the themes that have informed U.S. foreign policy since World War II. Francis Ford Coppola's film on Vietnam, *Apocalypse Now,* invokes the apocalyptic frame of reference as a means of interpretation; it also revives the older meaning of "prejudice" as material harm in the military order that, given to the main character, initiates the plot: "Terminate with extreme prejudice."

5 For a different view of the Puritan interpretation of space, see Sacvan Bercovitch, *The Puritan Origins of the American Self* (New Haven, Conn.: Yale University Press, 1975), esp. pp. 98–108. Bercovitch quotes an early New England letter from John Cotton to John Davenport in which Cotton uses the expression "New Heaven and New Earth" in reference to the peace and order of the colony (p. 94), but the Revelation sermons preached several years later do not employ the biblical phrase in this way.

6 See John Winthrop, "Christian Charitie. A Modell Hereof" [1630], in *Puritan Political Ideas, 1558–1794,* ed. Edmund S. Morgan (New York: Bobbs-Merrill, 1965), pp. 76–93. See esp. p. 93: "For wee must Consider that wee shall be as a Citty upon a Hill, the eies of all people are uppon us." Cotton uses the metaphor of the theater instead: "*God hath set us* (saith the Apostle [Paul]) *upon a Theatre* (as the word is in the originall 1 Cor. 4.9) *unto the world, and unto Angels, and unto men*" (6V.3.9).

7 Where Brightman discerned Luther, Cotton perceives the state power of English Protestantism.

8 That is, an end to the world that is the beginning of the millennium as the thousand-year reign of Christ. See, for example, Mason I. Lowance, Jr., *The Language of Canaan: Metaphor and Symbol in New England from the Puritans to the Transcendentalists* (Cambridge, Mass.: Harvard University Press, 1980), p. 130; and Everett Emerson, *John Cotton* (New York: Twayne, 1965), p. 97. Lowance and Emerson assume the traditional paradigm of apocalyptic thought. For a brief but helpful description of the paradigmatic narrative of last things, see Frank Kermode, "The End," in Kermode, *The Sense of an Ending: Studies in the Theory of Fiction* (New York: Oxford University Press, 1967; rpt. 1970), pp. 3–31.

9 Cotton's occasional declarations that Congregationalism is egalitarian mean very little from a social point of view. For example, he exhorts, "Leave every church Independant, [but] not Independant from brotherly counsell," warning that "when it comes to power, that one Church shall have power over the rest, then look for a Beast, which the Lord would have all his people to abhor" (R30–31). The "brotherly counsell" of Congregationalism in fact extends only to the Puritan elite. The sense of equality and peaceful, mutual counsel in the Congregational church is also prominent in his late tracts. See especially *Certain Queries tending to Accommodation and Communion of Presbyterian and Congregational Churches* (London, 1654), in which Cotton presents himself as a peacemaker as well as a spokesman for Congregational polity. These late tracts show some of the same pacifist sentiments as his much earlier, English sermon notes on First John, *A practicall commentary, or An exposition with observations, reasons, and uses upon the first epistle generall of John,* 2nd ed., corrected (London, 1658 [1656]). Both these notes and Cotton's brief defenses of Congregationalism seem less prejudicial than the Revelation sermons because they do not directly engage the social issues that disclose his predilection for elitism and violence. That is, Cotton appears far more egalitarian and pacifist than he actually was because these tracts tacitly assume that the religious elite constitutes, or at least represents, the whole of society.

10 Cotton probably had a specific recent event in mind, but it is not possible to identify it from the text.

11 The abrupt decline in immigration at the end of the first decade of settlement created a financial crisis in New England. On economic conditions in Boston in 1639–40, see Darrett B. Rutman, *Winthrop's Boston: Portrait of a Puritan Town, 1630–1649* (Chapel Hill: University of North Carolina Press, 1965), pp. 183–86. On the conditions in New England in general at this time, see Bernard Bailyn, *The New England Merchants in the Seventeenth Century* (New York: Harper & Row, 1964), pp. 45–74.

12 In this respect he follows the social theory of William Tyndale, *The Obedience of a Christian Man*. Cotton singles out women, again demanding an especially exacting obedience from them. As Sheila Rowbotham has pointed out, radical political movements, revolutionary though they claim to be, have often ignored the oppression of women in society and have frequently reinstated traditional means of controlling them, or devised new methods of control as part of their political revolutions. See Sheila Rowbotham, *Women, Resistance, and Revolution: A History of Women and Revolution in the Modern World* (New York: Random House, 1972; rpt. 1974), pp. 200–47. Rowbotham discusses only modern radicalism, but it appears that a similar phenomenon occurred in New England. Cotton's actions in the Hutchinson controversy and his sermons from 1637 to 1640 made an important contribution to the control of women in the name of radical church reform.

13 Cotton denounces both the Catholic church and the Church of England on these grounds. "Provinciall, Diocesan, Cathedrall, [and] National Churches" are all "the image of this first Beast" in their "forms" or "models" (R239, 244).

14 "Winthrop's Speech to the General Court, July 3, 1645," in *The Puritans,* ed. Perry Miller and Thomas H. Johnson, rev. ed., 2 vols. (New York: Harper & Row, 1963), vol. 1, p. 206.

15 Cotton elsewhere calls this the "bodily" sense of the text (3V.9, 13).

16 On the Pope see, e.g., R52.

17 On the harsh treatment of children by "evangelical" Protestants, see Philip J. Greven, *The Protestant Temperament: Patterns of Child-Rearing, Religious Experience, and the Self in Early America* (New York: New American Library, 1977), esp. pp. 21–54.

18 Cotton digresses at great length to discuss Christ and conversion in the exposition of Revelation 13. Once he introduces the subject, he seems to become confused about frames of reference, for he never quite makes his way back to the initial themes of his exposition.

19 E.g., see WL20–21, 124.

20 He identifies his references to death as the rhetorical figure of "antanaclesis" (CR6). The *Oxford English Dictionary* suggests that seventeenth-century authors tended to understand the repeated use not only as different but as contradictory: "*Antanaclesis* . . . Repeating a word in a different or even contradictory sense, 1657."

21 Cotton employs the same differentiation in another manner in his debate with Roger Williams. Against Williams, Cotton counter-proposed what he thought was a suitable frame for their debate, the figurative text of Revelation from which Cotton took the title of his reply. At the outset Cotton repeats the word "bloud" until he can finally secure it in the context he thinks will vindicate him, Rev. 7.14, undoing the literal significance Williams gave this word when he accused Cotton of favoring persecution: "But if this Tenet have any appearance of blood in it, It is because it is washed in the Bloud of the *Lambe, and sealed with his bloud*. And then though it may seem Bloudy to men of corrupt mindes destitute of truth, (as *Paul* seemed to such to be a Pestilent fellow) yet to faithful and upright soules, such things as are washed in the Bloud of the *Lambe,* are wont to come forth white, as did the followers of the *Lambe, who washed their Robes white in the Bloud of the Lambe,* Rev. 7.14" (John Cotton, *The Bloudy Tenant, Washed, and Made White in the Bloud of the Lambe* [London, 1647], p. 3). In his argument with Williams, Cotton takes refuge in the symbolical and parabolical passages of Scripture, appealing to the visionary figures of John's Revelation to transfer the debated meaning from a literal to a figurative signification.

22   On floating social signs, see Roland Barthes, *Mythologies,* trans. Annette Lavers (New York: Hill & Wang, 1972), pp. 109–59; Barthes analyzes this phenomenon in modern journalism. In the name of "Revolution," Barthes proposes a collapse of sign and referent, "a language thanks to which I 'act the object' " (pp. 145–46). Despite his political claims, Barthes's concept of language is very similar to Cotton's authoritarian theory of the enactment of tropes.

23   Cotton says that Catholics have the correct interpretation – his own – and he invokes the Catholics to convince the skeptics of his congregation of the validity of his own exposition.

24   He combines the language of the Geneva and King James translations of 2 Cor. 3, where ministers "of the spirit" are said to speak with "boldness" and with "plainness of speech."

25   Cotton's descriptive language, which repeats "abuse" several times, may be an allusion to tropes. On the trope of catachresis or abuse (*abusio*), see *The Institutio Oratoria of Quintilian,* with an English translation by H. E. Butler, 4 vols., Loeb Classical Library (Cambridge, Mass.: Harvard University Press, 1966–79), 8.6.34–36. See also the *Oxford English Dictionary,* which describes a broader range of meanings in English usage than appears in Quintilian, including "the misuse of a trope."

26   Cotton goes on to differentiate the "nature of wicked men," who enjoy abuse of power, from the nature of "godly men," for whom such abuses are a source of "shame," but this distinction does not undo his symbolic fusion of the "wilde" pope and the regenerate Puritan in the image of the abusive Beast. Cotton emphasizes that the figure of the Beast expresses the "nature" of both the regenerate and the wicked in the identical acts they commit, regardless of how they feel about what they do.

27   Cotton described the "Catholick" religion as, in effect, an absolute disbelief in Puritanism, creating a closed system of thought that co-opted any exterior perspective on New England religion by claiming that his "Catholick" *was* the ultimate exterior perspective. By asserting that there could be no point of view more different from his own than this one, he severely limited the social boundaries of the possible exponents of "Religion" and freed himself from the necessity of directly contending with the reality of his opposition. Unlike Winthrop, who found himself debating with Anne Hutchinson even though he did not "mean to," Cotton chose a projected object that conveniently enabled him to be exclusively concerned with the Puritan man's view of himself. He thus created a social closure that reproduced the isolated cave conditions of the Patmos world vision from which he took his cue. For the Puritan, the "Catholick" of his imagination would be the sole enemy everywhere until the end of time.

28 An armed French Catholic ship did arrive in 1643 in Massachusetts Bay, to the great surprise of the Bostonians. The colonists, confronted with the heretofore imaginary *res,* disagreed strongly about whether to treat the Catholics figuratively or literally. The harbor defenses were in complete disrepair, but as it turned out, the Catholic ship had no intention of attacking the Puritans. The captain was Charles de la Tour, who was on his way to claim the contended governorship of Arcadia. The French spent a month in Boston at the invitation of Winthrop, whose actions allied him with the Catholic hierarchy against the common people. He allowed the French to hold military drills on the common, and they feigned an attack on the crowd. Winthrop was voted out of office in the next election, probably for his hospitality to de la Tour. For an account of the events, see Edmund S. Morgan, *The Puritan Dilemma: The Story of John Winthrop* (Boston: Little, Brown, 1958), pp. 190-93.

29 Larzer Ziff, in *The Career of John Cotton: Puritanism and the American Experience* (Princeton, N.J.: Princeton University Press, 1962), chap. 6, esp. pp. 171-75, sees Cotton as essentially a displaced Elizabethan. Although Cotton often speaks as if he were in the thick of warfare between Protestants and Catholics, or else caught up in nostalgia for the era of Elizabethan Protestantism, he does not offer the context of Europe in these terms as a viable social frame of reference for American Puritans.

30 Moreover, Cotton suddenly reverts to a martyr's perception, warning his audience that "faith" is more powerful than "the arm of Flesh" (R111).

31 Cotton remarks at one point that the faith of the convert is a general principle of the Protestant mind, one that relies on words not only to define reality but also to generate and determine it: "The faith of the Elect is described to be a confidence, and evidence. . . . If we hold fast the confidence, the word is all one with subsistence, it is such a confidence as doth give a being, and subsistence unto the thing believed: it doth as truly make them to be as if they were actually extent" (R212). The language of Canaan, the language of the elect, does more than name the world. It gives "being" and "subsistence" to what it names, the "thing believed," because "the word is all one with subsistence." In Cotton's terms, his "confidence" exploited the geographical isolation of New England to create an "as if" referent, positing the being of Catholics "as if they were actually extent." Cotton privileges the ordained images of his own mind so strongly that he insists on their plainness as literal description.

APPENDIX

1 Julius H. Tuttle, "Writings of the Rev. John Cotton," in *Bibliographic Essays: A Tribute to Wilberforce Eames* (Cambridge, Mass.: Harvard University Press, 1924).

2 Cf. Larzer Ziff, *The Career of John Cotton: Puritanism and the American Experience* (Princeton, N.J.: Princeton University Press, 1962), p. 263. Ziff observes that the sermons date from Cotton's English career, but gives no evidence and makes no inferences about a more specific date of composition and delivery. A second, distinct commentary on Canticles was preached in New England in 1642 or later and published in 1655. See John Cotton, *A Brief Exposition With Practical Observations Upon the whole Book of Canticles* (London, 1655), p. 1, where the opening sermon refers to the publication of the first commentary in 1642: "the other notes already printed."

3 See Ziff, *Career of Cotton*, p. 44. For a summary of the historical background, and the importance of events on the Continent for the English, see Christopher Hill, *The Century of Revolution, 1603–1714* (New York: Norton, 1966), pp. 10–11. Hill summarizes: "In London and among Protestants all over the country there was strong support for the Elector Palatine, which was expressed in the Parliament of 1621" (p. 11).

4 *Career of Cotton*, p. 262.

5 [John Winthrop], Winthrop's *Journal History of New England*, ed. James Kendall Hosmer, 2 vols., Original Narratives of Early American History (New York: Barnes & Noble, 1959), vol. 2, pp. 187–88. The case is mentioned briefly in the records of the court of assistants, but no additional information is given except the prisoner's full name.

6 See Jesper Rosenmeier, "The Image of Christ: The Typology of John Cotton" (Ph.D. diss., Harvard University, 1966), p. 227.

7 See Jesper Rosenmeier, " 'Clearing the Medium': A Reevaluation of the Puritan Plain Style in Light of John Cotton's *A Practicall Commentary Upon the First Epistle Generall of John*" [London, 1656], *William and Mary Quarterly* 37 (1980), p. 580. These notes of Cotton's were published after his death. A transcript of a portion of the sermons delivered from the notes was published earlier as *Christ The Fountaine of Life* (London, 1651).

8 See "Cotton's Letter to His Wife" and "Cotton's Letter to the Bishop of Lincoln," in *Chronicles of the First Planters of the Colony of Massachusetts Bay, from 1623 to 1636*, ed. Alexander Young (Boston, 1846), pp. 432–33, 435. See also Ziff, *Career of John Cotton*, pp. 64–65.

9 Ziff, in *Career of Cotton*, p. 263, discusses only the first tract, attributing it to the period of Cotton's English career.

10 "Thomas Morton," in *Dictionary of National Biography* (London: Smith, Elder, 1909), vol. 13, pp. 1057–62. See esp. p. 1058.

11 Perry Miller, *The New England Mind: The Seventeenth Century* (1939; rpt. Boston: Beacon Press, 1965), pp. 331–32.

12 Samuel Whiting, "Concerning the Life of the Famous Mr.Cotton," in Young, *Chronicles*, pp. 419–31. There was a slightly earlier biography by John Davenport, to which Whiting refers at the beginning of his biography (p. 419), but Davenport's manuscript was never published and is now lost.

13 John Norton, *Abel Being Dead Yet Speaketh, Or, The Life and Death of that Deservedly Famous Man of God, Mr. John Cotton* (London, 1658); Cotton Mather, "The Life of Mr. John Cotton," in Mather, *Magnalia Christi Americana, or, The Ecclesiastical History of New-England*, 2 vols. (Hartford, Conn.: Silas Andrus, 1855), vol. 1, pp. 252–86.

14 Thomas Allen, "To the Reader," in R(n.p.).

15 Perry Miller, "The Plain Style," in *The New England Mind: The Seventeenth Century*, pp. 331–62. See esp. pp. 331–32; see also "Rhetoric," pp. 300–32. For Miller's sources on Cotton, see Perry Miller, *Sources for the New England Mind: The Seventeenth Century*, ed. James Hoopes (Williamsburg, Va.: Institute for Early American History and Culture, 1981), p. 84.

Index